DATE DUE 10/11

DEC 0 1 2011		
NOV 2 1 2012		
9102 8 7 AUG		
JAN 1 8 2017		
GAYLORD		PRINTED IN U.S.A.

THE
BACKLASH

THE
BACKLASH

RIGHT-WING RADICALS,
HI-DEF HUCKSTERS,
AND PARANOID POLITICS
IN THE AGE OF OBAMA

WILL BUNCH

HARPER

An Imprint of HarperCollins*Publishers*
www.harpercollins.com

HarperCollins books may be purchased for educational, business, or sales promotional use. For information, please write: Special Markets Department, HarperCollins Publishers, 10 East 53rd Street, New York, NY 10022.

FIRST EDITION

Designed by Renato Stanisic

Library of Congress Cataloging-in-Publication Data is available upon request.

ISBN: 978-0-06-199171-4

10 11 12 13 14 OV/RRD 10 9 8 7 6 5 4 3 2 1

FOR MY FAMILY, WHO ALWAYS REMIND ME THERE
REALLY IS NO PLACE LIKE HOME

Fear is the foundation of most governments; but it is so sordid and brutal a passion, and renders men in whose breasts it predominates so stupid and miserable, that Americans will not be likely to approve of any political institution which is founded on it.

—JOHN ADAMS, *Thoughts on Government*, 1776

I'm sorry. I just love my country. And I fear for it.

—GLENN BECK, MARCH 13, 2009

CONTENTS

PROLOGUE

The truth is—they don't surround us. We surround them.
This is our country.

        —GLENN BECK, FOX NEWS CHANNEL, MARCH 13, 2009

You are surrounded here in Section 107 of the UCF Arena—just about the only nonbeliever in the middle of what you thought was going to be a bland daylong political forum but instead has taken on all the trappings of an old-fashioned, rocking tent revival. They have come here to Orlando from up and down the East Coast, some 7,500 of them, and the demons they seek to cast out are the evil spirits they believe inhabit the United States—the socialists, the Marxists, the totalitarian wannabes and their imposter-in-chief, Barack Hussein Obama.

The preacher of the bad news for modern man, this hellish anti-gospel, is the politically themed entertainer Glenn Beck. In the fifteen months since Obama became the forty-fourth president and first African-American commander-in-chief of the United States, Beck has instinctively created, out of thin airwaves, this unlikely counterrevolution. And so you are in Florida now to see where Beck—writhing on the hard stage and grimacing and even weeping on several occasions—is taking this thing next.

"We stood when the odds were against us—maybe some of us were lost along the way," Beck is telling his audience now. "But we did our best, and when that happens we have a real chance."

Many in the audience are scribbling his words down on their legal pads, while others look toward the performer's sky-blue eyes on the stark stage. Yet Beck is not truly the star of the show. As is his style, he wants to put the audience at the center of the performance. What is new here in Orlando are these American revolutionaries who would man the barricades . . . of their gated retirement communities. They are speaking in violent language of retaking America—fueled not by the energetic folly of youth but by the distemper of middle age and the latest conspiracy fashions spreading like brushfire over the airwaves and across fiber-optic cables. And the flames are no longer tamped down by the politicians and the pundits but rather fanned, in a craven bid for ratings and votes and even cash from the lucky who still have spare dollars at the dawn of the 2010s.

You are not the kind of person who would ordinarily be at a place like this. You are one of the 53 percent of U.S. citizens who voted for Obama on November 3, 2008, quietly rejoicing in the apparent end of eight years of a torturing and preemptive-warmongering America that you suddenly did not recognize. And then you sat back—too comfortably, in hindsight—part of a way-too-silent majority that waited to see the green shoots of change, only to instead watch that program seemingly interrupted by this anger coming from the so-called heartland.

You expected the fury to fade away, and when it did not, you labored to understand it. There were more hard questions than easy answers— who were all these angry Americans, and where did they and some of their more out-there political notions come from? Finally, you ventured out to where they were—to the big gun show and the coffee-powered political confabs and the radio control rooms and the small-town political breakfasts, and after many months you have finally come to this Orlando revival tent disguised as a basketball palace, a theme park of exotic political ideas on the far side of Disney World, and everything you thought you knew was changing, right before your eyes.

The one constant during your odyssey to understand the backlash against Obama was this:

They would talk.

And you . . . would listen, following the trail of voices all the way back to figure out how the hell we got here in the first place.

CHAPTER ONE

The Cassandra of Lower Delaware

A t approximately 11 a.m. on June 30, 2009, inside a senior citizens' center in the rustic rural county seat of Georgetown, Delaware, a mysterious woman in red appeared with a disturbing message for the citizens of the United States of America.

No one seemed to even know her name. Few people glimpsed her face, either; most just saw her from behind or in silhouette. Yet her words would be heard by millions of people, and discussed at great length across the fifty states over the weeks that followed. This middle-aged siren wore a crimson blouse, and her reddish hair was clipped back. Fittingly, she addressed a direct descendent of one of America's Founding Fathers, a great-great-great-great-great grandson of Ben Franklin, a courtly seventy-year-old Republican U.S. congressman named Mike Castle. The stranger's tone was highly agitated, her words apocalyptic.

"Congressman, um, Castle!!!" The voice knob was cranked all the way up to eleven, and most of the heads in the senior center—about two hundred or so of them—whipped around to see who was raising the commotion. "I wanna know! . . ." Over the next couple of minutes, the stranger spoke of Dark Conspiracies and of Threats to the Republic, of a bastard prince born in Kenya and of soldiers fighting halfway around the world, of forged documents and an endangered flag—all amid knowing whoops of approval. Her cryptic sound waves were captured for posterity by an equally anonymous man with a digital camera, and they soon spread across America—uploaded and downloaded and embedded on blogs until they finally landed in the steel media palace of Rockefeller Center, where eager young producers edited them down and boomeranged them back across the heartland.

This all took little more than three weeks, and by then the woman had long disappeared—America's own Cassandra, vanished with the salt-flecked breezes that rustle the sea oats across this marshy, isolated corner of the eastern seaboard.

The original Cassandra had first appeared to the world in the fifth century B.C., another anxious time of great but fragile empire, with rivals to Greece—particularly Sparta—emerging across their pond. The nation's bards responded with great and lasting myths of national strength and righteousness. In 438 B.C., Aeschylus, the father of Greek tragedy, sent the Princess Cassandra, a beautiful vision in red silk, onto the national stage in Athens for the first time in *Agamemnon*, part of the Oresteia trilogy, all about vendetta and the search for justice in an unjust world. Cassandra has been toyed with by powerful gods for all of her life, and although she is convinced she will be killed for speaking out, the woman is determined to share her strange, incoherent visions with the world before she goes.

In the last 2,448 years, the red prophet has inspired writers ranging from William Faulkner to Florence Nightingale. The academic Seth L. Schein said Cassandra holds our imagination because "[s]he evokes the same awe, horror and pity as do schizophrenics, who often combine deep, true insight with utter helplessness and who retreat into madness." But you don't need a Ph.D. in the classics or English literature to see the story's relevance to our current moment, as the national nightmare of the 2000s that Big Media branded "The Decade from Hell" ended and threatened to morph into something worse—with roughly one out of six willing and able-bodied Americans not working and experts still unable to predict when the job market might fully recover from the economic near-death experience of 2008. You have only to flip on your car radio, where White Men in Mono talk nonstop on a daily basis of socialism and rage against the impending doom that our new president is ushering in.

This isn't the place you expected—not with the memories of November 3, 2008, still ringing in your ears, the car horns randomly and joyously bleating on the streets of Philadelphia at 2 in the morning, impromptu marches on city hall by boisterous college students with a beer in their right hand and hope in their hearts. They had achieved something historic, these seventy million—a new political coalition electrified not just by students but by blacks and white-collar eggheads and Latinos and old hippies and gays and Asians. They had done the incredible in coming together to elect Barack Obama as the forty-fourth president of the United States. It wasn't just that Obama was the first black president ever—sure, that was remarkable—but those honking cars were also reveling in the first grown-up American president in eight years. Here was a new leader who at least promised the nation he was going to take seriously things like global warming, threats to the American way of justice, and repairing a society that was weighted down by the heavy money vaults of all the penthouses up Park Avenue.

Then, in a matter of months, this brave new America seemed to evaporate, surrendering all of the psychic territory this new boisterous majority had fought so hard to win, practically ceding the political landscape to what came next:

The backlash.

It was a gathering force that came out of nowhere, seemingly before the echoes of Obama's inauguration address had even stopped reverberating against the granite boundaries of the National Mall. You and so many others had scoffed at first, at these "dead-enders" with their aimless protests with the misspelled signs and their bogus Internet conspiracy theories that Obama was really a Manchurian candidate born in Kenya and trained in the Muslim madrassas of Indonesia to destroy America from within.

But crazy as it sounds, the woman in red, her conspiratorial monologue, and the cheering Greek chorus behind her was a major turning point.

As her rant at Congressman Castle leapfrogged from an obscure link on YouTube and Internet discussion boards to the Drudge Report, and then to radio's *Rush Limbaugh Show*, and then to the *NBC Nightly News*, it became the most palpable symbol of the anger that was on display at similar town hall meetings from coast to coast—and with every report of public fury, Obama and the congressional Democrats saw their ambitious agenda for a major health-care overhaul lose momentum. The spillover from this backlash emboldened a congressional minority that had just barely enough votes to stymie action, and then it stalled equally bold plans to address climate change and reform immigration laws. One year into Obama's presidency, most of his agenda for "change" was on the ropes, with the GOP seemingly poised to win back at least some of the myriad seats they'd lost in 2006 and 2008.

In some polls, a mythical third party called the Tea Party of angry citizens like the one at Mike Castle's Delaware town hall meeting was even more popular than the Republican Party, as the anti-Obama crowd deserted even identifying with the GOP; in a few polls in late 2009, this nonexistent Tea Party outpolled both the Republicans and the Democrats. Republican stalwarts like Florida governor Charlie Crist, seeking a U.S. Senate seat; Texas senator Kay Bailey Hutchison, running for governor; and even the 2008 presidential nominee, Arizona's John McCain, either lost primaries or saw their authority challenged not from their left flank but from their right. Though these angry citizens were at most one-fourth of the national electorate, the collective tail they formed—a far-right majority within the 46-percent minority that had just voted for McCain and his running mate, Sarah Palin—seemed to be wagging the American dog. How could this happen?

Indeed, in the months that followed the outburst at Delaware's Mike Castle, these angry, loud people were everywhere in the twenty-four-hour news cycle, with a confusing array of groups that did not exist on January 20, 2009—not just the Tea Party but the 9-12 Project and even more fringe groups like the conspiratorial Oath Keepers, (mostly ex-)soldiers and cops who pledged—among other things—not to put Americans in concentration camps. Some extremists began aggressively and openly carrying their guns into the neighborhood Starbucks to make a point, while others stood at the Home Depot waving placards and intimidating Mexican day laborers.

But for all the hyperbolic news coverage, the public perception of the rank-and-file of this new reactionary movement remained incredibly polarized—they were common folk heroes to some, villains to others who defined them by the angry words on their signs, not by who they actually were or how they got to this strange moment in American history. How much of their anger was rooted in old-fashioned racism at the first black president, how much of it was new-fashioned and genuine—yet arguably misdirected—rage over an economy that increasingly had nothing to offer to its working class, and how much of it was the result of a political system that catered solely to the affluent or to the elite classes? And how come nobody was watching the vultures circling overhead—the media superstars whose ratings grew in proportion to their ability to scare regular Americans, the other hucksters making a quick buck on that fear, and the political opportunists quick to embrace radical and often bogus ideas to keep their elected positions?

As the first year of Obama's presidency morphed bumpily into the 2010 midterm elections, you traveled about the country seeking to dig into the roots of this new paranoid style in American life. Your quest would start in Delaware, the scene of Mike Castle's notorious confrontation with the mystery woman and the first state to ratify the U.S. Constitution. Despite its picture-postcard size, Delaware has become a remarkable microcosm of America in the twenty-first century, from the northern urban and liberal enclaves of Wilmington to the southern conservatism of its rural farmland, laced with upscale new communities of retirees on the Atlantic coastline and a growing downscale Latino population built up around a string of chicken-processing factories. Most of all though, you thought you could better understand what was going on if you could somehow track down not just Castle's Cassandra in red but, more importantly, the roomful of everyday people who cheered her on.

. . . .

THERE WAS NO traditional press coverage when Mike Castle, Dela-ware's congressman-at-large, came to Georgetown on June 30, 2009; he'd already had a couple of fairly low-key health-care confabs in the more populous northern reaches of the small state, where most of its journalists reside. The venue for what would prove to be such an angry gathering was the ironically named CHEER Center for senior citizens. One of the senior citizens in attendance this morning was the seventy-year-old Castle himself—one of the last of a dying American species known as the moderate Republican.

Castle's long career in state and local politics—he was a state law-maker and then governor before he made the leap to Congress in 1992 in a remarkable bipartisan deal with Democrat Tom Carper called "the swap," when each took the other's job—flourished through something called "The Delaware Consensus," or also "The Delaware Way." This meant that incumbents from both parties favored similar policies—conservatively pro-business but fairly liberal on social issues like the environment and abortion—and serious election battles were few. The mild-mannered Castle was not used to being challenged, politically or otherwise. A tall, bespectacled man with a sloping forehead, outsized ears, and a gentle patrician bearing, the Ben Franklin descendent gives off a weirdly colonial vibe.

Now, in the summer congressional recess of 2009, with Washing-ton fixated on Obama's push for health-care reform, Castle thought this would be a good moment for what he called a "listening tour" of the First State. As a sign of his commitment to improving health care, he even brought along a panel of knowledgeable and smartly attired doctors and nurses to join him onstage to address what he expected would be the practical health-care concerns of his constituents. Little did Castle know that hundreds of outraged Delawareans would instead be lying in wait, ready to tell the great-great-great-great-great grandson of Ben Franklin to go fly a kite.

Much of what transpired in Georgetown that morning wasn't so different from dozens of similar town hall meetings during 2009's Summer of Rage. The big crowd that packed the senior center—mostly over the age of fifty, mostly white—had been largely whipped up by a local radio station, WGMD (92.7, "The Talk of Delmarva"), and many were members of a newly formed Tea Party–like group called the Sussex County Community Organized Regiment, or SCCOR. There was booing and there was yelling and there were some heated questions about global warming as well as health care; unlike most of his more strident GOP colleagues, Castle had as of this date still left the door open to working with Democrats on compromise legislation. But most of what was said that morning would have been lost to history had it not been for YouTube.com, the video-sharing Web site that did not even exist before 2004.

It was eleven full days after the meeting that the short video—two minutes and fifty-five seconds, to be exact—went up on YouTube. It was uploaded by a brand-new, pseudonymous user named William-DawesinDE (inspired, obviously, by the 1775 American revolutionary who rode on the same night as Paul Revere). Entitled "Mike Castle on Barack H. Obama's birthcertificate," the video hit the trifecta over the dozen or so days that followed. The biggest break came when it received a coveted link on the ultra-popular and conservative-leaning Web aggregator the Drudge Report, which mainstream news junkies have watched like ravenous hawks ever since the Monica Lewinsky scandal broke there in early 1998.

The ensuing uproar led the video-maker "Dawes" to phone in and give a radio interview on the coast-to-coast, conspiracy-minded *Alex Jones Show*, which gave the incident both publicity and credibility on the extreme far right. But it reached an even wider audience as it filtered up to the attention of the nation's top conservative talker, Rush Limbaugh, who also played the clip and said, his voice smacking of approval, "There's all kinds of stuff bubbling up out there." The video kept climbing toward the one-million-hit mark on YouTube, but that doesn't count millions more who watched it the old-fashioned way, on left-wing MSNBC shows and right-wing Fox shows and finally the big-time, *NBC Nightly News*, on July 22, 2009.

And what exactly was so newsworthy about the clip, anyway? Good question. It starts with Castle, looking all funereal in a navy-blue suit, pointing into the crowd: "This lady in red has had her hand up for some time." The "lady in red" stands up, her back completely toward the camera, auburn hair tied back. Awkwardly in her left arm, she is holding a white document in a large Glad bag and one of those little American flags that you might buy in the front of the A.C. Moore around Independence Day. "Thank you," she mutters almost inaudibly before launching into her loud, nasal introduction.

" . . . I have a birth certificate here from the United States of America saying I am an American citizen, with a seal on it . . ." She briefly turns toward the paper, as if to make certain of what she just said, then continues: " . . . signed by my doctor and a hospital administrator stating my parents, my date of birth, stating the time, the date. I wanna go back to January twentieth"—the day that Barack Obama became president, the day that changed everything—"and I wanna know why are you people ignoring his birth certificate?!" The mention of the birth certificate gets a big roar and a couple of full-throat-and-belly cheers, and the uproar only grows in volume as the woman in red picks up verbal steam.

"He is not an American citizen!!! He is a citizen of Kenya!" Hands in front of the woman in red now smack together in fervent applause. "I am here because my father fought in World War Two with the Greatest Generation in the Pacific Theater for this country, and I don't want this flag to change!

"I want my country back!"

The crowd erupts one more time. Mike Castle, keeper of the Delaware Way and the established order, leans back toward his microphone, a befuddled professor, throwing his large hands apart. "Well, I don't know what comment that that invites. If you're referring to the, the president there, he is a citizen of the United States."

Cries of "No!" fill the air, amid a crescendo of boos.

The YouTube video cuts to a later scene from the same meeting, and the woman in red's unmistakable voice: ". . . . all the men and women that died in this country from 1776 till the present time, I think we should all stand up and give the Pledge of Allegiance to that wonderful flag, for all the people that sacrificed their lives for our freedom!"

"Whoooo!"

The woman in red waves both arms over her head, like an outside linebacker who just sacked the quarterback for a twelve-yard loss. "Okay, we're going to do this," says Castle, with an air of resignation pulling down his noblesse oblige. "Do you want me to lead?"

Now there was a political double entendre.

The whole thing was a rout. Representative Mike Castle, heir to America's colonial legacy, longtime public servant, and supporter of sensible, centrist policies on issues from environmental protection to stem-cell research, had been beaten back by an angry mob that had been whipped up by an emotional and anonymous woman. Five months later, this Delaware moderate who'd initially promised to seek a bipartisan compromise to improve health care joined 176 of his fellow Republicans—out of 177—to vote against the reform bill, just as he would later vote against a new jobs bill—just another faithful and faceless servant of "The Party of No," burnishing his newly minted right-wing credentials as he now prepared his run to fill the Senate seat vacated by the new vice president, Joe Biden.

No one expected this to be the big story as the 2000s came to an end—angry mobs armed with a political myth giving strength and renewal to a beaten-down conservative movement and frightening moderates like Castle in both parties. This was predicted to be the Age of Obama and his new coalition of college-educated professionals, students, African-Americans, the nation's fast-growing population of Latinos, gays, and urban and upscale coastal suburban people that seemed in 2008 to announce itself as a New American Majority, one that would only grow more powerful in the decades to come. The Obama voters were rational, numbers-minded people—with numbers on their side, and time. The U.S. Census Bureau, after all, is forecasting that whites will become a minority in America—outnumbered by blacks, Latinos, and Asians, who voted overwhelmingly for Obama in 2008—by the year 2050. The number of Americans with at least a bachelor's degree from college—also a strong predictor of voting for Obama and other Democrats—is also continuing to rise year after year; one study found that professionals in the American electorate had soared from about 7 percent in the 1950s to roughly 25 percent today, and Obama had swept the regions where these folks were moving, even high-tech and formerly "red" zones of America like the northern Virginia suburbs and North Carolina's Research Triangle. The veteran political journalist Ron Brownstein referred to Obama voters as "the coalition of the ascendant." At the height of the liberal euphoria in the weeks right after Obama's inauguration, the top progressive demographer Ruy Teixeira looked at his trend charts and flatly proclaimed, "A new progressive America is on the rise."

But everybody seemed to be forgetting about one thing: the other 47 percent of America—the folks who did not push the button for Barack Obama in pursuit of "transforming America" on November 3, 2008, including the people—some 59,934,818, if you believe in the mathematics—who wanted to see John McCain and Sarah Palin occupy the West Wing. They were, to paraphrase the nation's top-selling conservative author, the Christian-apocalyptic Tim LaHaye, the country's new "Left Behind"—and they weren't getting the demographic memos from Ruy Teixeira.

The full backlash wasn't really 47 percent. As the first weeks of the Obama administration dragged into months, the parameters of the hard-core resistance emerged, with a figure attached that was closer to 26 percent, maybe less. These were the 26 percent of Americans, according to *Newsweek*, who still approved of George W. Bush in the waning days of his presidency; the 26 percent who in 2009 said they'd like to see Sarah Palin as Obama's successor in 2012, according to CBS;

the 26 percent who reported to Fox News they were outraged when President Obama bowed to the Japanese emperor; and the 26 percent who believed that Obama's 2008 election was not legitimate, that the much-ballyhooed antipoverty group ACORN had somehow swooped down and "stolen" the contest by recruiting new voters in the heavily black and Latino inner cities.

Indeed, race shadowed every discussion. Times had changed—this was not 1968, when an avowed segregationist like George Wallace could still run credibly for president. But experts weighed a new term—"pararacial"—for a raft of issues that made people ponder Barack Obama's blackness even as race itself was never mentioned. That included specific issues like Obama's birth certificate, but also the more general sentiment of "I want my country back"—another coded statement uttered by the woman in red in reference to the inauguration of a black president. As CNN commentator Roland Martin said about the meaning of "I want my country back" after his network aired the Castle confrontation clip: "What that means is, 'All of a sudden how is this black guy running the country?! What's going on?!'"

IN A WAY, Richard Hofstadter saw all this coming—but in another sense he did not. The groundbreaking historian of the mid–twentieth century searched for and often found the not-so-sweet spots where social and even personal psychology connect with American politics. He was already on track for a Pulitzer Prize for studying "Anti-Intellectualism in American Life" when he started taking things to the next level in the early 1960s. Hofstadter and many of his leftist friends had already felt the sting of McCarthyism for their youthful dalliances with communism, and now he watched with some alarm the rise of a new fringe right-wing movement, the John Birch Society, which had gained thousands of ultraconservative followers even as its founder, Robert Welch, called ex-president Dwight Eisenhower a possible "conscious, dedicated agent of the Communist Conspiracy."

In November 1963, Hofstadter was asked by Oxford University to deliver the Herbert Spencer Lecture, where he discussed for the first time "the paranoid style in American politics." Hofstadter's timing was remarkable; just a few days after the talk, President John F. Kennedy was assassinated in Dallas. Paranoid speculation about a murder conspiracy continues nearly a half-century later, and nine months after the assassination the GOP would begin its rightward shuffle with the nomination of its 1964 presidential candidate, Barry Goldwater, whose delegates included a handful of Birchers.

Speaking across the Atlantic that day in November 1963 (his ideas were later popularized in a 1964 *Harper's* article that became the lead essay of a book), Hofstadter suggested that conspiracy theories were as American as apple pie and older than the republic itself, a straight line from anti-Freemasons to the anti-immigrant Know-Nothings through the Ku Klux Klan and finally to the Birchers. At the same time, Hofstadter noted that "[t]he paranoid spokesman sees the fate of conspiracy in apocalyptic terms—he traffics in the birth and death of whole worlds, whole political orders, whole systems of human values. He is always manning the barricades of civilization"—but he also observed that increasingly those barricades were manned by conservatives, fearful of social change and the unraveling of order. In one chilling passage of "The Paranoid Style in American Politics," Hofstadter chronicled the rise of the 1960s conservatives with remarkable prescience of what was to come:

> But the modern right wing, as Daniel Bell has put it, feels dispossessed: America has been largely taken away from them and their kind, though they are determined to try to repossess it and to prevent the final destructive act of subversion. The old American virtues have already been eaten away by cosmopolitans and intellectuals; the old competitive capitalism has been gradually undermined by socialistic and communistic schemers; the old

national security and independence have been destroyed by trea-
sonous plots, having as their most powerful agents not merely
outsiders and foreigners as of old but major statesmen who are at
the very centers of American power. Their predecessors had discovered conspiracies; the modern radical right finds conspiracy
to be betrayal from on high.

They want their country back. *Whooo!*
The thing people forget is that Hofstadter's words were supposed to
be oddly reassuring. While some Americans were alarmed at the arrival
of the John Birch Society, the gist of Hofstadter's message in the 1960s
was that these people have always been here, and while the paranoid
style is a fascinating historical case study, the republic has never truly
been threatened by these fringe groups.

But while Hofstadter was a genius, the man—who died from leu-
kemia in 1970 when he was only fifty-four—was not clairvoyant. His
research on anti-intellectualism and paranoid politics centered largely
on fears of an urban ethic destroying small-town America, and of intellectual elitism; while those things still exist, Hofstadter did not live
to gauge the even more explosive impacts of millions of non-English-
speaking arrivals, and a president who not only did not share perceived
rural values but didn't even share middle America's skin color. What's
more, the paranoid world that Hofstadter described was by definition a
fringe, a furtive place where conspiracy theories were spread by crude
pamphlets, in back rooms.

There is a photograph from the 1960s that reminds us how the paranoid fringe used to do business in America. It shows spectacularly tail-
finned U.S.-built automobiles cruising past a stark billboard with an
American flag that reads "Save Our Republic! Impeach Earl Warren.
For Information Write P.O. Box 1337." Compare that snail-mail suggestion to today's universe of conspiracy and political intrigue that is only
a mouse click away. A half-century ago, Hofstadter's paranoid fringe

had neither the multiplier effect of the Internet—able to spread false-hoods and slurs at the speed of light—nor the big-media reinforcing mechanisms of talk radio and cable's Fox News Channel. Hofstadter's fringe was restrained by a world of three channels and trusted anchors like Walter Cronkite, where TV conveyed enormous authority.

In 1963, a town-hall confrontation with a congressman from the small state of Delaware would have been a tree falling in the American political forest. Try to imagine a John Birch Society back then with a simpatico TV network, available in living rooms coast-to-coast, entertaining frequent discussions of the communist tendencies of JFK or Ike or boosting the impeach-Earl-Warren movement—and the very notion seems absurd. But as the age of Obama dawned, the highest-rated cable TV network was the rightward-slanted Fox, where some hosts—echoed occasionally by outliers on other channels such as CNN's Lou Dobbs—spoke openly about topics like the validity of Obama's birth certificate, the theory that the Federal Emergency Management Agency (FEMA) had built camps that could detain American citizens, and claims that there were "Maoists" in the White House. They were outlandish charges equal to or beyond anything that Senator Joe McCarthy put out there in the 1950s.

What's more, the new media environment—with its own self-contained ecosystems of the political right and left—led to the flourishing of what social scientists over the last four decades have come to call "group polarization," the tendency of viewpoints and even "facts" to grow more extreme among people who are, in essence, talking only to themselves. By April 2010, a *New York Times*/CBS News poll would find that 84 percent of Tea Party supporters claimed that their beliefs "generally reflect the views of most Americans"—even though only 25 percent of all Americans said they felt that way. Exhibit A was the notion that the just-elected president was not a U.S. citizen, which didn't seem so far-fetched to people sharing their views online with so many others.

But far-fetched it was.

. . . .

BARACK HUSSEIN OBAMA was born on August 4, 1961, in Honolulu, Hawaii; his mother, S. Ann Dunham, was a student at the University of Hawaii and his father, also named Barack Obama, was a Kenyan native with a Harvard degree doing postgraduate work at the school. Their child's birth certificate in Hawaii has been validated there by state officials working for a Republican governor. Lest any of the more conspiracy-minded express suspicion of governmental record tampering, both daily newspapers in Honolulu also printed young Barack Obama's birth announcement—supplied by the local hospital—a couple of days later. The idea of an elaborate ruse to cover up a birth that took place in Kenya or anywhere else—all in order to make the dark-skinned kid of an interracial marriage, born in humble circumstances in an era when segregation was still common, legally eligible to become the president of the United States decades later—is beyond ludicrous.

So where did the "birther theory" come from? Its roots were planted in a related bogus idea from the 2008 campaign—that Obama, who joined the United Church of Christ as an adult, was really a secret Muslim. As the then Illinois senator started winning a string of Democratic primaries in the spring of that year, an email by two well-known Christian missionaries working in Kenya, Celeste and Loren Davis, circulated widely among conservative evangelical voters here in the United States. It repeated the secret Muslim claim and said the would-be forty-fourth president was bent on starting a race war, adding:

He is not an American as we know it. Please encourage your friends and associates not to be taken in by those that are promoting him. It is world wide Jihad. All our friends in Europe are very disturbed by the Muslim infiltration into their countries. By the way, his true name is Barak Hussein Muhammad Obama. Won't that sound sweet to our enemies as they swear him in on the Koran!

The email from the Davises—who've actually made even more outlandish charges in the past, including a claim that the Super Bowl was a conduit for Satanist messages—nevertheless gained enough steam that the people at PolitiFact.com, as part of their fact-checking journalism that led to a Pulitzer Prize in 2009, published an article debunking the specific claim that Obama's real name is "Barak Hussein Muhammad Obama." But that same article also noted that the Obama campaign had not yet released a birth certificate, and that—under Hawaii law—journalists could not obtain it directly. On June 9, 2008, a conservative activist and journalist named Jim Geraghty, writing for *National Review Online*, noted this passage in a short posting that said Obama could "debunk a bunch of [rumors] with a simple step: Could they release a copy of his birth certificate?"

The Geraghty article—read with a year and a half of hindsight—does not come off as unreasonable: after all, Obama's documentation had indeed not been released at that time, and the conservative journalist notes the improbability of the candidate having been born outside of the United States, the one serious issue since the Constitution requires that the president be a natural-born U.S. citizen. Even Geraghty noted that scenario "would require everyone in his family to lie about this in every interview and discussion with those outside the family since young Obama appeared on the scene."

Yet in a matter of weeks, millions of Americans would come to believe exactly that—even with the online publication of Obama's certification papers just three days after the first Geraghty article. Various hucksters appeared on the scene. They included Philip Berg, a former prosecutor from Pennsylvania who had become a 9/11 conspiracy buff but now gravitated toward theories about Obama and filed an unsuccessful lawsuit seeking to prevent his election, and Andy Martin, a politician—if you can call him that—who launched his career back in 1986 running for Congress with a committee officially titled "The Anthony R. Martin-Trigona Congressional Campaign to Exterminate Jew Power in America." Incredibly, Martin—who like Berg whipsawed between seemingly conflicting conspiracies, having run a 2000 campaign commercial in Connecticut about George W. Bush and cocaine use—and Berg were able to receive valuable face time on national cable powerhouses like CNN, in reports that may have intended to tamp down the rumors yet clearly fueled them. A week before the election, Martin went back on CNN—"America's most trusted name in news"—with a new outlandish claim, that Obama's real father was not the Kenyan academic Barack Obama Sr. but a leftist black journalist named Frank Marshall Davis.

This was typical of the ever-shifting goalpost on the Obama birth rumors. There were claims that the future president's stepgrandmother, Kenyan Sarah Obama, had said in a taped interview that she had been present for the birth, as the Berg-promoted tape omitted her later insistence that Barack Obama was born in Hawaii, and that Obama couldn't be a citizen because he'd traveled to Pakistan in 1981 and that wasn't possible with a U.S. passport (short debunking: it was possible). Some documents that purported to disprove Obama's U.S. citizenship—and that were about as valid as a $3 bill—began to appear. Most famously, Southern California dentist-and-real-estate-agent-turned-attorney Orly Taitz, the bleach-blond, Zsa Zsa Gabor talk-alike and self-appointed leader of the "birther" movement, claimed to have uncovered the Holy Grail, a Kenya-issued 1961 Obama birth certificate. Never mind that it purported to be from the "Republic of Kenya" when the African land was still under British rule, or that its city of issue, Mombasa, was actually part of Zanzibar at that time, or—most importantly—that Internet sleuths using Google learned in a matter of hours that this was just an altered version of a 1959 Australian birth certificate that was available on the Web.

And yet, weeks after Obama became president, the seemingly trashed theories were echoed by high-ranking elected officials. U.S. Senator Richard Shelby, a former Democratic good ol' boy turned Republican and ranking member of the Senate Intelligence Committee, was asked about the birth certificate at a town meeting of his Alabama constituents and replied, "Well his father was Kenyan and they said he was born in Hawaii, but I haven't seen any birth certificate." In the House, a newly elected Republican from Florida, Bill Posey, gained at least ten GOP co-sponsors for legislation that would require any White House hopeful to produce a birth certificate and supporting documentation; he claimed it wasn't a direct assault on Obama but to "prevent something like this [controversy] from happening in the future." By September 2009, a Public Policy Polling survey found that 23 percent of Americans did not believe that Obama is a U.S. citizen, while another 18 percent were not sure; those two categories of doubt included nearly two-thirds of all Republicans.

Now, one could look at all this and ask . . . so what? Obama was now ensconced in the White House, and every thinly documented lawsuit by the birthers had been unceremoniously tossed out of court so far. But a shared belief in the invalidity of Obama's citizenship and indeed his presidency had a certain power for millions that defied reason or logic. It was about legitimacy—if Obama himself was illegitimate, then so was everything he stood for, and therefore they had to unite against him and challenge everything. It was a shared article of faith that helped to recruit new members to a movement making itself felt in other, very concrete ways—such as the debate over national health care.

What exactly was it about the psychology of the birther movement that gave it this political power? Some academics struggled to give it names like "implicit social cognition"—that's what writer Steve Mirsky called it in *Scientific American*, describing it as the way that our past experiences and our stereotypes affect our judgments. Here, that would be our past experience of forty-three straight presidents with white skin. However, some observers said that these fancy academic terms for the paranoid opposition to Obama were just highfalutin words for old-fashioned, all-American racism. J. Richard Cohen, president of the hate-group-tracking Southern Poverty Law Center, wrote to his supporters that "[t]his conspiracy theory was concocted by an anti-Semite"—referring to Andy Martin—"and circulated by racist extremists who cannot accept the fact that a black man has been elected president."

That's a simple explanation, and one that was no doubt true for some of the foot soldiers in this uprising against Barack Obama. But the racist tag is also a bit simplistic. While the rise of the conservative movement in America was initially rooted in deep discomfort with the increased empowerment of blacks—and, later, of Spanish-speaking immigrants—during the glory days of this movement's iconic figure, Ronald Reagan, this reactionary right wing had also acquired a messianic streak because of its arm-in-arm linkage with a new era of Christian fundamentalism. Together, the movement's followers truly believed that a conservative revolution had saved America from the godless, hedonistic, and socialist rule of 1960s hippies and fellow travelers.

Time proved the God-granted permanence of the conservative counterrevolution to be a myth. In reality, America was growing more diverse; more liberal, especially on social issues like gay rights; and less religious. Reagan was not the beginning of something but the end of something: between January 20, 1989, the day that the Gipper retreated to the hills of west Los Angeles, and the present, the GOP has won a plurality of popular votes for president exactly one time, in 2004, when the commander of two wars, with a terror-obsessed citizenry, won reelection with 51 percent of the vote. To modern conservatives, the elevation of a Democrat who was both black and a product of the nation's most elite law school at Harvard was not just a political event; it represented the destruction of their elaborate if cheaply constructed conservative temple of belief. The only answer that made any sense to the true believers was total denial.

But frankly, this new cottage industry of pop-psychoanalyzing—from a safe distance—the birthers or their cousins the Tea Partiers seemed like a hollow exercise. The best way to understand precisely what was making them so angry was to go out and ask them.

YOU WEREN'T THE only one trying to track down Delaware's woman in red. There was a time back in the summer of 2009 when a lot of people were on her trail—even the folks from TV's *Inside Edition*, arguably the keepers of America's fifteen-minute egg timer of fame.

Surely somebody else in that room that day knew the identity of the auburn-haired oracle. And after a few days, clues did begin to emerge. That nasal tone—someone online compared it to the intentionally annoying comedian Bobcat Goldthwait—of "I want my country back" was indeed familiar to some of the talkers and listeners of the locally popular Voice of Delmarva, radio station WGMD. It was the voice of a woman who called there all the time, or at least until they had to shut her down.

Her name was Eileen—but people at the station called her "Crazy Eileen."

Crazy? According to the folks at WGMD, conservative politics wasn't even Eileen's favorite topic, although she did opine on occasion that Obama was "the Antichrist" or that the would-be forty-fourth president would be assassinated before taking office and that Hillary Clinton would somehow assume the position, regardless of what the Constitution actually says about presidential succession. She was primarily a psychic; a WGMD talk-show host, Jared Morris, posted his own videos on YouTube about Eileen, including a call from New Year's Day of 2009 in which she predicted "alien contact in the southwestern United States in October of this year" and that in the year ahead "[t]here will be peace among men and negativity will end"—a bit ironic in the wake of the Mike Castle moment. That was actually an example of relative clarity—at other times Eileen would just make prank calls consisting of fart noises (WGMD was too small to have producers who screened the calls, and it lost its caller ID after a lightning strike) or fax angry threats to the station when the hosts wouldn't pick up the phone. She was banned from WGMD, and host Morris actually had an on-air "intervention" for Eileen less than two weeks before the infamous showdown in Georgetown.

Morris also spoke of their one in-person meeting, before all the angry faxes and the fart calls, when he asked Eileen to come in as an in-studio psychic; he said he knew instantly he'd made a huge mistake. Said Morris: "I saw there in this person's eyes, a madness." After he had posted his YouTube response to Eileen, the trail had gone cold. Yet you still remained determined to find her.

You thought it would be easy—starting late that summer by poking around this grassroots group with the odd name, the Sussex County Community Organized Regiment, or SCCOR. From what you could gather, SCCOR was a group eager to adopt all the facile trappings of an armed revolt against the government—as long as it didn't do anything that might actually get it into trouble. It was a "regiment" whose logo was formed by a couple of old-fashioned muskets over the words "The Second Amendment isn't a suggestion. It's a right!!"

But it was clear this Sussex County Regiment wasn't a militia off shooting guns out in the woods. Instead it was having lots of talky meetings about subjects like how $7.5 million in Obama-backed stimulus dollars to redo the boardwalk down on Rehoboth Beach could be the Jenga block that caused this whole wobbly republic to collapse. Its members were also growing a large victory garden down in Georgetown—tomatoes, corn, potatoes, you name it. One of the SCCOR members told a local paper, "This is a hedge against uncertain times and the high price of food. We want to learn to be self-sufficient."

Another SCCOR member who was at the Georgetown seniors' center that night was Eric Bodenweiser, identified as the regiment chaplain, who had also told the newspapers that the real purpose of the group with the rifle logo and the mildly scary name was to recruit "good, conservative, godly people" to run for office and "get the bad people out and get the good people in."

Bodenweiser was where you find most twenty-first-century American revolutionaries—on Facebook—and so after an exchange of emails you are on the phone with a gentle-speaking, part-time do-it-yourself Christian minister who had not one but two pieces of bad news. First, he didn't really know much more about Eileen other than what he'd read in the paper. And second, SCCOR was already out of commission, just six months after it had formed. It had been absorbed by the new alpha Obama-backlash group in Delaware—the Delaware 9-12

Patriots, which had behind it both the national cachet of right-wing icon Glenn Beck and the blessing of the main political voice on local talk radio, WGMD's Bill Colley.

The Regiment had launched almost spontaneously back in the winter—when a south Delaware UPS driver named Chuck had called up Colley's show to voice his frustration over the new president and then asked, in so many words, "Isn't there something we can do about this?" Soon there were more than two hundred people at its meetings— a testament largely to the power of Colley's show and the megaphone of talk radio. But as with a lot of Tea Party groups that sprouted across America, there was also acrimony and infighting. The Regiment fell apart when Colley abruptly quit after Bodenweiser insisted on start-ing a SCCOR meeting with the Lord's Prayer, and not the version that Colley knew from his Catholic upbringing. Colley later blogged that he thought people were joining SCCOR "out of concerns they no longer had a voice in affairs of state" but that apparently "[y]ou're eligible for these concerns unless you happen to be a Catholic, Mormon or Jew."

Other right-wing bloggers and local politics-watchers didn't know Eileen, either. The only hope for finding her identity was under the 420-foot tower in the middle of a barren cornfield, the political right field of dreams in the Delmarva Peninsula, WGMD. This radio station with so much local political clout could not be any more physically anonymous, based in a tiny white ranch house on a rural road, miles from its ritzy mailing address in Rehoboth Beach. The man behind the curtain there is the stocky, avuncular, and mild-mannered Bill Colley.

For every Rush Limbaugh or Glenn Beck, there are hundreds of Bill Colleys dotting the radio-towered cornfields of America, and collec-tively, under the radar, they have as much influence, maybe more. These are guys who bounced around a string of stations, lacking the snark power that made a national superstar out of a Limbaugh or a Michael Savage but with the patience to deal with the latest small-town school-board outrage and the variety of not-ready-for-prime-time callers, the "Crazy Eileens" of a Conservative Talk Nation. Frankly, it's hard to know whether the political backlash in southern Delaware ever could have come together without Colley—who'd started at WGMD in 2008—to connect, cajole, and hype, to take the isolated fearful electrons of angry and frustrated callers and send out a warm security blanket to anyone in range of that 420-foot tower—the frustrated guy in the UPS truck, the part-time preacher tilling the survival-oriented victory garden, and the shut-in psychic. It was this self-reinforcing community of the airwaves that convinced the people who thought Barack Hussein Obama was a citizen of Kenya hell-bent on a socialist one-world government and "changing the flag" that they were not alone, and if they were not alone then they could not be crazy for thinking such thoughts—even if Colley did not believe it all himself. (On July 22, 2009, when the "Eileen" video went viral, Colley said via Twitter: "I know this makes me sound an egoist. The Obama birth certificate spat unfolding can be traced to me and I don't doubt he was born in USA.")

It was Colley who launched and then killed the SCCOR, and it was Colley who'd stoked the fires of the big angry mob that confronted the genteel great-great-great-great-great grandson of Benjamin Franklin at the CHEER Center. For weeks, Colley had aroused radio ire toward the GOP moderate and his betrayal of Delaware conservatives by voting for Obama's global warming legislation. The day before, he had written on his Twitter account: "Cap&Trade Castle in Georgetown at Cheer Tuesday. Can we get a time and a 'greeting' committee?" That he did.

Colley hardly seems the vanguard of a revolution. He is forty-seven years old, a soft man with square wire-rimmed glasses topped by a neat salt-and-pepper buzz cut, and on this day he is wearing a plaid button-down shirt and an incongruously liberal-looking World Wildlife Foundation tie emblazoned with a gray wolf. He is working without a net under the old-fashioned setup inside the WGMD studio where he greets you—there is no engineer to work the dials for him, no one to screen the next call that could just as easily be about anthropogenic global warming as it could be a fart noise. He is armed only with an ever-open laptop computer, a stack of news clippings with talking points under-lined in yellow marker, and a copy of *The Catholic Bible* with a slightly tattered cover.

There was a time when Bill Colley was a progressive. His dad in rural western New York was a Democrat—a union guy in an auto plant, liberal on economics but conservative on all the social change going on as the son was growing up in the late 1960s and the '70s. Bill Colley went off to college and one-upped his old man, marching against apart-heid in South Africa and weighing a job offer in New York from the progressive writer and activist Michael Harrington. Instead, he went with journalism and changed his party ID to independent—a radio guy pounding the snowplowed sidewalks of Syracuse and covering house fires in the frigid air for WSYR, AM 570, the local news-talk leader ("won a stack of hardware," he says). But Colley apparently wasn't winning awards for the not-for-broadcast side of life; deeply troubled, in 1996 he went to a priest friend who convinced him to redouble his commitment to Catholicism—"I jumped back in with both feet," he says, adding, "I used to be in a tavern four or five nights a week—now it's been four or five nights in the last two years."

It is a familiar story. For so many conservatives, especially the zeal-ous converts like Colley, it is hard to say how much of their right turn on life's road map was the result of a change in political beliefs and how much of it was really seeking clarity and light in a dark night of the soul, fighting demons that don't appear on CNN but instead at the bottom of a bottle or the top of a stocking. Even Colley acknowledges that right-wing talk radio can have simplistic answers for complex prob-lems—which he likens to guys he remembers from his tavern days who sat at the end of the bar and who when the news came on pronounced, "Criminals? Hang 'em! Terrorists? Hang 'em!"

But Colley—in looking for answers, just like his listeners—gravi-tated to where they were being offered. There was his ever-present *Catholic Bible*—and then came 9/11. "That was an eye opener," he says. More and more, he found himself daydreaming about the small-town parades that his dad used to take him to in the hollows of western New York, with soldiers marching and old men saluting. "Maybe America wasn't the way we remember it as—sure there were problems, there was Jim Crow," Colley tells you. "But I think America was better. I think that we're missing something."

So Colley wants his country back, too. But he is at heart—like a Beck or a Limbaugh—just a radio guy, and everything, including the political stuff, flows from that, not the other way around. When Syracuse AM rival WFBL amped up to five thousand watts at the start of 2004 and offered Colley a prime-time talk gig, he jumped at the chance, and promised he was going to inform and entertain, telling the local newspaper that "[a] lot of talk radio these days is about shouting . . . I can't imagine doing that." But in the months that followed, he learned that his conservative listeners got worked up when he dared to even interview liberal guests, that they instead wanted a kind of "water cooler" of like-minded ideas and people; soon, Colley was meeting with as many as 150 of them in an old VFW hall in a group that called itself the Patriot League of Central New York.

So organizing the locals was a skill he brought down to Delmarva in the fall of 2007 when he was fired from WFBL. He started the same shtick that had worked for a time up in Syracuse—he encouraged the local "patriots" to meet up, first as a "regiment," until they were swamped by the blue-eyed tsunami of TV-and-radio's Glenn Beck and his so-called 9-12 movement. Indeed, Colley himself was there at the door to greet Mike Castle that fateful morning at the CHEER Center in Georgetown, carrying a global-warming–inspired sign that read "China Thanks Mike Castle."

WHICH BRINGS YOU back to the trail, back to Eileen. Through Bill Colley, you learned a little bit about Eileen—most notably her full name, even if you decided that maybe it's not such a great idea to publish it; let's just call her Eileen M. Eileen M. was fifty-four years old when "the incident" happened, with roots back in Philadelphia and the working-class suburbs immediately north in Bucks County. You were told she'd moved fairly recently to Millsboro at the southern end of Delaware right near the Maryland border, now something of a retiree hotbed, to take care of her ailing eighty-something mother. Confronting middle age in a new and strange town so far from all the red highways, Eileen M. had made friends with the local people who would listen to her . . . a radio station. You also learned that she hadn't completely disappeared since that fateful summer day, that she had taken to calling WGMD again, though maybe not as much as before, just once or twice a week—but she wasn't talking about Castle.

Eileen M.'s America—the one that she so emotionally wanted to take back—is Millsboro, Delaware, a town of just 2,300 souls at the marshy mouth of the Indian River, where the economy has bounced around from grist mills to making holly wreaths to the big cash-register factory for NCR that abruptly shuttered, only to become a nexus of lower-paying jobs at a bank call center for First Omni Bank, which became Allfirst Financial Center, which in 2003 became M&T Bank, constantly shedding jobs all along the way.

Eileen M.'s home is in a small, looping subdivision behind an unsightly boat store with big sea cruisers covered in blue tarps. These are factory-built homes, the kind you imagine John Mellencamp was singing about in "Little Pink Houses," except the pastels are much duller, faded, sea-shanty gray and colonial-pewter faint blue. Eileen M.'s house is marked on a December afternoon by its clutter, things Christmas-related and not—a row of candy canes here, a partially deflated Santa there, a tiny grotto with a Virgin Mary statue in the center of it all, and the ultimate symbol of belief-against-all-odds, a Philadelphia Eagles flag, all flopped up and whipped around by incessant sea breezes. There is a big pickup truck in the driveway and a sloped, wheelchair-ready ramp up to the front door.

A fiftyish man, with a thick beard and a trucker-type cap reading "Lower, Slower Delaware" with a cartoon turtle, opens the door.

Awkwardly, you begin a rambling explanation of how you came to this particular spot in America when Eileen appears on the perimeter, in sight but staying far from the door. Her auburn hair is up, and her skin is milky pale—in a baggy college sweatshirt and jeans she looks younger than you perceived from the YouTube video, but frail, drained of energy as well as color. It is as if the raw anger of her national Cassandra moment had sapped her of all strength.

You tell Eileen that this is a chance to tell the story of what her confrontation with the congressman was all about, that she hadn't offered her side of things.

"That's because I didn't want to."

The man with the beard and the Delaware cap takes a half-step closer. "She's got a lot of problems right now . . . with her health. So I don't think it would be a good idea." Eileen M. and the bearded man agree that it's okay, however, for you to leave your contact info, your phone and email address—but a phone call from the professional radio caller Eileen never comes. In the weeks after, you wonder how Eileen's difficult situation might have been helped by a national health-care system—one that would cover people who quit working to care for an elderly relative, for example. But like the rest of Eileen's story, that question would have to remain unanswered for now.

Cassandra had left the building. People like Eileen M. and her channelers Bill Colley and "WilliamDawesinDE" may have been the avatars of anger, but the new American Revolution needed more than emotional rage; it needed leaders, and a new breed of right-wing radical was rising to fill that void in the early months of Obama's presidency.

This is where Eileen's fellow Delawarean—Russ Murphy, ex-Marine, leather-jacketed biker, retired trucker, and self-styled American patriot—enters the picture.

CHAPTER TWO

The Incredible Story of How Obama Lost in 2008

Kirby & Holloway's Family Restaurant on the DuPont Highway in Dover, Delaware, seems as good a place as any to plot out a new American Revolution. It's a diner-kitsch time machine, an Eisenhower-era oasis plopped down in an endless desert of big-box stores and fast-food joints. Built in 1948, its fifty-foot-high sign is a great thing of American beauty, a trapezoidal beacon burning the word "Family" in neon pinkish-red, with a gentle arrow of flashing white dots to beckon hungry travelers—yet this faded calling card is easy to miss now, swamped as it is by the tidal waves of Lowe's, Wal-Marts, and Taco Bells that have overtaken these marshy flatlands of the Atlantic coastal plain.

It is in the shadow of this America at the dawn of the 2010s that the Kirby & Holloway sits, with no public green anymore, no Lexington and no Concord—just this diner with its $7.99 chicken-fried steak special at a neon relic shoehorned between the hacienda orange of the Home Depot and the crimson façade of the Red Roof Inn. And so instead of the hoof-beats of a Paul Revere, here now is Alex Garcia and his massive Ford 150, the one with National Rifle Association bumper stickers festooned across the back. It is here that the linebacker-sized, goateed Garcia, his commercially perky blond real-estate-agent wife, Theresa, and the thin, ruddy-faced Russ Murphy have agreed to meet you. Murphy is the founder and executive director of the Delaware 9-12 Patriots and thus the de facto local commander of a radical right-wing movement.

The patriots say they are rushed, because their next appointed round awaits them—a biweekly confab with the other 9-12 Patriots of surrounding Kent County, Delaware. There, they will discuss their plans to stop Obama's health-care bill and to prevent the teaching of global warming in schools and also hear from a conservative pundit who wants to challenge Mike Castle for the open U.S. Senate seat from Castle's right flank.

But now before the plentiful ovals of spaghetti and meatballs and gravy-smothered meatloaf have even appeared, the Garcias and Murphy are patiently explaining to you something remarkable, a sacred, core belief that seems to drive their newfound political awakening: that Barack Obama didn't actually win the presidential election of 2008.

"I think people voted for him just because he was black—that's my opinion," says Murphy. "Because they thought they were making history." Murphy is sixty-five years old, still rolling full throttle with no brakes on a long, strange odyssey that has taken him from the crowded working-class baby-boomer-created suburbs just south of Philadelphia to the jungles of Vietnam to working security at a nuclear-power plant to driving a long-haul rig, with unscheduled pit stops in taverns and AA meetings and divorce court. There is an ever-present intensity in his voice—searing, occasionally offering some dark hints of the violence he has seen before and says he hopes to avoid now. His words carry a heightened sense of melodrama, regardless of whether he's invoking the spirit of the Founding Fathers or his adventures driving a Jeep near the front lines over in 'Nam—or simply ordering the veal parm special. Murphy gives off the vibe of a wild-eyed Irish poet from this so-called Lower, Slower Delaware—dark, piercing eyes set high on craggy and perpetually ruddy cheeks, attired in his biker vest with the ever-present metal Vietnam Veteran clip.

This is when Theresa Garcia, the organizational force of the 9-12

Patriots of Delaware, seller of houses by day and T-shirt paraphernalia for the revolution by night, who seems a slightly sunnier foil to the hard-edged Murphy, pipes up. "He did not win the popular vote," she says, an air of defiance in her voice. "He won the electoral vote. If you took into account the popular vote, he lost by a landslide."

There is a brief moment of silence. You don't have the numbers at your immediate disposal, but you know for a fact that Barack Obama defeated the Republican candidate, John McCain, on November 3, 2008—in fact, whupped him from Kauai to Key West. You could look it up, which you later do: the final tally was 69,456,897 for the Illinois Democrat and 59,934,814 for the Republican from Arizona. You ask them how their theory—that Obama didn't win the popular vote—is even possible.

So Alex Garcia, the big-time gun enthusiast, tries to explain to you how Obama really lost the election in a landslide. "California has twenty-seven electoral votes"—actually, it has fifty-five—"where Delaware only has three," Garcia begins, launching into a lecture on how Obama could get more electoral votes even as McCain was winning more states, which indeed could technically happen. Except that it did not in 2008, when Obama won twenty-eight states (and the District of Columbia) while McCain won only twenty-two. But there was no stopping Alex Garcia now. He was rolling.

"Statewise, if you look at the maps. . . . Statewise, how they went . . . McCain actually won more states, more ground, more people than Obama did," Garcia tells you. "He [Obama] just had more electoral votes." Here, Garcia actually gets one out of three right, since McCain actually did win more land—2,310,315 square miles, much of it in the nation's most sparsely populated turf from the majestic mountaintops of Sarah Palin's Alaska to the barren bend of the Rio Grande down in Texas, while Obama won just 1,483,702 square miles, much of that in the densely populated cities and suburbs where the majority of citizens in this democratic republic actually live and vote.

But this urban nature of Obama's support was exactly the point that the Garcias and Russ Murphy were awkwardly trying to make. When Alex Garcia has finished his monologue about the big states and the small states, you sheepishly note—more of a question than a statement, really—that Obama and his native-son running mate Joe Biden actually carried Delaware, did they not? (By a landslide margin of more than 100,000 votes, in fact.)

"What it is," said Alex Garcia, " . . . is Wilmington."

"Wilmington!" chimes his wife, Theresa.

Wilmington, with 72,826 people, an hour north of your diner booth, is the largest city in Delaware by far—capital of the American credit-card industry and also plagued by more violent criminal enterprises, a crowded world apart from the marshy spaces of lower Delaware. The city of Wilmington is roughly 10 percent Latino and about 35 percent black; in 2008, Obama carried New Castle County—Wilmington and its surrounding suburbs—by a two-to-one margin while McCain narrowly won the rest of the state, including small towns that his running mate Sarah Palin once called "the pro-America parts of the country."

Wilmington?

"They get a lot of influence from New Jersey and New York because a lot of the New York and New Jersey people live in Wilmington, and that's a big influence," Alex is saying, "and they're really into the welfare state—it's a handout area up there. When you start coming down below the [Delaware] Canal into Kent County and Sussex County, it's a total different way they voted."

A long silence settles in over the table. Plates clink. Toddlers babble in the background, as soft rock descends from a speaker overhead. The big platters of spaghetti and meatloaf arrive, and the once talkative Murphy is bent over his mound of pasta, handing off to the Garcias the task of further explaining McCain's glorious 2008 victory.

But, you finally stutter, should votes from Wilmington actually count less?

"There's more of them," Theresa says.

"It's population," adds Alex.

"They're in the big cities," says Theresa. "That's what the problem is."

So are you saying that voters from Wilmington aren't the real America?

"They represent the welfare America, the handout America—what do they call it, the nanny state, everybody is taken care of," explains Alex. "When you get into the big areas like that, everybody is expecting their free handout . . . You have a lot more of the . . . how would I put it . . . a lot more of the welfare recipients, stuff like that."

There is a famous and somewhat apocryphal anecdote about the *New Yorker* film critic Pauline Kael saying from her liberal bastion in Manhattan that Richard Nixon could not have won the 1972 election because every single person she knew voted for George McGovern. Here is the flip side: that looking out on the "pro-America" horizon from the Kirby & Holloway, it is impossible to imagine that someone like Barack Hussein Obama could have won a presidential election—or even that he is a United States citizen. These things are the pillars of a shared faith.

You initially had been told to seek out Russ Murphy—the de facto Delaware leader of the right-wing revolution, in alliance nationally with the so-called Tea Party—here in the fall of 2009 when you were first looking for Eileen M. Now Murphy had agreed to open up his 9-12 Patriots in his small and quirky but oddly representative state—and to provide a window into how the paranoid style was infusing practical politics. Their uprising was something the likes of which America had never seen before—whiter, older, and more affluent, yet angrier than anyone could have expected, whipsawed into rebellion not by the hormonally raised expectations of youth but instead by a nonstop sedentary couch-potato bombardment of unfiltered fear. Eileen M. had merely voiced out loud—unfiltered, with raw emotional directness—the kind of wild things that Russ, Alex, Theresa, and the rest of the Tea Party movement were thinking as they sought respectability in lobbying state lawmakers and rallying against health-care reform.

The proof came in conversations like this one—with their search for a Pyrrhic victory, their contention that Obama's win couldn't be legit because it sprang instead from the "handout areas" like Wilmington, that the real America would be killed by majority rule as opposed to the Constitution-embodied values that their movement embraced. The more that you talked to people like Theresa Garcia, the clearer it became that the deep-seated psychological roots of this quest to deny the legitimacy of the forty-fourth president arose from a first vague and then growing discomfort that a man like Barack Hussein Obama had the audacity to put himself forward as the face of their America.

"The first time I heard Obama speak, I felt very, very uncomfortable," Theresa Garcia tells you, and then she pauses a bit, careful to think about how she wants to elaborate on this: "And I didn't like what I was hearing. I mean, he wasn't giving us any clear idea other than that he was going to change everything. It was very, very concerning. He was just being, I don't know, what's the word?—he wasn't giving us anything, any information, and that was scary to me."

Russ Murphy chimes in to add that Obama was "being disingenuous" when he talked to American voters during the 2008 campaign. But for the older Murphy, what that means is the feeling that Obama—because of his Chicago acquaintance with the former 1960s bomb-making radical William Ayers and some of his other reported friendships—is heir to a direct line from the hippies who he insists abused him after his return from Vietnam.

"All the people that they turned everybody against us . . . was all the people that Obama was associated with, and it doesn't take a rocket scientist to put two and two together," Murphy says in his slow-burn style. "He is not American."

Literally?

"I believe that literally . . . not American."

Theresa Garcia mutters in the background, "Useless."

"Let me put it this way, he's the commander-in-chief of our armed forces, he's the person that makes the decision to send our people into war," Murphy explains. "A man of honor, sending our people to their death, an unknown future, would at least have the integrity to present all of his documentation to prove that he is without a doubt eligible to be the commander-in-chief."

ALL THROUGHOUT THE tumultuous first year of the Obama presidency, Americans of every political stripe were asking questions. Just who were these 9-12ers, these Tea Partiers, these complete unknowns like Russ Murphy or Theresa Garcia who appeared from nowhere with their signs and their slogans, on the Capitol Mall or sometimes at your shopping mall? Where did they come from? And why are they so angry?

In some ways, the Delaware 9-12 Patriots looked pretty tame compared to the news reports that were filtering in from some of the far-flung regions of the country, such as the big blue libertarian skies of the Far West. Consider the 350 Tea Party activists and members of a new outfit called the Second Amendment Task Force who gathered on the first Saturday of 2010 along the main drag in Alamogordo, New Mexico, to wave their handguns and semi-automatics in the air—perfectly legal in New Mexico—at passing cars in a show of force against a bogus but popular notion that the Obama administration had a plan for confiscating the guns of regular Americans. One of the New Mexico protestors was Korean War veteran Jim Kizer, who was packing a .444 Marlin and a holstered .41 Smith and Wesson Magnum and told the local newspaper, "I've fought Communists all my life, and now our government is being taken over by them. That's why I'm here." (Indeed, it was hard to disagree with the editor of another local paper who wrote, "Nothing will 'put a positive light on gun ownership' quite like inviting every yahoo with a weapon in southern New Mexico to gather at the busiest intersection in Alamogordo and wave their firearms at the passing traffic.")

Meanwhile, some thousand miles due north in Montana, a fast-growing outfit in rural Ravalli County with the innocuous-enough-sounding name of Celebrating Conservatism presented a list of demands to local officials in early 2010 that instructed them to create mandatory militia service in the county and prevent forced inoculations as well as any attempts at enforcement of federal gun laws. The list of demands stated that federal employees could not approach citizens without written permission from the county sheriff and that 2010 federal census takers be allowed to ask only about the number of people in each home. No local pols actually signed on, but by the spring of 2010 the group had reportedly swelled to nearly one thousand supporters.

You'd think such revolutionary events might have made national news. But by 2010 the arrival of these angry gatherings—even those armed to the teeth like the one in New Mexico—didn't feel so unusual anymore. It seemed hard to believe that it was only April 2009 when America and the world got its first glimpse of this Tea Party Patriot-9-12 Regiment movement—a spontaneous combustion less than three months after Obama was inaugurated.

The rise of the Tea Party movement depended on three factors. The first and the most important was genuine anger and panic by rank-and-file conservatives who were not only deeply frustrated by the 2008 outcome but suddenly saw a world in which—thanks to a growing electoral base that did not think or look like them—their Reaganist conservative philosophy might be shut out of power for good. They were mad at big government, to be sure. But quite frankly you didn't see gun-holstered fifty-five-year-old white dudes taking to the streets during the years of Bush 43—even as that president created massive debt through two wars, impractical tax cuts for the rich, and even expanded spending on federal "handout" programs like Medicare. What the base of the Tea Party movement really feared most was not a random big government but a particular big government that was run by The Others, the inhabitants of that vast crumbling "welfare state" that was a world apart from their familiar well-manicured landscape of Lowe's and Red Roof Inns.

Still, in an earlier century such anger would likely have had a slow fuse. Enter the second element: the electronic media. That included not just the usual suspects—the Glenn Becks and the Rush Limbaughs whipping up fury and creating shared daily talking points—but also local talk stations just like Delaware's WGMD, as well as the ability of the Web and now social networking sites such as Facebook and Twitter to connect these like-minded Obama naysayers and quickly bring them together, without actual journalists intervening to filter out untrue information like the canard about the president's birth certificate.

Thirdly, there were the ever-circling capitalists—the policy pushers who saw a new grassroots movement as a back-door way to revive the big-business agenda that had won so many victories using the old-school techniques from the 1980s right through the Bush 43 era, quickly joined by the pure-profit hucksters who realized that in the Tea Party they were working with a different kind of revolutionary—consumerist freedom fighters who, if they hadn't lost their jobs yet, still had some disposable cash in the bank. As the Tea Party movement grew, there were some days it was hard to tell the phony profiteers and the true prophets of this revolution apart from each other.

The origins of the Tea Party are instructive. The popular right-wing blogger Michelle Malkin claims it all came together just twenty-six days after Obama's inauguration when "a young conservative mom who blogs"—a woman named Keli Carender who writes in Seattle under the handle "Liberty Belle"—started calling in to local talk radio shows as well as working the Web; her goal was to drum up just one hundred people to hit the streets against the $787 billion economic stimulus plan that was backed by Obama and the Democrats in Congress. During the Obama transition, many economists, most Democrats, and even some moderate Republicans saw such an aid package as a logical last line of defense against the brutal recession turning into America's second Great Depression, an echo of the kind of successful emergency spending measures that Franklin Roosevelt undertook in the 1930s.

Notably, the stimulus debate also came just a couple of months after a nearly similar dollar amount, $700 billion, had bailed out banks where multimillionaire CEOs and traders had made ridiculous bets on housing-related securities; when the bank bailout happened—proposed by President George W. Bush and backed by John McCain and Sarah Palin as well as Barack Obama—some conservatives did get mad enough about it to call talk radio, rant, and then hang up and go back to their lives. Now, when the Democrats tried to spend a similar amount not to rescue lifestyles of the rich and famous but to pay for working-class jobs pouring concrete on bridges and keeping local cops walking the beat, they called it "generational theft" and took to the barricades.

And the big money took notice right away. Just two days after "Liberty Belle" and her impromptu Seattle rally, Americans for Prosperity, a lobbying group started by the second-richest man in all of New York City, the oil-and-gas billionaire David Koch, threw its clout and some of its cash behind the new grassroots movement. This was not exactly a new tactic; in fact, the billionaire's equally wealthy father, Fred Koch, had been one of the founders of the John Birch Society in the late 1950s. Still, the mainstream media narrative was that after the financial crisis of 2008, the public would be most angry toward the departed Bush administration and rich people like Koch and his Wall Street neighbors. That narrative was wrong, as usual. Instead, resistance flowed down the well-worn path first trod during the Nixon years, with rage moving toward those lower on the economic ladder rather than the people above them.

On February 19, 2009, a CNBC futures-trading-floor correspondent named Rick Santelli, who'd also not said a peep about the CEO-benefitting bank bailout, ranted on live TV for several minutes about an Obama-backed plan to help those devastated by housing foreclosures, turning to a swelling mob of traders behind him on camera and asking, "How many of you people want to pay for your neighbor's mortgage that has an extra bathroom and can't pay their bills?" Santelli's plaintive cry was like a pitch-perfect dog whistle to the brand of resentment felt by the nation's white working class toward "the handout areas." On this winter's day, Santelli then turned to the in-studio hosts and announced, "We're thinking of having a Chicago Tea Party in July. All you capitalists that want to show up to Lake Michigan, I'm gonna start organizing."

The rest, as they say, is history.

But history of . . . what? At first it was clear to anyone paying attention only what the Tea Party movement opposed—anything that involved government spending and anything that involved Barack Obama, and not necessarily in that order. There was nothing about what it was for. When the first large-scale Tea Parties were held on April 15, 2009, or Tax Day, many of the marchers adopted the mantra of the 1760s and decried "taxation without representation," a bizarre claim considering that 130 million Americans had voted democratically for Obama and the 111th Congress just weeks earlier. A liberal columnist, Dan Gerstein, spoke for a relatively silent majority (indeed, he noted that the number of Americans believing they pay the right amount of taxes was the highest since the mid–Eisenhower administration) in early 2009 when he wrote dismissively that the initial Tea Parties "are not the stirrings of a broad movement. They're just a mishmash of misunderstandings of a shrinking conservative minority—about the import of the last election, the mood of the country now and our economic and budgetary needs going forward."

Gerstein, and those who expressed similar views right after Obama's inauguration, badly underestimated both the intensity of the right-wing anger and the new media environment in which the conservative-oriented Fox News Channel, wall-to-wall right-wing talk radio, the blogosphere, and social networking could amplify their message to a level where the mainstream media would re-report it and make it the loudest voice in the room, "shrinking minority" or not.

Even the ugly extremism at the new edges of the old paranoid fringe didn't derail the Tea Party movement's rapid growth. At the initial Tea Party in Chicago, for example, marchers carried signs with messages such as "The American Taxpayers Are the Jews for Obama's Ovens" or a placard depicting the new president in a Nazi uniform with a Hitler mustache and swastika armbands, "The New

Face of Hitler," in what would become a commonly recurring theme in the months that followed.

Meanwhile, political vultures were already circling the angry mob, trying to channel this unanticipated surge of negative electricity into their own wall outlets. For example, an offshoot of billionaire Koch's Americans for Prosperity called FreedomWorks—also backed by the likes of multinational corporations such as Phillip Morris and Verizon as well as family members of the ultraconservative billionaire Richard Mellon Scaife, and run by GOP *über*-leader and ex-congressman Dick Armey—stepped forward to provide cash and direction, meaning that a movement supposedly rooted in anger over government bailouts of Wall Street was linked instantly with a pro-big-business lobby.

On the less-polished side of the same coin, some far-right militias or extremist groups worked to recruit new members on the fringes of these early Tea Parties—groups such as the military-and-law-enforcement-oriented Oath Keepers, claiming their allegiance was to the U.S. Constitution and not the president, or the Ohio Valley Freedom Fighters of rural Shelby County, Kentucky, an outfit that also organized "open carry" church services and held paramilitary training exercises in the woods.

Despite the newfound sway that these groups possessed, there was one man who arguably had more influence over this new movement than any other individual: Glenn Beck. The Fox News Channel host, whose TV show, which had been on CNN Headline News, serendipitously debuted on FNC exactly one day before the Obama presidency, seemed plugged into the raw emotional zeitgeist of the Tea Party. Beck's core political philosophy was hard to pin down—it seemed to be one-third "Morning Zoo" radio-libertarian nihilism of the 1980s, one-third alcohol-recovery-finding-Jesus, and one-third naked career-advancement calculation, or what many would less charitably call unvarnished hucksterism.

That may not sound like a promising formula for a political revolution or its leader, but Beck emerged as living proof of Marshall McLuhan's most famous maxim: that the media is the message; while most journalists were still drooling at Obama's inauguration over the Netroots and at how the campaign used tools like Facebook and Twitter (both not even invented until the middle of the Bush 43 presidency), Beck found an audience that was old-school, fifty-something and older, which fooled around with the Web but was most comfortable heating up dinner at 5 p.m. with the big-screen TV blaring from the living room. The *New York Times*/CBS News poll of Tea Party activists in April 2010 found that while 24 percent named the Internet as a main source of info—an impressive number—a plurality of 47 percent named TV as their main news source, and the overwhelming majority said their television information was mainly from the Fox News Channel. Most were already watching FNC when Beck arrived on the scene, but the new host had a remarkable skill for whipping up anxieties that were already heightened by the economic chaos and societal change of the moment. Of course, he then would claim he alone had the answers to these fears that he had just driven sky-high in the first place.

Appropriately, a pivotal moment in the Obama backlash came on a Friday the thirteenth—March 13, 2009, to be exact—when Beck took to the airwaves to announce a plan that even George Orwell might have found an extreme exercise in double-speak, with a feel-good label for a massive political endeavor that would instantly become a vehicle for promoting unmitigated rage toward the president and his supporters: the 9-12 Project. This is how the ambitious Fox News newcomer shamelessly cloaked his anti-Obama endeavor in the patriotic afterglow of the September 11, 2001, attacks:

> We came together. We promised ourselves that we would never forget. On September 12th, and for a short time after that, we really promised ourselves that we would focus on the things that were important—our family, our friends, the eternal principles that allowed America to become the world's beacon of freedom.

What Beck promised on the air that night was not an unfamiliar theme—the notion that while the deaths of nearly three thousand U.S. citizens in the terrorist attacks of September 11, 2001, were truly horrific, the spirit of national unity, the American flags that magnetically sprouted from so many cars and the rallying behind the president and his "bullhorn moment" in lower Manhattan and his decision to send troops on their way to Afghanistan in the weeks that followed was nonetheless a special time, especially when viewed through the prism of political discord that followed.

But here's the funny thing: the 9-12 Project never seemed to be about any of that, not from day one, when it instead emerged as an angry bullhorn that was pointed not at outside enemies but directly at, and against, the new president of the United States. As political passions boiled in those early months of Obama, the home page of Beck's 9-12 Project proclaimed, "The day after America was attacked we were not obsessed with Red States, Blue States or political parties." Yet right behind that, on message boards, Beck fans posted links to articles like "President Obama Gets Booed at AMA Speech" or a video "Wondering if we are a Christian Nation or a Muslim Nation: WATCH THIS!" On chat areas of the site, a commenter named "spec4pat" declared, "I'm ashamed that the tyranny we fight is growing on native soil," while "dsame" wrote, "Obama Is Satan I now believe it." A photo gallery of pictures of a later rally in Washington on September 12, 2009, shows an array of White House–directed anger, such as a woman with a sign reading, "YOU STOP lying, and we will stop calling you a Liar."

Free speech? Sure. Beyond that, what did this Internet-mutating rage have to do with "our family, our friends, the eternal principles that allowed America to become the world's beacon of freedom"? The answer was locked away in the inscrutable mind of Glenn Beck.

IT DIDN'T TAKE much to see Beck's thinly veiled hypocrisy, yet his muddled message resonated in living rooms across America. One of them was in a small trailer on some farmland just off Highway 1, the wide thoroughfare bisecting central Delaware, the relatively new home of this battle-tested retired Vietnam vet named Russ Murphy. He was one of the many looking for an outlet to channel his anger at what he saw happening to America—and he found it on the television that night.

"This goes back to when Glenn Beck had his infamous show of March thirteenth," Murphy says months later. "I'd been pretty well upset and depressed about the ways things were—and when I saw that, I said 'that's what we need to do.'"

Retired now for several years after a career that had included his Marine service in Vietnam, guarding the Limerick nuclear power plant outside Philadelphia, and finally long-haul trucking, Murphy had already found one vehicle for his boundless energies by motoring around America with the Patriot Guard Riders, motorcyclists who attend military and law-enforcement memorials all over the country, but this ex–fighting man clearly needed bigger battles. Then, in the 2008 autumn of his initial unease over the ascension of Obama, amid hearing all the allegations on TV of unsavory ties to 1960s radicals like William Ayers of the bomb-making Weather Underground, Murphy found two people who would give a voice to all these fears and provide a philosophical framework—if arguably not a particularly coherent one—to explain it all. That would be Glenn Beck and a recently deceased author named W. Cleon Skousen, a nearly forgotten commie-fighter and John Birch Society ally from back in the 1960s.

Murphy says he wasn't even a large Beck fan—the entertainer was still on CNN Headline News and getting low ratings in 2008—when his nephew urged him to read Skousen's tome *The 5000 Year Leap*. This is a once obscure book that had been brought back from the dead through relentless pimping by Beck—who several years earlier had converted to the Mormon faith, in which Skousen had also been a leader for many years. Murphy took Skousen's book with him on a visit to his son in North Carolina.

He says, "I'm not a big reader but I couldn't put the book down—I finished it and then I reread it; then I was really upset and angry with myself."

Why?

"For not paying attention to what was going on and not realizing what our Founding Fathers had done—and I didn't take an active role to protect that," Murphy tells you in the Dover diner. "I was frustrated because I couldn't figure out how to get active."

Murphy wasn't the only one. Journalists at the first mass rally to arise from the 9-12 Project, which took place on that date in 2009 in Washington, D.C., were mildly surprised to hear how many of the marchers said they'd been drawn into the movement by *The 5000 Year Leap*. Mainstream reporters had not even heard of this book that was initially, and obscurely, published in 1981—the first year of a differently transformative presidency, that of Ronald Reagan. Now, the nearly thirty-year-old tome unsurprisingly received no serious media attention or book reviews, even as it spent weeks at or near the top of the best-seller lists, in a revived edition with a foreword naturally written by Glenn Beck himself. Only one writer, Alexander Zaitchik on Salon.com, delved deeply into the book's bizarre backstory.

The 5000 Year Leap itself is rather insipid far-right-wing boiler-plate, arguing that the roots of the U.S. Constitution lay in the devout Christianity of the Founding Fathers (an idea that numerous scholars have debunked) and that the document's blend of Jesus-based inspiration and a conservative natural-law ideology was so different from any system of government developed before the late 1700s that the United States was, in Skousen's view, a 5,000-year leap forward for mankind.

But even more alarming than the popular book is the story of Skousen himself, a man who pulled off the remarkable achievement of being seen as a dangerous wacko of the extreme far right both by J. Edgar Hoover's FBI and by the elders of Skousen's own ultraconservative Mormon religion, who formally disavowed Skousen's writings in 1979—two years before *The 5000 Year Leap* was published. During a somewhat checkered career highlighted by a best-selling book of the McCarthy era called *The Naked Communist*, Skousen reached his career peak as police chief of Salt Lake City and went on to found a clone of the John Birch Society called the All-America Society. A *Time* article from 1961—the first year of John F. Kennedy's presidency—cited Skousen as one of "the rightwing ultras," quoted the rationally conservative mayor of Salt Lake City as saying Skousen "operated the police department like a Gestapo," and stated that Skousen "freely quotes the Bible, constantly plugs his book, *The Naked Communist*, [and] presses for a full congressional investigation of the State Department." The very year after Skousen published *The 5000 Year Leap*, he produced a history textbook for schoolchildren that called early-American black children "pickaninnies" and made the bizarre argument that U.S. slave owners were the "worst victims" of the slavery system.

Cleon Skousen died in early 2006 and thus didn't live to see his resurrection by Beck, a Mormon convert in the late 1990s who apparently had been turned on to Skousen's books a few years after that by a never-to-this-date-named Toronto lawyer friend. What did Beck, a newly minted multimillionaire, see in a dying, forgotten right-wing extremist author of the John Birch era? You might want to ponder this quote from the early 1960s about Skousen from the judge advocate general of the U.S. Navy, who called the Birch-era conservative "money mad . . . totally unqualified and interested solely in furthering his own personal ends."

Sound familiar?

Beck, Skousen, and the wooing of new rank-and-file converts like Delaware's Russ Murphy were closely intertwined; the Fox News and radio star had even urged listeners to read Skousen in a December 2008 show in which he'd talked about something he called "the September 12 man," a trial run for the project.

After that Friday-the-thirteenth show in March, Murphy knew that he had to become active. He asked a few people he knew to come to his trailer; two of them were Alex Garcia, an NRA activist who knew Murphy's brother, and his wife, Theresa, the real-estate agent with a passion for "branding." Both Alex and Theresa are retired from the Air Force, where they met, and in the end, it was just seven or eight attendees who hatched the Delaware 9-12 Project and who—working the open phone lines of local talk radio, putting up signs "at the gun shop" (as Alex Garcia put it), and handing out fliers to small businesses—turned out 650 people for a Tax Day rally at the state capitol in Dover. Now, just eight months later, the Delaware 9-12 Patriots are getting anywhere from one hundred to two hundred people for their routine meetings in each of the state's two rural counties every two weeks. The crowd, as Murphy and the Garcias acknowledge, is heavily comprised of retirees who are plugged into local talk radio like WGMD and into Fox News.

"I have elderly people come up at meetings and hug me, crying, thanking me—because they feel so alone," Murphy says. "They say, 'Nobody's looking out for us, we're so scared.' I say, 'Don't worry, we're here.'"

"We're so scared . . ." The official title of that Glenn Beck show back on Fright Night, March 13, 2009, was "You Are Not Alone," his oxymoronic medley of terrifying words and reassuring ones glowing in atomized living rooms and retirement trailers across America.

With hearty dinners at the Kirby & Holloway concluded, you pulled in behind Alex Garcia's bulked-up truck and followed the revolutionary vanguard to see the Kent County contingent of the Delaware 9-12 Patriots in action. They meet in the low-slung, corrugated aluminum Bowers Beach Fire Hall, where everything is bone white—the Spartan cinder-block walls, the row of long plastic tables and matching chairs, even the glow from the humming fluorescent lights in the pale drop ceiling.

The audience was bone white as well: all Caucasian and overwhelmingly over the age of fifty, at least until the arrival of the ready-for-cable-primetime-cheery, forty-year-old Sarah Palin-esque conservative Republican candidate for the U.S. Senate—a woman named Christine O'Donnell—and her small cadre of aides, one of whom was black. The regulars started trickling in a few minutes after six o'clock, right after the nightly fade-out of *The Glenn Beck Program,* and soon were lining up for coffee or a slice of homemade chocolate cake, several leaning on their canes, gray hair reflecting the pale fluorescence.

Not only did it turn out that the revolution *was* televised after all, but it also needed assistance out to its car.

By the time Murphy called the meeting to order a few minutes after 7 p.m., there were 107 people crowding the big ivory-colored room—retirees in blue-fleece windbreakers who'd fled New Jersey, New York, and Pennsylvania in search of affordable housing on the eastern seaboard and fifty-somethings who'd recently walked away from a career at Dover Air Force Base or one of the area's other military bases, as well as small business owners who insist on handing you a business card. Outside, there was virtually no sign of human life in tiny and eerily quiet Bowers Beach, a once thriving fishing village on Delaware Bay where mist cascaded over reedy marshes and paint-peeled Victorian homes, none of them with lights on. The 9-12 Patriots are the only game in town.

Here inside the packed room, Theresa Garcia is explaining to the baby boomers who had sat out the protests of the 1960s how they could use the famed "Rules for Radicals" tactics of the mid-twentieth-century American socialist Saul Alinsky to promote their conservative, antisocialist causes such as blocking health-care reform, which was the cornerstone issue at that time. "We're basically using their playbook against them," she says. Several earnestly write it all down in notebooks.

The first attendee you'd met at the fire hall was a tall man under a spanking-new "Don't Tread on Me" cap. In his late fifties, semiretired, he said his name was Mike—unlike most of those you spoke with, he wasn't all that eager to give his full name to a stranger with a notebook. Mike and another man named Mike, also fifty-something, retired from the post office, traded small talk over cake about the ups and downs of their newfangled patriot movement, about their frustration after a few dozen of them went down to lobby their Democratic U.S. senator Tom Carper, who told them it was the citizens' job to row the ship of government and it was the job of elected officials like him to steer. Not surprisingly, Carper's comment was like a lighted match tossed into a gasoline ocean of anti-elitist resentment. They had already trusted the Tom Carpers and the Mike Castles of the world to steer for them once, and look at what happened.

"I want my kids to grow up in the kind of America that existed when I was twenty," the first Mike tells you, and when you ask him what was going on when he was twenty, he says it was 1972 and he was in the U.S. Air Force in Thailand making war against Asians—the year that back home the president and all his henchmen were caught bugging the opposition party. It was your first exposure to a notion that became familiar over the coming weeks: that unlike Reagan conservatism, which promised a misty-eyed return to small-town values, this was the yin to the yang of liberal protests in the 1960s, an equal and opposite force some forty years in the making. Mike does little to disabuse you of this idea; he says that the big anti-Obama rally on September 12 "was just like Woodstock." And there's also a "generation gap" all over again—Mike complains to you about how his recent University of Delaware grad son is pro-Obama, like most of the son's friends. But now it's the old-timers taking to the streets, as the kids are too busy, the slackers playing their xBox while the go-getters frantically search for a job.

A 9-12 Project gathering is a little surreal, a quasi-revolutionary cell that at times operates more like a PTA meeting. "We've got to think like them, but better than them," Murphy tells the room, adding later: "Apathy, complacency, and ignorance—that's how they've been getting away with this for all these years." A minute later, he's announcing that there will be a deejay at the group's Christmas party at the American Legion hall in Dover. Then, at different intervals, there are updates on legislation, anger over the Obama administration's just-announced plan to try some 9/11 detainees in a civilian court in New York, and a break where the activists split off into committees. You catch a bit of the education committee, where there is much concern that school kids in Delaware are getting taught only the arguments in favor of man-made global warming. "Global warming is already being taught in the schools," bemoans 9-12 activist Tim Pancoast, "but there is another side of the story."

In addition to two hours of yakking and baked goods, a nexus of 9-12 Patriots activity is a long table in the back of the room where T-shirts and other paraphernalia are for sale to support the cause. It's not surprising that a capitalist counterrevolution of the twenty-first century brings with it a lot of bizno-babble about marketing and even "branding," the concept that the real-estate agent Theresa Garcia had been pushing since that very first meeting in Murphy's trailer. So there are shirts and hats with a nifty logo based on Benjamin Franklin's famed 1754 "Join or Die" woodcut, but the item that really catches your eye is a long, framed horizontal poster of the crowd in D.C. at the September 12, 2009, rally, an audience that Theresa Garcia and every other activist you would meet over six months will insist was 1.7 million or maybe 2 million people and not the 70,000 estimated by the experts actually familiar with the subject, the District of Columbia Fire Department.

The inscription on the poster is attributed to John Adams: "It does not require a majority to prevail, but rather an irate, tireless minority keen to set brush fires in people's minds." This quotation has in fact been adopted as a mantra by the Tea Party–9-12 movement, with 64,600 search results on Google, most on Tea Party Web sites.

The quote is also completely bogus—apparently an indirect effort at a paraphrase from a 1987 article in *Parade* magazine that somehow wrongly morphed into a direct quotation from Adams over the years, even though the source, tellingly, is never cited. (In fact, the word "irate" was not common usage in the 1770s, and the term "brush fire" was not popularized until the twentieth century.) Now here's something that Adams really did say: "Facts are stubborn things."

But the fact-free quote—underneath a bogus crowd estimate—pretty much summed up the true philosophy of "the 9-12 American" perfectly: the majority was no longer worthy of power in this great experiment of a democratic republic, since the majority was now "the handout people" from up near Wilmington.

The one thing that is clear after two hours in Bowers Beach is that Russ Murphy—cowboy boots, one-toothed smile, voice knob always turned to high simmer—is the leader of this sea-oat brush fire down in Delaware. You watched the room pay rapt attention when he spoke, and you heard Theresa Garcia declare admiringly that "Russ is inspirational." You determine to learn more, meeting with him again in a different cozy, big-portion diner, and his journey to this American moment takes shape.

Murphy was always one half-step ahead of the baby boom—born in 1944, dispatched as a twenty-year-old Marine to Okinawa and then to Vietnam in the confusing months surrounding the bogus Gulf of Tonkin incident, when his unit initially operated under rules of engagement that they could not shoot at the enemy unless the enemy shot at them first. He almost died in Vietnam—not from a Viet Cong bullet but from a bout of encephalitis. The Marines initially told Murphy's family he was unlikely to survive. He did just that, of course, but he was also a changed man after his close brush with mortality. Despite having a wife and two young sons at home, the returned Vietnam vet began to drink heavily. He burned through that first marriage and then another and then another before he found sobriety and his resulting fondness for diners. Even then, there was a restlessness in Murphy. He became a king of the road—a biker for fun and, after collecting his early retirement from the Philadelphia Electric Company, an independent long-haul trucker for a living. He wasn't much on politics then—he didn't seem to have much of a thought-out ideology, just a lingering anger from the way he was treated when he came home from the war.

"When we came back from Vietnam, our own country turned on us," Murphy says. "Our own country rejected us."

How so?

"I heard one time a fellow was writing a book and he was dispelling a lot of what he called 'myths' and he said troops weren't spit on when they came back. I'm looking you right in the eye and I'm telling you it's a damn lie." He is indeed looking you in the eye as he speaks, with an uncomfortable intensity.

"I . . . got . . . spit . . . on. . . .

"And the only reason I didn't go to jail was because my ex-wife's uncle was the chief of police," he said. "I laid up six college students in Swarthmore, P-A." Swarthmore College—Quaker bastion and hotbed of 1960s protest—is supposedly pacifist, but not so according to Murphy on a night that he, wearing his dress blues, went with some fellow Marines by train to an event over in Cherry Hill, New Jersey. He insists that when he came back, the alleged college punks spit down on him from a platform above. What happened in the moments that followed is lost in the purple haze of a tumultuous decade, but the facts are frankly less important now than the rage so evident in Murphy today when he talks about it. And so when he heard those news stories on Fox and saw on the Internet that our next president allegedly had ties to 1960s radicals, it felt as if those kids from the fancy, high-priced college were spitting on him all over again.

The late 1960s were an emotional time for Russ Murphy with his near-death experience in the jungle and his confrontation with those hippies when he came home, but the thing that seems to bother him the most is his lingering regret over a decision he made at the behest of his ex-wife regarding their young children: to refuse a potential commission to second lieutenant, which would have meant a second tour in Vietnam. The ex-Marine feels that he left his comrades behind. "I've always regretted not going back," he says. "It was my friends, my comrades, the people I went over there with. I belonged with them. We were in that together."

Russ Murphy was a difficult puzzle to solve. As long as you talked about growing up in the early '60s and stayed away from hot-button topics such as Barack Obama's citizenship, it was hard not to like the guy and his somewhat mischievous pluck. Politically, he seemed like the product of the traditional Betty Crocker recipe for a modern right-wing reactionary: a cauldron of resentments and rage, boiled for a lifetime, with a splash of twelve-step recovery and a pinch of dubious book-learning via the extremist Cleon Skousen—with a TV demagogue serving as the electric stove top.

But that still didn't answer the more important question; now that they were organized, where were Murphy and his legion of newfound followers planning to take this whole thing, anyway? Asked about his party politics, the leader of the Delaware 9-12 Patriots said he was actually a Democrat for most of his life—a socially conservative, pro-union one, the kind that used to dominate the blue-collar row houses in and around Philly—and was very briefly a Republican but into the last year had switched again into something called the Constitution Party.

"They're more in line with the Constitution," Murphy tells you vaguely. "I wanted to make a statement. I wanted to tell these Republicans and these Democrats they aren't doing what they're supposed to be doing."

The Constitution Party traces its roots all the way back to the ultimate angry, white, blue-collar reactionary, Alabama's George Wallace, and the American Independence Party that the once-segregationist had formed to run for president in 1968. Not unlike your typical American corporation, there had been a convoluted trail of political mergers over the years, and some halfway-respectable figures including Representative Ron Paul, a GOP White House hopeful in 2008, and Nixon-era warhorse Pat Buchanan.

But at day's end, the Constitution Party was an extremist band that could make a familiar conservative like Dick Cheney look more like a Berkeley barista. One of its predecessors, the U.S. Taxpayers Party, had ties in the 1990s to the burgeoning militia movement, according to the progressive writer David Neiwert, and the preamble to the platform of the Constitution Party "gratefully acknowledges the blessing of our Lord and Savior Jesus Christ as Creator, Preserver and Ruler of the Universe and of these United States." The party has also been tagged by the Southern Poverty Law Center on its list of "Patriot groups" that are "opposed to the 'New World Order,' engage in groundless conspiracy theorizing, or advocate or adhere to extreme antigovernment doctrines."

You are still pondering Murphy and his movement one snowbound December night when you realize that he has sent you an email— asking kindly if you'd made it home ahead of the blizzard and wanting to shore up a point he'd omitted from your earlier conversations, that "as Christians we absolutely will no longer tolerate attacks or attempts to disparage us or deny the importance of Christianities [*sic*] role in the Founding of the United States of America. This is, and always will be 'One Nation Under GOD.'"

But nothing defined Murphy right now more than his fanatical devotion not to the Lord but to Glenn Beck. In the summer of 2009, Murphy even went online with a plea to the TV host and his people to assist with an event he was planning for the state capitol in Dover:

I humbly ask for his help. You know how people ask if you could talk to anyone special "who would it be"? For me it used to be John Wayne, then Leck Walinsa (speeled [*sic*] wrong). Now, I would give any thing to talk with Glenn Beck, to me he is the most Patriotic American, next to George Washington (whom I'll have to wait to meet).

The Becklash

All that has happened is that the public has adjusted to incoher-
ence and been amused into indifference. Which is why Aldous
Huxley would not in the least be surprised by the story. Indeed,
he prophesied its coming. He believed that it is far more likely
that the Western democracies will dance and dream themselves
into oblivion than march into it single file and manacled. Huxley
grasped, as Orwell did not, that it is not necessary to conceal
anything from a public insensible to contradiction and narcoti-
cized by technological diversions. Although Huxley did not
specify that television would be our main line to the drug, he
would have no difficulty accepting Robert MacNeil's observation that "Television is the soma of Aldous Huxley's Brave New
World." Big Brother turns out to be Howdy Doody.

Neil Postman, *Amusing Ourselves to Death*, 1985

Glenn Beck said famously on TV in the summer of 2009 that Barack
Obama had "a deep-seated hatred" of white people—and also something that he called "white culture." It wasn't clear at the time what
that second bit was about—but maybe he meant this place called
Main Street at Exton, a twenty-first-century extreme makeover of the

strip mall, with every chain store known to mankind plopped down in a cornfield near an exurban Philadelphia exit ramp, and a few new narrow shop-lined "streets" with honest-to-goodness parallel-parking spaces, although almost everyone parks in the massive old-school lot on the other side. On a rather nippy October evening, there is a line of people that starts right at the front door of the Barnes & Noble, and you decide to follow it to the very end. That takes you past the Rolex watch store and the front of the Buca di Beppo "authentic Italian restaurant" and the Radiance Medspa and down the street to Eastern Mountain Sports and beyond, while the line stretches from here to retail eternity. Months later, you still wonder whether there was ever an end, or if this rush of people waiting to meet Glenn Beck in person just faded off into an unseen horizon like the headlights in *Field of Dreams*.

"Beck zombies," laughs a man named Al Buono, who is the only resident of urban Philadelphia (population 1.4 million, just 25 miles away) that you find among a couple of dozen folks you spoke with at the shopping theme park. The purpose of this line—ultimately estimated at well over two thousand people—is to whiz past the extraordinarily popular TV-and-radio host Beck when the bookstore lets them inside at 7 p.m., get his signature on his book *Arguing with Idiots* (incongruously depicting the author in Red Army garb on the cover), shake his hand, and then keep moving. It is one of only a handful of book signings that the *über*-busy Beck has scheduled across the country, most not in downtowns but in scattershot exurbs like this one. There is mild snark in Buono's voice as he puns, "They come out because they come out at his beck and call, whenever he says anything."

Despite this apparently reflexive response to Beck's words, it soon becomes apparent that many of those in attendance are fixated on convincing people their resentment is genuine.

"I have to say that I'm a very normal person," Suellen Hahn says calmly, matter-of-factly, as if responding to a question—except that none had been asked. She turns to some people listening to the conversation. "Aren't you guys normal people?"

Hahn is sixty-six years old, with short light-brown hair, straightly cut, wearing a heavy knit American-flag sweater, co-owner with her husband of a beverage business, so salt-of-the-silty-Pennsylvania-earth that it's hard to imagine she'd ever before felt the need to defend her normalcy. Maybe she does so because she'd driven about an hour and a half east to this far western fringe of the Philadelphia exurbs from Womelsdorf, Pennsylvania—a town of exactly 2,599 souls (according to the last census), where the biggest employer, the M. H. Schmaltz cigar plant, closed long ago and they now make American flags inside the old building—to stand in line for more than three additional hours, all for an encounter that would literally last less than three seconds.

Or maybe it is because she was standing near the front of the line behind a guy with a T-shirt that read "Russian Socialism," depicting Communism's Murderer's Row of Marx, Lenin, and Stalin right above a parallel line of Nancy Pelosi, Barack Obama, and Harry Reid, " . . . American Socialism." (Such things still had the ability to shock back in October 2009.) About ten people back, casually interspersed between the motorized wheelchairs and well-dressed moms with their baby strollers, another gentleman wore on his chest the famous quote from Ann Coulter right after 9/11: "We should invade their countries, kill their leaders and convert them to Christianity."

The bookstore throng felt like a bit of a coronation for Beck after he went in just eight months from low-rated host on a low-rated cable network (CNN Headline News) to the new king of all right-wing media, in-your-face on the cover of *Time* magazine asking "Is Glenn Beck Bad for America," a former Top 40 "Morning Zoo" guy now wielding enough political clout to take down the Obama administration's so-called "green jobs czar." After the angry health-care town halls of the summer and sudden appearance of new protest groups like the Beck-inspired 9-12 Project and the various Tea Parties, reporters investigating the source of this anger and energy found quite frequently—as you had in Delaware with Russ Murphy—that when you peeled away the layers, there was Beck at the core. (In a much-talked-about article on the movement by David Barstow of the *New York Times* in February 2010, he described the eureka moment for the scores of economically battered working-class Americans that he interviewed: "That is often the point when Tea Party supporters say they began listening to Glenn Beck.") In just the twenty-four hours before the book signing, Beck had earned a personal condemnation from both the press office of the Democratic president and the stalwart GOP senator Lindsey Graham of the bleeding-red state of South Carolina, who charged in a speech that Beck is "aligned with cynicism. And there's always been a market for cynicism."

And now you are standing in the crowded square of that market. You feel compelled to identify yourself as a writer who also works for a Philadelphia newspaper to a Barnes & Noble employee walking down the line with a bullhorn shouting, "Who here's excited about meeting Glenn Beck?!," as whoops and hollers echo across the miniature canyon of the contrived Main Street. As you unsuccessfully wave your arm for her to stop, she quickly adds, "Somebody from the newspaper is here!" Hundreds of happily chattering voices suddenly fall silent all at once, leaving only the sound of the autumn breeze and trucks rumbling nearby on U.S. 30.

But then, individually and in small groups, the "Beck zombies" on the infinite line are actually eager—maybe desperate—to tell their story to someone who will listen, even someone from the loathsome mainstream media. They insist they are the heirs to Richard Nixon's "silent majority"—as Robert Lloyd of nearby West Chester, Pennsylvania, the guy with the loud shirt calling Obama a socialist, puts it. Indeed, this is why they are here on a crisp fall weeknight: because they want to rise up from their couches and show the world they are here. The book—even though they've just paid $21 for a hardcover tome padded with pictures and white space—is an afterthought. Watching Glenn Beck and hearing him say that "you are not alone" provided the first step toward validating their unease over the new president and the uncertainty of a changing America, and now group events like this one in

Exton or the big 9-12 Project rally in Washington a few weeks earlier are the second step: witnessing the others who share the same fears, the same complaints, the same anger. They are not alone! The real event is not Beck but the line itself—and being counted. And for the miracle of bringing them all together in this one place, they ascribe almost mystical qualities to their leader.

Hahn, the woman who continues to vouch for her normalcy ("I'm still married, I'm not strange, I've never been arrested.") tells you that Beck's virtue is "fairness—it's fairness, he's very fair." This causes the newly formed community on this corner of the line to almost play can-you-top-this on the entertainer's special qualities.

"He's the only person doing any investigative reporting!" Lloyd pipes in.

"What it is, is that he's an honest person," pipes in Buono, the Philadelphian. "He believes what he says."

"He loves this country," Suellen Hahn adds, softly, in the background.

"And he will go to the wall for what he believes in," adds Lloyd.

For the next few minutes, you will struggle to engage the gaggle of Beck fans on more specifics regarding just what exactly it is that Beck—and they—believe in. What you know about Beck's accumulated record so far suggests a man whose political philosophy could be summed up as this: What will sound the most entertaining coming out of my mouth at this particular moment? For just one glaring example, he'd called the government's $700 billion bank bailout "necessary" and "also not nearly enough" just six months before it became a cornerstone of his crusade against "socialism" in Washington.

To Buono, the main Beck-inspired answer to any of America's problems could be summed up in just two words: "Stop spending." Under that lay the deeper fear that government's goal was to take away what they had—or what they had left, in some cases—and dole it out to the have-nots. The Beckinistas trashed every single government program that had been launched as a response to the economic crisis—the government takeover of General Motors and the just-concluded "cash for clunkers" car buyback program, but especially health-care reform. "They're worried about the thirty million who don't have it," says Buono of health insurance, "but what about the three hundred million who do have it?" The Medicare-eligible Hahn then chimes in about the "death panels" in the Obama plan, which weren't really in the Obama plan, saying that "they're getting a needle ready for me, and I don't need that!" She added: "I want to be responsible for me. Not everyone." Her new friend from the line, Buono, says that sounds exactly right. "When everybody contributes to the rest, that's good—but all in all, you've got to take care of yourself first."

You are curious what these other Beck fans do for a living. Buono says he is self-employed, like Hahn. You turn to Lloyd, wearer of the "American Socialism" T-shirt.

"I'm unemployed," he says. The others around him chuckle, perhaps uncomfortably—it is a jarring note amid the talk of self-reliance, even though unemployment clearly is one major factor in boosting the Tea Parties. "I've been unemployed for over a year. They outsourced my department. But I've got job interviews lined up—I'm flying out to Chicago on Monday."

After a year of joblessness, doesn't Lloyd think the government should be doing more to create jobs? "The concern I have is whether things like cap and trade"—the proposal for eliminating greenhouse gas emissions—"is going to be sending jobs overseas." The cold fact that his last job had already been sent abroad, pre-Obama, is irrelevant.

Lloyd isn't the only unemployed man spending his late afternoon at the book signing—perhaps not so surprising among diehard fans of a TV show that airs at 5 p.m. on the East Coast, an hour when those without a job or a commute home are desperate to be entertained, and when a host peddling doom is well suited to their sour mood. As the line of book buyers begins snaking into the store, an older man stands off to the side, all by himself, an American Legion cap on his head, holding a Navy Jack flag, stars and stripes underneath a snake with the slogan "Don't Tread on Me," a symbol born out of colonial resistance.

His name is Al Whayland. He tells you he has already attended several Tea Party events—his first protests in a life that has spanned seventy-four years and included a stint in the U.S. Army during the peacetime of the late 1950s.

"I don't believe this is what people voted for," he says of the Obama administration. "We're moving too far from the direction of our Founding Fathers." He echoes some of the common themes of the Fox News Channel, that the new president had appointed too many unaccountable "czars," that Obama has shamed America by "apologizing to Europe."

You ask the septuagenarian Whayland if he's retired now.

"I was laid off last year," he says. He explains he had worked for a large mortgage company that had collapsed along with the housing market, and he says that despite his age he would love to work again.

"But I'm seventy-four." He shrugs. Now he is a part of something bigger than one job—a movement.

The ghost of unemployment hovered over this event, just as it hovered over the intertwined Tea Party and the 9-12 Project. The numbers were grim—the "real" unemployment rate that included folks who were so discouraged that they'd stopped bothering to go out and look for a job continued to hover at roughly 17 percent, or one of every six able-bodied would-be workers. But even most people who still held jobs knew family members or close friends who were unemployed, and according to one 2010 survey, more than one-third of Americans knew someone who had given up trying to find a job. This bred considerable fear and anxiety that the U.S. economy and societal order might collapse—if it hadn't already. There was always a cast of bottom-feeders like cult radio figure Alex Jones to feed on the deepest paranoia, but Beck had taken it to another level. Beck reached out for the same dark places, but he smoothed out the rough edges of hosts like Jones, who toyed with 9/11 as a government inside job and railed against "the Bilderbergers," an internationalist group he targets with conspiracy theories. Blessed with the already large platform provided by Fox, Beck rarely mentioned unemployment directly—the real problems and real solutions would have been a buzz-kill—but spoke directly to fears of an apocalypse and to nationalistic pride. He appealed to the unemployed like Al Whayland by grabbing those emotions and moving them someplace else.

Asked what he got from Beck, Whayland says, "He's bringing America back together."

What Whayland said actually made sense—if your view of America started at the front door of the Barnes & Noble and ended at the stucco subdivisions and fallow farmlands just past your limited horizon. This was not all America, just *an* America, one that mostly stretched on a radius that started with cookie-cutter chain Italian restaurants and swept past dead-factory Victorian towns like Womelsdorf but abruptly came to a stop at the urban netherlands like West Philadelphia that were less than an hour east on Route 30.

From 1976 to 2004 in America, according to the 2008 book *The Big Sort*, the ambitions of Americans to live in communities of like-minded people were such a compelling force that the number of landslide counties where either the Democratic or GOP presidential candidate won by more than 20 percentage points went from less than one-quarter to nearly half. Here tonight, it is the overwhelmingly Republican and overwhelmingly white areas from exurban Chester County to its west that are out in force. Inside the Barnes & Noble you find a tableau that looks a lot like it was painted by Norman Rockwell. Call it "The Book Signing."

Beck—tall and lanky, in a plaid shirt and a sports jacket—is back-lit to the level of angelic, his blond hair practically radiant white. He moves with animatronic efficiency, signing a book literally every two seconds with his left hand while shaking hands with his right and mouthing "Thank you" with an occasional "God bless you." A few feet from the line, gawkers strain to get a good cell-phone picture of the gangly superstar, and one woman gushes loudly, "He's so cute."

Beck is totally exposed here and yet impenetrable at the same time. Just an hour earlier, nearly three million Americans watched this earthly cherub as he ripped into Obama, his wife, the American city of Chicago, and their soon-to-be-spectacularly-unsuccessful in-person pitch for the 2016 Olympics. "Chicago is good at . . . organized Mafi—oops, did I say that out loud?" But that was on videotape; in real time he was here at the mall, a cheery salesman moving the product at a rate—even at the discounted retail price—of roughly $250 a minute. When the end of the line finally weaved its way into the store, a few reporters huddled at the front door. But Beck slipped out the back.

The next morning, Beck went on his coast-to-coast radio show to wax effusively about the people that he'd met on his brief road trip. "Last night, I went to Philadelphia [*sic*] and Cherry Hill, New Jersey. I had a couple of book signings to do, and something struck me. The crowds were enormous. They went all the way around—I don't mean like out the door and kind of around the corner. I mean out the door, around the corner, around the corner, around the corner, all the way around the block . . .

"And there was an unusual number of females in the audience. Now, sure, it could be because of my molten hotness. I mean—who doesn't want a slice of this, huh, ladies." No matter how many magazine covers featured Beck and his influence in this tumultuous time in American history, no matter how much Beck began talking about his "Plan" that would both balance the budget and renew the soul of the nation, there was just something impulsive that kept pulling him back to his raw roots, back to the "Morning Zoo."

To understand the odd origins of Beck's pseudopolitical movement, it's good to start back in 1985. That was the year that an academic named Neil Postman, a renowned media theorist, published the book for which the academic (who died in 2002) is still best known, *Amusing Ourselves to Death*. The book argues that the arrival of television to replace the printed word was destroying knowledge in our society, by creating a top-down communication system that increasingly valued sheer entertainment over education, even in the few hours of the day that were devoted to reporting the news.

It was a time of great debate over whether the dire predictions of George Orwell had come to pass, but now that the real year of *1984* had just come and gone, Postman argued that society was at risk not from Orwellian censorship but from the type of babble warned about by a different well-known futurist, Aldous Huxley of *Brave New World*. Wrote Postman: "Censorship, after all, is the tribute tyrants pay to the assumption that a public knows the difference between serious discourse and entertainment—and cares. How delighted would be all the kings, czars and fuhrers of the past and commissars of the present to know that censorship is not a necessity when all political discourse takes the form of a jest."

Postman focused on the medium of television, and he was clearly correct in seeing this as the paramount form of communication—even with the impending arrival of the Internet. However, important things were also happening outside the box, the idiot box, in the pivotal year of 1985. This was the time, after all, when Ronald Reagan, an actor turned politician, was at the peak of his popularity as he reinvented the American presidency around entertainment values, giving life to notions like the "photo op" and the "thirty-second sound bite" that had not existed in politics before. And although Postman touched somewhat on developments in radio—"such language as radio allows us to hear is increasingly primitive, fragmented, and largely aimed at invoking visceral response," he wrote in 1985—it is not clear that he saw the rapid changes in that medium that would reshape the ways in which Americans communicate with each other. Radio was becoming a manic, nihilistic place—self-aware enough to know that the best and maybe only way it could cut through the clutter was to shock people.

Hence, the "shock jock." These became the glory days of Howard Stern, the disc jockey who kept getting himself fired up the ladder until he was based in New York and nationally syndicated with an audience of millions. Stern built that listenership through outrageous stunts and held onto it through humor that was sometimes hilarious and sometimes a thinly disguised assault on gays, blacks, or other minorities. Stern's following was heavily larded with young white middle-class males who believed that the shock jock cut through the hypocrisy of post-1960s political correctness but were not drawn to the prudish Sun Belt–styled social conservatism that was fueling the so-called Reagan revolution of that era. Many wondered at the time what would happen if the likes of a Howard Stern, or the like-minded Don Imus, converted his growing following into a political movement, but his young working-class audience relished their distrust of politics. Not surprisingly, the only core political value of a shock jock was unfettered free speech—anything else that flowed from that was a loose version of libertarianism. "I'm for personal freedom," Stern was quoted as saying in 1984. "I'm for freedom of the marketplace."

While Stern and Imus were taking root in the media epicenter of New York, out in the secondary metro markets a related phenomenon was taking the radio world by storm. Although they were not the inventors of the format, the "Morning Zoo" had been perfected by the mid-1980s by two drive-time disc jockeys in Tampa, Florida—Scott Shannon and Cleveland Wheeler. As described years later by Glenn Beck's unauthorized biographer Alexander Zaitchik, the Shannon-Wheeler radio zoo—copied in most markets across America—absorbed elements from the broader culture like the biting satire of *Saturday Night Live* and remixed it into tiny and often unconnected skits, parody songs, imitations, and caricatures, usually with a cast of local (sometimes self-appointed) comedians, frequently—as Zaitchik chronicles—fueled by a cocaine-based lifestyle off the air that mirrored the frenetic pace heard by listeners. When tossed together with the traditional drive-time elements of traffic and weather and even an occasional Top-40 song, the "Morning Zoo" was the disconnected world of noninformational entertainment that Neil Postman deplored . . . on steroids.

This was the universe that created Glenn Beck.

In 1985, Beck was working the morning show in the unlikely out-post of Louisville, Kentucky. He was a twenty-four-year-old kid with a gold Rolex watch and a $70,000 salary, which back then was big-time money for a twenty-something. He was also a nonstop—by his own later account—pot-smoker with libertarian views, such as supporting abortion rights and opposing the death penalty, that would have been in line with Stern's simplistic personal-freedom agenda of that era. Except no one cared what Glenn Beck's politics were. His shtick was comedy, "Captain Beck and the A-Team," with lots of voices, including an alter ego named Clydie Clyde and—according to Zaitchik's exten-sive reporting—the obligatory "black guy." His only cause at the time seemed to be the nonstop hounding of an overweight female talk host on a local AM station—which got so nasty it may have led to the poor ratings that led to Beck's eventual firing from Louisville's WRKA. For Beck, it was just one more stop in a decade-long barnstorming tour of mostly Sun Belt markets. He wasn't trying to change the world. Beck didn't want power, only money and fame; he didn't want to be Ronald Reagan or a radio rabble-rouser like Father Charles Coughlin, who was FDR's bête noir of the airwaves during the New Deal. His hero was Orson Welles, a man who had electrified, frightened, and entertained the nation once with the sound of his voice—and with something that was not real.

On October 30, 1938, Welles—perhaps by accident, or perhaps in-tentionally, if you believe some conspiracy theorists—conducted the first real massive test of how the airwaves could be used to generate fear and an intense public response. Welles's special Halloween broadcast of his *Mercury Theatre of the Air* over the CBS radio network was based on H. G. Wells's classic alien-invasion novel *The War of the Worlds*. Not only did the up-and-coming artistic giant move the setting from England to the more prosaic Grover's Mill, New Jersey, but he built the narrative around the conventions of radio news reporting, inspired in part by the strong listener reaction to the live broadcast of the recent *Hindenburg* air disaster. The alien landing and ensuing battles are portrayed as breaking news reports, including a poisonous gas attack that apparently fells the live reporter, giving way to a ham-radio operator in the background saying, "Isn't there anyone on the air? Isn't there . . . anyone?" Some listeners were savvy enough to hear the several disclaimers in the Welles broadcast, but thousands did not—some frantically called the police or local radio stations, and a huge throng descended on the real Grover's Mill (one of the biggest panics, coincidentally, was in a small town called Concrete, Washington, not too far from where Glenn Beck later grew up, in the Bellingham area, because a real-life electrical explosion and power outage took place there at the same time as the broadcast).

In the days following *The War of the Worlds*, there was an overheated debate over the ability of such a broadcast to mislead and frighten a susceptible public. One of the most pointed critiques came from overseas; "*The War of the Worlds*" controversy was "evidence of the decadence and corrupt condition of democracy"—according to Adolf Hitler. Many listeners had a hard time admitting they'd been conned, in a fashion, by Welles's skillful manipulation, as a young Cleveland radio deejay—the future *Tonight Show* host Jack Parr—found out; when he told his panicked callers that the CBS broadcast had all been a hoax, some of his enraged audience accused him of "covering up the truth."

Orson Welles and his epic 1938 radio broadcast figures prominently in one of the two major events that shaped the young Glenn Beck. On February 10, 1972, in the smallish town of Mt. Vernon, Washington, Beck turned eight years old and his mother gave him a birthday present, a double LP record called *The Golden Years of Radio* that left the boy spellbound listening to the radio broadcasts of comedy and drama from the 1930s and 1940s. "[I was] mesmerized by the magic radio was, how it could create pictures in my head," Beck would write in his autobiography. By the time Beck was thirteen, he'd won an amateur deejay contest at a small local radio station, and two years later—still too young for his driver's license—the teenager convinced the grownups at a new FM station in Seattle to give him an on-air job, which he

reached by a long and circuitous Greyhound-and-city-bus route when
he wasn't sleeping there on the weekends to do the overnight shift for
minimum wage. He knew what he wanted, according to later news accounts, telling his best friend, Robert Shelton, that he planned to make
big money in radio someday.

"I always felt like he judged people on how useful they were going
to be to him," another high school friend, Pat Wolken, would tell the
newspapers years later. "That seemed to be his main thing, getting
. . . Glenn Beck moving forward." He was student director of his high
school play, Molière's *The Miser*, another clue as to Beck's love of performing. He didn't spend a day in college, since he already had a career
doing what he loved in radio. By then, his mother, who'd triggered the
whole thing with the birthday present, was gone. Mary Beck, divorced
from Beck's father and struggling with alcohol and perhaps mental illness, drowned with a male friend in a never-well-explained boating incident in Puget Sound around the time her son was starting at KUBE,
when Glenn was fifteen.

The Christmas Sweater, a book that Beck published in 2008, is the
now superstar's attempt to come to terms with his mother's death in the
usual fashion—in front of millions of people, creating fiction from fact
(intentionally, for a change), laden with teary-eyed bathos; *Publisher's
Weekly* said the book "cruises on predictability, repetition, and sen-
timentality," an epitaph perhaps for Beck's larger body of work. After
the novel's twelve-year-old protagonist gets and rejects a homemade
sweater—the only Christmas present his mother could afford, not the
cool bike that the boy wanted—the mom is killed in a horrific car crash
(although in a later theatrical production and children's book, that grim
part of the saga becomes a dream) and the hero deals with his anger and
guilt. Beck later told Don Imus in an interview that the meat of the story,
regarding the sweater, is true, although he repeats for Imus his apparently
self-mythologized tale that his mother's boating death was a suicide.

"And then shortly after that, she died and that was kind of the turning point in my life," Beck said. "That was the first kind of real rocky

area that kind of screwed me up for many years. And then I started to repeat my mom's life and . . ."

This time, what Beck says is pretty much true. Most of the next two decades after his mother's death in 1979 would be spent on what certainly looks like a quest to both please his late mother—bearer of the gift of Orson Welles—and follow Mary Beck's pathway to an early grave. Beck's career in radio during the "Morning Zoo" era of the 1980s and into the 1990s is pretty much a blur of cities that sounds a bit like some obscure Amtrak route—Salt Lake City, Phoenix, and Louisville, among others, and finally close to a decade in southern Connecticut. But his odyssey is also a high-speed line of high hopes blurred by ugly episodes and a series of firings, mostly against a backdrop of cocaine and booze. An admitted sufferer from attention-deficit disorder, Beck clearly struggles with impulse control, even after he finally stopped drinking and doing drugs in 1994 and with the help of a then-friend, Senator Joe Lieberman, enrolled in a religion course at Yale, the only brief time he's ever spent on a college campus.

The low moments that brought Beck to this point were many. This was especially true in the late 1980s in Phoenix when, desperate to get his "Morning Zoo" out of a deep ratings rut, he staged a series of inane pranks against the show's number-one drive-time rival—crashing the wedding of its program director to plaster his own show's bumper stickers on the bridal car, for example, and finally, unbelievably, calling the wife of his rival deejay to make fun of . . . her recent miscarriage. But the truth is that even sobering up, finding God and a new wife, and adopting conservative-or-libertarian-or-whatever politics didn't stop Beck from blurting out things on the air against all better judgment. One morning in Philadelphia in September 2005, after Beck had moved there to launch his nationally syndicated talk-radio career, you were cruising through a blighted section of West Philly—near the gates of the zoo, appropriately—when you pushed the button for 1210, The Big Talker, and there was Beck holding court on the big topic of the day, the aftermath of Hurricane Katrina. The worst was over in New Orleans but thousands were adapting to the life of an American refugee, some at the Houston Astrodome.

"Let me be real honest with you. I don't think anybody on talk radio—I don't think anybody in their right mind is going to say this out loud—but I wonder if I'm the only one that feels this way." Here it comes, you're thinking. Sure enough, Beck brings up the chaos at the Astrodome when the government handed out ATM cards as a form of relief payment. "When you are rioting for these tickets, or these ATM cards, the second thing that came to mind was—and this is horrible to say, and I wonder if I'm alone in this—you know it took me about a year to start hating the 9/11 victims' families? Took me about a year." He wasn't done. He went on to call the New Orleans survivors, the people who had lost their life's possessions and watched neighbors or loved ones drown, "scumbags." That morning, you blogged about what you heard and sent it along to the people at Media Matters, thinking correctly that it would be a big deal for a day, thinking incorrectly it might even stop Beck's relentless march toward stardom. Just a few months later, he was snatched up for a national gig on CNN Headline News.

How did that happen? Beck's rise from obscure mid-market deejay at a Connecticut Top-40 station called "KC–101" to driver of the great national debate took less than a decade. But his gravitation toward politics was a slow one. Working his Sun Belt gigs in the 1980s during a time that Beck now fondly remembers as Reagan's "Morning in America," he didn't talk much about his then-liberal-to-libertarian social views, but when Reagan bombed Libya in a terrorism-related retaliatory attack in 1986, it did awaken a jingoistic response in Beck that dovetailed with his sense of grabbing and wringing the emotions of his listeners. As re-created by Zaitchik, Beck's show that morning was an unexpected burst of patriotic bombast, interspersing Lee Greenwood's "God Bless the USA" and a New Wave-y parody with the Zoo-friendly title of "Qaddafi Sucks" with Beck observations like "I personally don't think we did enough. We should've went over there and bombed the hell out of 'em."

Beck's twelve-step recovery from drugs and alcohol led by 1999 to a new wife, Tonia, two new children (he also has two from his first marriage), and an unlikely religious conversion to Mormonism, recommended by a former radio co-host and lifelong best friend, Pat Gray (who rejoined Beck on his radio show in 2009). The language of AA-style recovery and self-control had become surprisingly central to modern conservatism by the end of the twentieth century, as right-wing politics coupled with Christianity offered stability and a renewed faith to many aging baby boomers who'd been battered by the temptations, some generational and some eternal, of sex and drugs and booze. The personal recovery of Glenn Beck created a new form of verbal entertainment that gyrated all over the place—from the church-basement sharing in the tradition of AA founder Bill W to crude shock-jock blasts of words like "vomit" and "crap" to pseudo-intellectualism, featuring a kind of revisionist three-credit Early Twentieth-Century American History class that created villains out of figures like Woodrow Wilson too dead to defend themselves.

This didn't happen by accident—Beck spent much of the mid-1990s inspired by the success of then *Time* magazine cover boy Rush Limbaugh and scheming to remake himself in the increasing popularity of AM talk radio, even hiring the best-known talk-radio agent, George Hiltzik. The formal unveiling came in that impeachment summer of 1998, when Beck began filling in on New York's 50,000-watt talker, the legendary WABC. His emotional and sometimes fact-free approach to the news quickly took shape, as described by Zaitchik through this anecdote that the AM newcomer told over the air about an unnamed friend who he claims had served in 'Nam. "He got off the plane from Vietnam and a woman spat in his face and called him 'baby killer,'" Beck told his New York audience. "Then he left his medal of honor in a trash can." You can almost feel the bonds of patriotism and resentment that would form with future viewers like Delaware's Russ Murphy, who claims that he, too, was spit on by Swarthmore hippies at the height of the 1960s. This new Beck was the blue-eyed bastard child of Richard

Nixon and Howard Stern, and the combination worked well enough to launch his new career path.

The genius of Glenn Beck—and make no mistake, there is genius amid the mayhem—lies in a remarkable ability to synthesize disconnected yet iconic American sound bites, both from real pop-culture heroes and from fictional ones, from the gripping narratives of Welles to the cathartic madness of the out-of-control Howard Beale in Hollywood's *Network*. The character of Glenn Beck manages to be 100 percent derivative yet an American original.

The horrific events of September 11, 2001, played a key role in the development of the Beck character to a higher level. The terror attack ushered in an American decade of fear, raw emotions, and jingoistic impulses of patriotism and revenge—Beck's sweet spot. He was all over the new patriotic fervor, even donating an American flag to Tampa International Airport that summer that he claimed was given to him by troops from 1991's Operation Desert Storm. Within days of the attacks, a raft of large-market stations dumped the suddenly dated sex talk of Dr. Laura Schlessinger and plugged in Beck. Said a Milwaukee program director: "I thought it would be best to put on, in the here and now, a program that could address the biggest news story in at least the last thirty years."

But in reinventing himself as more of a political personality, Beck also turned—perhaps unconsciously—toward a growing world of underground conspiratorial radio that drew little attention in the mainstream media. After the mainstream conservative heavy hitters like Rush Limbaugh and Sean Hannity remade AM radio in the 1990s, a second wave of more fringe voices came in their wake. This was partly a function of there being more airtime to fill, as most AM mono frequencies ditched music for talk, and it was augmented by the ability of radio shows—even and perhaps especially those with extreme points of view—to now build a national audience via the Internet. During the late 1990s came middle-of-the-night, UFO-minded gabbers like Art

Bell and George Noory, and the floodgates seemed to open for conspiracy-minded political talkers as well.

Over the course of the early years of the new century, the Austin, Texas–based Alex Jones emerged as the leader of this new pack. Born in 1974 and emerging into the media-saturated era of the 1990s, Jones used vehicles with a low barrier to entry—most notably local cable-TV public access, which was booming in Austin at the time—as a tool for building an audience despite views that were way outside the mainstream, starting with a campaign for a memorial for the followers of cult figure David Koresh who were killed in the encounter with federal agents at Waco. Jones blended pure politics—he even ran for Congress briefly in 2000, as a Republican—with a knack for ambushing members of Congress and other entertaining stunts, including a couple that led to his arrest. As with Beck, albeit in a much different style, Jones's career took off in the paranoia-gripped era kicked off by 9/11.

In the mode of many followers of White House hopeful Ron Paul, Jones's muddled view mixed ideas of both conventional liberals and the far left—the 9/11 "truther" view of the attacks as a U.S. government inside job and disagreement with the Patriot Act and the two wars launched under George W. Bush—with hard-right views, especially after Obama's 2008 election. A generation ago, someone like Jones might be rolling diatribes off a mimeograph machine, but today he's aired on roughly sixty stations (it used to be more before his 9/11 inside-job rants)—with a weekly audience estimated at two million—and is heard everywhere streaming over the Internet, with two popular Web sites, PrisonPlanet.com and InfoWars.com. His highly conspiratorial tone and Web-oriented approach brings in a younger demographic than do Beck and other well-known talkers. It has been reported that more people visit Jones's Web sites than Rush Limbaugh's, for example. The Internet has also proved a fruitful incubator for the fringe ideas that have both broadened Jones's influence and seeped into the groundwater of mainstream discourse as conspiracy theories about everything from a nonexistent "Obama gun confiscation" to the fictitious "FEMA detention camps" where law-abiding Americans would be herded.

Beck, naturally, synthesized the parts of the Alex Jones–inspired paranoid style that worked for him while ditching those aspects that would have gotten him in hot water with his bosses at Fox or his radio syndicators at Clear Channel—not to mention his mass audience. As conspiracy theories became more fashionable in the post–9/11 world, Beck became a master at knowing which ones he could flaunt (broad warnings of societal breakdown, the collapse of the dollar, or U.S. dictatorship), which ones he could tease (the Alex Jones–driven "FEMA camps" fiction, which he promoted and then debunked), and which ones he could score points with by dismissing (notably, the Obama birther theory, with Beck's denial providing him cover for other equally out-there ideas). Beck had a skill for pushing and stretching limits in the public arena that lesser figures like Jones could never match. It shouldn't shock that Jones himself is a tad bitter about Beck and considers him a copycat; Jones even told *Texas Monthly*, "Glenn Beck is literally word for word taking everything I do and twisting it and turning it into a Roger Ailes Fox News evil doppelgänger of my show."

Broadly, Beck now described the shtick that he alone had perfected as "[t]he fusion of entertainment and enlightenment." Say what you want about Beck's lack of college education, about his occasional non-rocket-scientist moments such as his famed TV blackboard lecture based on the misspelled acronym "OLIGARH"; Beck's unifying theory of twenty-first-century media bombast and politics is practically Einsteinian in its complex simplicity.

It would be Glenn Beck, and Beck alone, who would take everything that he had seen and learned since the start of the 1980s to temper the nihilistic libertarian style of all of the shock jocks and "Morning-Zoo"-keepers with newfound faith and patriotism, and to moderate the heavy-handed and didactic GOP-talking-point conservatism of the pure-politics boys, Limbaugh and Hannity, with entertaining mood swings of teary emotion and biting sarcasm. His audacious goal was nothing less than taking the entire nation on the same kind of emotional, one-hour-long roller-coaster ride of fear and deliverance it experienced on October 30, 1938, and sustaining that high five times a week in high definition in living rooms across the country. Beck had already named his production company in honor of Orson Welles's radio drama: Mercury Radio Arts.

"These people see themselves as entertainers—privately they're stunned and uncomprehending of the degree to which people in politics take them seriously," says Marc Fisher, a longtime *Washington Post* journalist considered a leading radio historian. He is speaking primarily of Beck, whom he considers more of a master storyteller of the airwaves than any kind of ideological thinker. Like other broadcasting experts, Fisher believes that Beck is a product of perfect timing, because radio was moving away from pure shock in the early 2000s—as the Federal Communications Commission cracked down—and Beck could see the new quasi-political direction. Beck's stage-managed earnestness and attempts to connect emotionally, Fisher argues, are a reflection of the new twenty-first-century zeitgeist. He notes, "What really distinguishes Beck is his manner—there's none of the meanness and sour-curdling tone that even a Limbaugh has."

What's more, Beck's rise gave the conservative movement a new kind of voice infused with some of the ironic vibe so familiar to his own generation of tail-end baby boomers born in the late 1950s and early 1960s, who grew up first on *Saturday Night Live* and later on Stern. By the 2000s, the best-known avatars of ironies were comedians who generally tackled politics with a liberal worldview—most notably Comedy Central's Jon Stewart and Stephen Colbert—but now Beck and his flights into sarcasm and a kind of humor gave the right wing its own warped brand of Jon Stewart to claim as its own.

Still, Beck's upward path was not a straight line. CNN Headline News was an odd fit, and the ratings were poor even in comparison to that network's legal eagle Nancy Grace; when it was announced in late

2008 that he would be moving to Fox News, it felt less like a promotion than a lifeline. The 5 p.m. Eastern slot in particular sounded like
a dead zone, but it would prove perfect placement for Beck's audience
that combined retirees, the unemployed, and small-towners who were
home from work or didn't work at all.

Some wondered why Beck's move to Fox took so long in the first
place. In the 1970s and '80s, when so many Americans were on the
move, especially from cities to suburbs and even exurbs, there was a
tendency for people to sort their environs by politics—from the cappuc-
cino-laced liberal enclaves of San Francisco to the conservative mega-
church belt of Texas. Well, by the 1990s that "big sort" had moved
on—thanks to technology and other factors—to include the ways that
we communicate. Talk radio, personified by Limbaugh, took root in the
first years of the decade after Ronald Reagan had pushed to eliminate
the federal equal-time rule known as the Fairness Doctrine; in 1996,
Internet usage began to soar, and in October of that year, the Fox News
Channel first aired. FNC was the brainchild of the Australian-born
billionaire and conservative-leaning media mogul Rupert Murdoch;
his first and only hire to run the network was a doozy—the longtime
GOP-strategist-turned-broadcast-executive Roger Ailes. Ailes's major
contribution to American politics had been helping to craft and market
the white working-class resentment policies that elected his then boss
Richard Nixon in 1968. That resentment wasn't just something that
Ailes manipulated for profit—he felt it in his bones, a graduate of Ohio
University who, according to biographers, still retains a suspicion of Ivy
League coastal elites.

But as Ailes's income soared with his successful launch of Fox, the
FNC boss grew suspicious, period. According to a 2010 profile in the
New York Times, Ailes is obsessed with both national security and
personal security, traveling with two security SUVs and always keeping his office blinds closed while buying up all the property around
his house in exurban Putnam County, then surrounding it with posted
warnings of guns and video surveillance. When the 9/11 attacks took

place, Ailes sent home all but a bare-bones staff and reportedly told a co-worker: "I've got a bad leg, I'm a little overweight, so I can't run fast, but I will fight." The audience for Fox News grew slowly in the '90s rollout, as hard-core conservatives reveled in a friendlier medium with simpatico talking heads like Bill O'Reilly, and it became and stayed the number-one U.S. cable news channel in the flag-waving days after 9/11. According to news accounts, Ailes didn't always approve of Beck's most outlandish verbal stunts, but in other ways the two men were clearly soul mates, and Fox was the ideal fit for Beck's paranoid reinvention of the notion of political entertainment.

The tsunami hit on January 19, 2009, the Martin Luther King holiday, with Sarah Palin as one of his first guests; the next day, of course, Barack Obama was inaugurated as the forty-fourth president, and over the course of the coming two months the economic mess that Obama inherited seemed only to worsen, with the Dow Jones average closing on March 9 at 6,547, having lost more than half its value since the housing bubble burst in 2007. Mortgages were underwater by the boatload, and unemployment was continuing to rise despite the speedy enactment of the roughly $800 billion stimulus plan that the right-wing talk-o-sphere had quickly and successfully rebranded as liberal pork spending. Panic was in the air—about the future of the economy and the future of America, as evidenced by a survey by Barclay Global Investors that April that showed 58 percent of Americans now expected not to retire but to work until they died, assuming they could find a job or hold onto one. For a while, liberals and conservatives even shared something: anger that Wall Street had been bailed out to the tune of $700 billion by the pols in both parties, when the little guy seemed to get nothing.

This was the cauldron of fear that Glenn Beck showed up to ignite for the early-supper crowd on Fox. It was the role of a lifetime. Viewers of the most-watched cable news network had never seen anything like this before. They were used to its jingoistic patriotism from the heartland to Iraq, and the "What Would Reagan Do?" Republican National Committee–inspired dogma of Sean Hannity, but Beck was an audacious remix of conservatism, a Fox host who wasn't just angry but could feel your pain in the fashion of that bleeding-heart liberal Bill Clinton. Fox viewers had never seen anything like Beck's twelve-step-flavored rawness, his nonlinear lessons in American history, his bursts of anger, his crude language, or his tendency to have tears roll down his cheeks. It was a train wreck of an emotional roller-coaster crash from which no one could turn away—"politics" for the entertainment-besotted baby boomers who'd managed to avoid politics their whole lives but now wanted guidance on whom exactly to tar and feather.

It all came together not on Halloween, as it had for Welles, but on Friday the thirteenth—March 13, 2009, the night that propelled Beck into a new orbit. Just as humans had outnumbered and worn down the fictional aliens that attacked Grover's Mill, New Jersey, that night in 1938, Beck told his audience that they had the power to "surround" the small number of elites, to "pull away the curtain" and expose their true weakness:

> Meanwhile, over 4 million friends and neighbors have lost their jobs in the last four months alone—names that we always thought described American strength, and stocks that are now worth less than a frappachino. And we're all told they're just too big to fail. Yet 70 percent of all jobs are created by the small businessman and nobody seems to even notice him. What happened to the country that loved the underdog and stood up for the little guy? What happened to the voice of the "forgotten man"? The "forgotten" man is you. The voice that no one seems to hear just quietly saying, 'Enforce the law. Take responsibility for yourself. You can't have it all, and anybody who promised that was a liar.'

It was just a few moments later that Beck pulled the maneuver that made him famous, choking back a tear and wiping his eye socket before he uttered, "I'm sorry. I just love my country. And I fear for it." But the tears probably weren't even necessary—he had them at "the little guy."

That night, Beck also managed to make the 9/11 attacks sound like a real-life alien attack on New York, when "[t]he skies were filled with black clouds and our hearts were full of terror and fear. We realized— for the first time—how fragile we really were." As Beck addressed his coast-to-coast audience, viewers saw images of anguished, tearful women, heads in hands, mouths agape, staring at the hellish fires of the World Trade Center, then a mother racing down a Manhattan byway pushing two children in a stroller, away from the deadly dust. But now Beck was here to rally the people of earth—American soil, anyway—to the way the nation felt in responding to the 2001 attack. Although he originally called the March 13, 2009, event "We Surround Them" and the "You Are Not Alone Project," the episode is remembered for the political action group that arose from that day, the 9-12 Project, forever commemorating the day that Americans were both most patriotic and most fearful—the ultimate Glenn Beck state of mind.

IN THE MONTHS that followed, a cottage industry sprang up, all centered on trying to understand and interpret Beck. There were un- authorized biographies and a Mormon-produced DVD about his conversion and more magazine covers and national TV interviews and entire blogs that hung on Beck's every word, many searching for the deep inner meaning of something that may never have been there in the first place. In reality, Beck's place in the great political discourse of the twenty-first century is best defined not by what's going on behind his blue eyes but by the hopes and fears—especially fears—that mil- lions of fans project onto those pupils five nights a week. The real story of Glenn Beck was not taking place in a studio in Midtown Manhattan. It was happening in living rooms up and down the vast contours of the United States, where viewers talked back to the TV screen and wept in tandem with the host and where the most hearty went out to form chapters of the 9-12 Patriots, as Russ Murphy did, or to attend a con- gressman's town hall meeting or a protest march and express outrage over the unbelievable things Beck was teaching them. Beck could take the vague and deeply held fears of so many Americans in this time of economic upheaval and accelerated political change and weave them into a shared experience for millions.

Of the folks that you met over an American winter of discontent, there was one who stayed with you. It took a long time to reconnect, thanks to an unlisted phone and a low Internet profile, to a man unknown to the local Tea Party activists. But after more digging, you pinpointed an address in the rolling hillsides an hour west of Philadelphia, amid a jumble of nineteenth-century barns and newer fortress-like executive homes under massive power lines from the nuclear plant that Russ Murphy had once guarded. Not too far from the Barnes & Noble where Beck had signed books that fall, you drove along a scenic creek and then up a ridiculously steep driveway, where there was a modest ranch house surrounded by ferns and tall pine trees and the shade of deep forest—and that unmistakable Navy Jack flag out front. You ring the doorbell and Al Whayland—seventy-four-year-old job-seeking casualty of the global economic crisis—lets you in.

Whayland says he's still checking the help-wanted ads every day, still looking for a firm that might give an opportunity to a senior citizen whose primary expertise is in mortgage banking, a field that had practically collapsed along with U.S. home prices. He is gruff in tone but unfailingly courteous, a bald man with a white mustache and glasses and the bearing of a ship captain, although his military experience came in the 1950s with the Army Signal Corps, where he eye-witnessed the first air drop of a hydrogen bomb in the South Pacific. He then worked his way through college and rose to a high-ranking position with a venerable Philadelphia savings-and-loan, PSFS, which collapsed in the 1990s; Whayland landed on his feet at GMAC Mortgage, which was spun off as Capmark Financial but then spun out of control from its bad commercial real-estate loans from Ireland to the United States. The firm filed for bankruptcy in 2009, but Whayland had already been laid off by then. Had Whayland not been jobless, he might never have discovered Beck and his show on Fox, since it airs at 5 p.m. and he used to come home from the office around 7 o'clock.

As Whayland spoke, his more effusive wife, Larraine, wandered in in her bathrobe and slippers. The three of you sat around a coffee table with a tall pile of conservative books by Michelle Malkin and Dick Morris, with Beck's *Arguing with Idiots* on top, its pages stuffed with political articles that Whayland has printed out from the Internet. The centerpiece of their stylishly decorated living room—with polished antiques and a large fish tank—was a thirty-two-inch high-def television. You asked if you could return there next week and watch an episode of *The Glenn Beck Program* with them, and they said okay.

In the minutes before 5 p.m. on the appointed night, Al and Larraine Whayland fill in some of the blanks of their sudden, late-in-life interest in conservative politics. Al is the serious one, who traffics in facts and says he's a fan of Beck because the show has researchers who report stories that aren't on the other channels—"he tells you things about this administration." Larraine, who once volunteered for a conservation-minded Democratic state legislator who represented their scenic stretch of the Philly exurbs, is the more outspoken one, and a lot more emotional—she tells you that watching Beck "stirs a lot of emotions for me that I haven't felt for a long time."

"For me, my feeling was that I had to learn so much about him— about Obama—before the election," she says. "I was fearful of what his policies were going to do. I was fearful of the word 'transformation'— that's a very strong word." Larraine Whayland had started watching commentators like Fox News's Sean Hannity by 2008—Beck hadn't joined the cable network yet—and was even more alarmed at the things he and other conservative hosts were saying. "He [Obama] made a statement that the Constitution was no longer valid to him, that it was outdated!" Her voice rises in tone and intensity as she remembers some of the things that she learned from Fox and from talk radio. "He was offered a car and a limo by a big mob boss—a BIG MOB BOSS! Their Chicago house was also given to them!" A moment later, she adds that

Obama "may be an illegitimate heir to the presidency because he wasn't born in this country." At several points, her husband tries to change the flow of her monologue, unsuccessfully.

The conspiratorial political diatribe is interspersed with chatter about the Whaylands' two grown children; at several moments as Larraine talks her way into a frenzy about Obama's supposed ties to the Chicago mob, her two dogs rub her leg or come to her lap, as their black cat scurries past. Since day one, Tea Partiers have bitterly complained about their being stereotyped as cartoonish haters, and this is a point well taken here in the cordial Whayland home. They are generous hosts and they are expressing something that isn't hate but something deeper, anxiety and anger over the things they have heard coming from their television, and a sense that something must be done.

On April 15, 2009, the senior citizens went to their first protest, ever—a Tea Party at the county courthouse in West Chester, Pennsylvania, that attracted three hundred people, and they were caught up in the camaraderie, the passersby honking their horns and giving the thumbs-up. That was what brought Al Whayland back to the Beck book signing in Exton—in fact, he tells you he was having such a good time with the big crowd that night, he never even made it inside to get his book signed. Instead, he hung outside Beck's parked tour bus and snapped pictures with the flag and about sixty or so fans. "I enjoyed it so much, just the people who were interested in the flag," said the lifelong history buff. It sounded like the time of his life.

Al Whayland now has almost a sixth sense when it is 5 p.m., and he clicks on the big screen. The couple adopts their stance for the show. Al sits at an improbable right-angle to the screen—the kind of thing only a guy would do—and holds the remote in his right hand and pointed out the whole time, as if the former signal corpsman is going to shoot off a flare. But Larraine sits square-on to the screen and leans forward a bit in rapt attention, placing a small pillow from the sofa on her lap.

Beck is in mid-season form. Many weeks have passed since that book signing, and so there have been monumental developments in health-care reform and mounting concern that violence is edging its way into the body politic, and he is warning his audience that patriots like Beck's fans—and even Beck himself—are going to take the blame. "America is angry," Beck intones. "The progressives in Washington, the liberal Democrats, they've always said, well, we should understand those in the Middle East and we should talk to them. And yet, they don't want to do that with the Tea Party members. They don't want to do that with about sixty percent." As Beck speaks, his boyish face twisting from sarcastic to sad and back in a matter of seconds, the hot-red and cool-blue graphics are ever radiating, moving, gyrating, doing their part to make sure the people on the couch do not relax too much.

"Can you sell your house?" Beck asks. "Do you have a job?"

Al smiles wanly. "No, and no," he says back to the flat screen.

Beck is running through a series of nightmare news headlines about debt and foreclosures and even the disruption of a terror plot in Saudi Arabia. "Hey, how would you like to add six-dollar-a-gallon gasoline on?" he asks the audience. "How would that be for you?"

Then there is a commercial break.

"I just feel we are on quicksand," Larraine tells you, her voice tinged with angst and despair, voicing her fears that "government oppression and corruption" are going to destroy everything, that the nation faces "death by drowning." Al has muted the volume, and there is a commercial on the screen touting gold coins as the only defense against an economic collapse. Larraine is repeating the same phrases— "quicksand" and "corruption" and "death by drowning"—except now tears are softly welling up in her eyes.

The show comes back, and Beck is still preaching his gospel, one man connecting eye-to-eye with Al and Larraine and with three million other like-minded Americans. "I'm telling you the way to solve this is with faith, hope, and charity," Beck says. "We're under attack unlike anything ever before from multiple fronts. I've talked about almost—gosh, probably eight years now. A perfect storm would come.

"It's here."

There is a short segment with an author, a kind of cool-down period, and then the hour is over. The main thing you still want to know is what Al Whayland says in response to those who say that Beck's emoting is nothing more than contrived fearmongering.

"Yeah, there is fear—but he [Beck] backs up everything he says with facts," Al responds. "There *is* fear out there—in fact, I'm scared to death—but he's not generating it. He's bringing things to our attention—things that we ought to be aware of."

CHAPTER FOUR
_____

Fear and Loathing at Knob Creek

The first good look you have at heavy weaponry comes a few weeks after the Beck book-signing extravaganza. It is at a mildly famous event called the Knob Creek Machine Gun Shoot—held down in a Kentucky holler that you reach by renting a car at the Louisville airport and aiming south, down the old Dixie Highway where lush, oak-covered knobs singed with autumn rise on your left while on your right, the view of the sturdy, white-roofed Kosmodale Baptist Church is obscured by the crooked, goofy neon of Al's Beer Bait Depot. The beer, bait, and Bibles come just a few yards before the Rivergirls Lounge, whose mysteries are hidden behind hot-pink, windowless cinder block, heralded by roadside letters reading "Welcome Knob Creek Machine Gun Shoot."

At the height of a Kentucky rain far more savage than the one Elvis once sang about, you wedge a tiny gray Hyundai rental into a miniature gap in the line of bulked-up, performance-enhanced pickup trucks that run for about a mile down both sides of Highway 44. The behemoths sport Kentucky's "Choose Life" state-sanctioned license-plate slogan or are festooned with stickers like "Got a Birth Certificate" or the recent 2008 official McCain-Palin campaign bumper sticker—except with McCain scraped away to leave just the name of the ex–Alaska governor, now a patron saint to America's gun aficionados. It's a long walk to the ten-dollar ticket booth, and marching toward the rear hills, you see a payloader moving slowing across the muck with its cargo of fresh fall pumpkins, which might have been a bucolic harbinger of fall had the machinery not been zigzagging past a real-life Grand Theft Auto screen shot of bombed-out Buicks and simmering, bullet-riddled refrigerators.

Welcome to the Knob Creek Machine Gun Shoot, indeed. For America's enthusiastic fans of light artillery and heavy firepower, this is pretty much like the Super Bowl . . . if the Super Bowl were played every six months, with a shattered, smoldering sedan straddling the forty-yard-line and if the halftime show wasn't Paul McCartney or Tom Petty but a band from the Poconos singing ditties about the Zionist occupation of America. Every October and again in April, they swarm here by the thousands, south from half-empty Wisconsin paper-mill towns and north from the Tennessee foothills, transporting their M–3 submachine guns with their tripods in the back of a Ford Explorer over the highways of red states with loose gun laws, or else they just bring enough cash for a couple of forays down the quite consciously Vietnam-styled Jungle Walk, forking over thirty-five dollars for fifty rounds of ammo and a chance to ding some metal.

On this gray and soggy October afternoon, many attendees seek refuge under a tent for gun and military-collectible merchants that has grown steadily over a couple of decades to where this lethal mall is now nearly the size of a football field. It is a place where you might find a genuine Vickers machine gun from World War I or a Soviet SA7 or Brazilian bayonets or a case of various and sundry machine-gun triggers with a "Nobama" sticker on the side or the spent shell from a Patriot anti-Scud missile, which retails for $1,550 at an event where gawking is widespread but actual money-changing in this year of the Great Recession seems pretty rare. Hundreds more sit shell-shocked and awestruck in four rows of bleachers overlooking the main shooting range, where at about ten minutes past every hour a horn goes off and a line of machine-gunners crouches behind tripods, broken up by a lone gunman picking up his AK–47 and even the occasional sonic boom of a Vietnam-era cannon.

On the second afternoon, they take down the rope and let agog bystanders trample onto the firing range, into the muck of what you could now call Gunstock, three days of slugs and music and mud galore—even as gray smoke still sizzles with an eerie hiss and rises in a column from what was once a boxy, mid-'60s-style sedan, propped six feet in the air atop a massive industrial spool. The crisp fall air is filled with the odor of gunpowder and charred pumpkin flesh as dozens of folks slosh around a few identifiable car parts that had been blown back to earth—a pockmarked muffler here, a smoldering tire there. A teenager—wearing a shirt that reads "America's Bible Belt" over a black-and-white picture of a gun holster—peers inside the hollowed-out interior, while a few others comb the ground like crime-scene investigators, looking for bullet fragments around an old refrigerator riddled with hundreds of holes. While this is going on, workers tow a large, virgin RV to the back of the range. "See that?" says one of the onlookers, eyes widening. "Fresh meat!"

Eventually, the line of bystanders works its way back to Machine Gun Row, where a seventy-year-old Vietnam vet is showing off his MG 42, a rare, rapid-fire machine gun that was developed by the Nazis at the height of World War II. Despite his insistence that he doesn't want to be named or even interviewed, he launches into a thirty-minute monologue that jumps from the dangers of a more liberal Supreme Court to his worries that an eighty-eight-year-old man couldn't get a knee replacement under "Obamacare" to listing the states through which he cannot drive his valuable weapons, such as California ("A communist state!" his gun-line neighbor chimes in). His main message to Knob Creek newcomers is that you haven't seen anything yet, not until the heavy firepower of the famous Saturday Night Shoot. "It looks like Baghdad on the first night of the Gulf War!" the gray-maned septuagenarian exalts. "God bless America. This is something that could only happen in this country—the greatest country in the world!"

Then you stroll back over to the pole tent, where two men are selling a Photoshopped photo of a boyish Barack Obama comforted by a paternal Adolf Hitler.

Their booth is called the Bazooka Brothers. At a long table, underneath a relic of the famous World War II–era rocket launcher, the two guys from Kokomo, Indiana, are also selling a rapid-fire variant of the lower part of the AR–15 semiautomatic assault rifle, a type of heavy-firepower component that was outlawed in America for a decade before then-president George W. Bush and a Republican-controlled Congress allowed the assault-weapon ban to expire in 2004. And at the front counter, it is just two dollars for this black-and-white glossy Photoshop job depicting Obama in an adolescent guise, in a plain white T-shirt, upright in a kitchen chair, while with his hands on our future president's youthful shoulder, in a soft parental pose, is the casually dressed Nazi Führer.

"I've sold a stack of them—they did a good job," one of the Bazooka Brothers (okay, not really brothers), Brian Kitts, says, gradually warming up to the topic. He says he doesn't know who had produced the Obama-Hitler Photoshop and was vague as to how exactly he came to be selling it alongside a card of the now semi-famous poster of Obama as The Joker, over the word "Socialism"—ironically, the very same image that the finance chief of the Republican National Committee would use just six months later in a presentation on using fear to raise campaign cash.

Why does he think the Nazi comparison is valid?

"At the very core, he's un-American," the gun merchant says of Obama. "The rest of the world sees him as weak and that's going to bite us in the ass." Kitts says he's been selling his brand of heavy firepower at Knob Creek for more than two decades, and—despite nary a word from Obama in support of gun control in the initial months of his presidency—he doesn't think it's far-fetched that his government would someday come knocking for people's weapons.

"There will have to be an emergency, or to compare it to Germany, a Reichstag event," Kitts continues, referring to the 1933 blaze at the German Parliament that Hitler blamed on Communists and used as an excuse to suspend civil liberties and consolidate power. "So here's a problem—we've got to declare martial law and suspend the Constitution indefinitely. . . . Will that happen? I don't know. It's possible. That's what a lot of people are afraid of. A lot of people here are really into military history, and history can repeat itself." As he speaks, a man who looks to be in his eighties strolls by, grins at the Obama-Hitler picture, and makes a disparaging remark about the president winning the Nobel Peace Prize, which had been announced the day before.

"You know damn well what he did to get it," the man mutters. "Look around. What's the majority here, and what's the minority."

Back in the 1970s, when the real guns of Vietnam were still ringing in the nation's ears, the Knob Creek Machine Gun Shoot was about nothing more than a bunch of guys taking advantage of this old abandoned naval firing range, six hundred acres way back up in the woods, to fire off their automatic weapons without hurting anybody (hopefully). The event even went away for a few years, but it roared back in 1984— that "Morning in America" year, when gas prices came down and the lure of massive firepower went up. People from around the country and even overseas kept bringing more and more cowbell to the knobby hills of northwestern Kentucky—the deadly mini-guns that had been fired from the helicopters in 'Nam, Civil War–style cannons, even a fondly remembered figure known to all as "the flamethrower man." But over these years, a darker political undercurrent began to swirl at Knob Creek—especially when Democrat Bill Clinton took office and worked with Congress to pass a middling gun-control law in 1994.

The new law had no practical effect on the party at Knob Creek, but the now-growing militias on the paranoid fringe found that the shooting hoedown was also an effective recruiting spot, a place where concern over the rights of gun owners simmered and then boiled into anger at the government—a flame that was rekindled in 2008 with the looming election of Obama. In April 2009, young journalist Dave Weigel, then of the *Washington Independent*, ventured out to Knob Creek on a last-minute whim and was alarmed by the level of what he described as "panic" over the first Democratic president in eight years and the first African-American president ever. In addition to a predictable array of anti-Obama T-shirts and slogans like "Hitler Gave Great Speeches, Too," he found that the Obama-citizenship-denying birthers had set up their own table right next to the National Rifle Association—with a surprise appearance by the woman who was at that time the blond, combative face of the so-called birther movement, Los Angeles dentist/realtor/attorney Orly Taitz. Meanwhile, her ally—Carl Swensson of Georgia—was gathering signatures for his "citizen's grand jury" that he hoped would indict the sitting president for faking his birth certificate, despite the overwhelming evidence that no such thing had taken place. It was the start of spring, and these were the first green, poisonous shoots hinting that a counterrevolution was in the April breeze.

This is why you have come to Knob Creek six months later. The world is just now, this fall, getting its arms around the notion and the paranoid stylings of the Obama backlash and noticing what is on the surface, the newcomers to politics like laid-off Al Whayland and the movement activist Russ Murphy and their public protests. But this place tucked far back in the Appalachian hills has long been a hidden incubator, where radical ideas about the government and about elite-driven conspiracies cross-pollinate, and then every six months get blown back across the heartland like wind-driven apple seeds, finding their way onto the Internet and local call-in shows and then slowly blossoming into the national conversation. And Knob Creek is also a place that reveals to its true believers that nothing is more central to the roots of American rights and exceptionalism than the guns that speak freely here in a steady roar. This notion is now embedded in the Tea Party movement, quickly becoming a core issue even among the party's new arrivals who might not know the difference between a semiautomatic and a flamethrower.

By October 2009, the leaves are beginning to die, and the high-profile vanguard of the anti-Obama reactionaries have mostly moved on—Taitz is now a cable-TV mini-celebrity embroiled in a web of lawsuits. The initial shock of Obama has worn off, too, to be replaced by a certain background buzz of rage and resentment, and with some hopes among the gun-bangers and militia recruiters that a dipping White House approval rating means that more of America beyond the firing range is seeing things their way. Yet their discontent still hovers over things like the black smoke from a flaming refrigerator. You can feel it the very second you first pass through the ticket booths, when the hawker of the *Shotgun News* hollers, "Win the Nobel Peace Prize in two easy steps!," causing knowing guffaws to cascade back down the line.

It is here in the Kentucky hills that you can see the roots of an idea that has animated the anti-Obama movement from day one: a new ultraliberal Democratic administration hailing from the gun-control capital of Chicago will tackle a variety of anti-gun initiatives. These presumed Obama initiatives range from the minimal (pushing through strict new laws that would restore the ban on automatic weapons that expired under George W. Bush, or placing a painful new government tax on ammunition) to the severe (taking advantage of a national emergency to adopt dictatorial powers that would begin with confiscating the legally owned guns of law-abiding Americans). Indeed, the widespread fear of the "Obama gun confiscation"—the polar opposite of the actual policy approach that the forty-fourth president adopted toward gun issues in the first fifteen months of his presidency—was such an irrational force that it became a kind of policy-oriented twin to the birther theory, helping to propel anti-Obama sentiment, not to mention the fear that Glenn Beck spoke of so frequently, into the zeitgeist. Both ideas gained their strength from the same heart of human darkness: that the Harvard-schooled, first black president in U.S. history simply did not share their values and therefore could not be trusted. For the birthers, this meant that his presidency had to be illegitimate; for the pro-gun zealots, this meant not just gun control but full-blown gun confiscation just had to be coming.

And so from the start, the backlash was fueled with an almost religious pro-gun fervor, and again it bubbled up toward the top of the national discourse. Starting somewhere around January 20, 2009, there were Americans who wanted the world to know that their right to bear arms even included at rallies with the president of the United States; one man who showed up outside a New Hampshire church where Obama was speaking that August had a pistol in his holster and a sign that quoted Thomas Jefferson: "The tree of liberty must be refreshed from time to time, with the blood of patriots and tyrants." A few months later, a conservative activist named Kitty Werthmann spoke at the Take Back America conference in St. Louis—a heavily female event organized by right-wing warhorse Phyllis Schafly of the Eagle Forum—and compared Obama's policies on guns to what she'd witnessed as a child in Hitler's 1930s Austria. "If we had our guns, we would have fought a bloody battle. So, keep your guns, and buy more guns, and buy ammunition." By 2010, an "open carry" movement of folks carrying their Glocks into their corner Starbucks in the forty-three states where unconcealed weapons are legal would gain tens of thousands of adherents—firearms chic.

All this despite the fact that since Obama became president the only law that he'd signed that related to guns was one that made American weapons restrictions even more lax, by allowing citizens to bring their weapons to national parks and on Amtrak trains. Indeed, throughout the first couple of years of Obama's presidency, the movement in state capitals and in courtrooms across America and even in a Democrat-controlled Congress was to make it easier to bear arms, not harder. These victories for the gun lobby rarely showed up on the media radar screen, but the "Obama gun confiscation" or a federal tax on ammo or other things that were not happening remained a source of nonstop chatter on the Internet.

And so, rational or not, it was under this banner of gun rights that this group of angry, conservative Americans gathered together to voice their collective fear of this administration, straining to shout their complaints about "losing their gun rights" over the high-decibel jack-hammer pounding of a row of .50-caliber machine guns strafing the Kentucky woodlands.

"IF YOU HAVE just a passing interest in guns, you've got to come to the crick," John Grant tells you. "Because it's like a Mos-lem going to Mecca."

You are sitting on the hard wood bleachers, resting your ears during a lull in the firing. You'd been talking with the only other journalist you encountered at Knob Creek, when Grant, amused, overheard you discussing the paucity of black faces at Knob Creek (for the record, you spotted six African-Americans among thousands over two days). Grant—sixtyish, a Vietnam veteran with a salt-and-pepper beard covering a face weathered over years spent up north in his hometown of New London, Wisconsin, wearing a camouflage jacket and a "Mohican Nation" baseball cap, clutching a pack of Camels in one hand—is eager to talk about the shoot and even to mock some of its more paranoid style. He positions himself as the voice of reason, here to explain Knob Creek in an accent melted with Wisconsin cheddar. "It's a guy thing," he continues. "You get down here, you have a few drinks with your buddies in the motel, and you come out to the range to see this. You see the guns that you've only read about!"

Grant says that he's shot in previous years at Knob Creek, but like a lot of regular folks (he used to be a sheriff's deputy back home) he finds that basic ammunition is getting too pricey, especially after the run on bullets that took place after the Democrats reclaimed the federal government in the 2008 elections. But he said he's here because he still gets off, after all these years, on the "unfrickingbelieveable" fireworks of the night shoot, which vividly remind him of his eighteen months with an Army cavalry unit in Southeast Asia, "The tracers, the pyrotechnics—about the only thing you don't have is somebody in the background screaming." He knows all about the fringe factor here. His first time here five years ago, Grant says, there was a rock band singing, "'We're white guys, we're Masons and we have guns' . . . *Okay, we're in Redneck heaven.*"

But he also admits he's increasingly alarmed by the radicalism of some of his buddies back home. One of them used to come along with him to Knob Creek every six months but now wants no part of it. "He says, 'That place is crawling with ATF [federal Alcohol, Tobacco and Firearms] agents.'" Grant's friend used to be consumed with his job as a police officer, but a few years ago he retired and instead started spending his days combing the Internet for conspiracy theories. The absent pal now believes that some 100,000 Russian troops are hiding in an underground base below Denver—"eating McDonald's" and preparing for God knows what. "He's gotten so paranoid that you can't talk to him anymore—you're afraid of the conversation," Grant says—and he's not the only one. A second friend called Grant in a panic the other day, he tells you, because he swore he'd seen "an East German army convoy" rumbling through the streets of Neenah, Wisconsin. Grant says he had to remind his pal that (a) East Germany no longer exists, and (b) it probably was just the newest vehicles from the nearby Oshkosh Truck factory rolling off the line.

Grant tells you his own political philosophy is rooted in "common sense," but in the land of the machine gun, the commonsense guy is still pretty far to the right. "We have a Secretary of Health, Education and Welfare who's advocating for gay rights," says Grant, using the old title for the cabinet post and seemingly also unaware that support for at least basic gay rights had grown pretty mainstream. "We've got a black president who today, I found out, is nominated for the Nobel Peace Prize—what the hell is that for?" (Grant was still unaware that Obama wasn't just nominated but actually won.)

He is the first of a number of folks you spoke to with the same verbal tic, describing Obama as "a black president" while quickly adding that their problem with him was competence, not race. "There's a useless guy in office who got elected because a lot of people felt because he's blaaaaack, quote unquote," he says, dragging out the syllable while making an air quote, "that, 'Well, he'll be a good president.' The man is an idiot. I'm sorry."

At Knob Creek, the manly aroma of gunpowder frequently masks the scent of fear, and as he speaks, Grant, an inhabitant of Wisconsin's Paper Valley, where good jobs are fading fast, manages to cover all the grand themes of the current anxieties, reflecting the paranoia and the insecurity of small towns and fading Rust Belt cities that felt under assault by both economic and cultural changes. As with so many of the folks who had too few hours of work and too many hours for talk radio and Fox News, his words all bleed together into the largely hypothetical and often illogical notion that the government is coming for their guns. And not just the big ones that rip apart Frigidaires, but also the small handguns that are the only thing making them feel safe in a big city or even in a small town in the Badger State.

"I today carry a loaded firearm, which I would not have done ten years ago," Grant says. You start to ask him what he is afraid of, but stumble as you wonder whether "afraid" is the right word. Grant assures you it is the right word. "What am I afraid of? I do not know—but I feel far more comfortable knowing that I have my nine-millimeter in my car. I stay in a cheap motel and the first thing I do when I unpack is I set my nine-millimeter where I can reach it."

That undercurrent of fear runs from general threats like a rise in crime (even as rates were actually falling) to specific worries about supposedly government-sponsored plans to infringe on gun rights. Right after Obama became president, reports began circulating that ammo had grown exorbitantly expensive, or was flat-out impossible to find. To people who lived on America's east and west coasts, the news sounded alarming, presented along the lines of "there's a black guy in the White House for the first time, and suddenly America is running out of bullets." It sounded crazy, but it really did happen, for reasons that—like anything to do with the laws of economics—defied a simple explanation.

First came the anecdotes—Wal-Mart was limiting its customers at some stores to just one box of fifty bullets per month—and then the apologetic public statements from the leading makers of bullets ("We have added extra shifts, machinery and we are also in the process of expanding our manufacturing plant," the ammo company Hornady assured its customers), followed by the almost complete unavailability of .380 ammo, the kind that's used in cheaper concealed handguns; and finally a Manassas, Virginia, gun-shop owner telling USA Today that he'd never seen anything like this, and "I was here for Y2K, September 11, Katrina." Then statistics proved it wasn't just hype. In the first quarter of 2009—the time period that included Obama's inauguration—the excise tax that gun and ammunition makers pay to the federal government based on what they sell rose by a whopping 43 percent over the same period in 2008. And that rise in business came during the nadir of the worst economy America had seen since the Great Depression.

Much of the news coverage of the ammo crisis in the early days of the Obama presidency implied that all the extra bullets floating around (some two billion—with a "B"!—extra, according to the NRA) were pointed at the head of America's first African-American president, or maybe fueling an armed uprising against him. But that wasn't it, not really. Millions of those bullets today are still out in the garage under the tool box, or maybe under the bed of some guy like John Grant who was afraid of something in 2009 that didn't have a name.

That's because the rumors had started during the 2008 campaign that Obama and the congressional Democrats knew they couldn't outlaw guns so they would tax the bejeezus out of bullets instead. In reality, there was no such plan—during 2007 and 2008 candidate Obama had almost never talked about guns, except when asked, and then recited the predictable pro–Second Amendment mantra you might expect from an incumbent senator from the deer-hunting prairie state of Illinois. For example, Obama—albeit in remarkably vague language—positioned himself to the right of many gun-control advocates who were his progressive political supporters in 2008, by asserting that the Second Amendment right to bear arms applies to individuals and not just to "a well-regulated militia."

However misguided the paranoia about Obama's stance on guns may have been, the unyielding laws of supply and demand combined with this anxiety to create a very real effect on America's gun-industrial complex. Weekend warriors of the shooting range and your garden-variety "Saturday night special" owners started hoarding bullets—and with that, the rumors grew more outlandish. As with so many other things about the backlash, the Internet was critical in spreading information—bad information, on this occasion—and reinforcing views that had no basis in reality. Did Wal-Mart running out of bullets really reflect just a huge rush of customers, anonymous posters speculated—or was the government already secretly cracking down? As one poster on the conspiracy Web site Abovetopsecret.com wrote at the height of the .380 bullet shortage: "One has to wonder if a certain percentage of the 'citizens' who were buying up all the ammo and weapons in record numbers were actually government agents?" Meanwhile, a gun-store owner in Fort Worth, Texas, reported that a box of nine-millimeter bullets that had once sold for $14.98 was now selling for $39. In a panic that the federal government was going to tax their bullets, America's gun owners effectively taxed themselves. Prices and public paranoia spiraled upward in tandem.

And that is the mind-boggling reality: while citizens already hurting from the worst U.S. economy in seventy-five years were riled up about the government confiscating their guns, the gun companies were busy confiscating their cash—to the tune of millions of dollars. Take the nation's largest and most iconic firearms company, Smith and Wesson; during the first full quarter under the Obama administration, the Massachusetts-based maker of pistols and revolvers said that its profits had more than doubled from the year before, from $3.3 million up to $7.4 million, and over the course of 2009 the shares of Smith and Wesson would triple in value, a huge windfall for gun-company owners in the face of a president who was rumored to be shutting them down while doing no such thing. Profits were also doubling at Olin Corporation—the parent company of Winchester and maker of ammunition—and some dealers were accusing the big companies of gouging, saying that boxes of some types of bullets that sold for $10 were coming in at closer to $100 by the first Obama summer.

"When you do find it, it's basically highway robbery," a local gun owner told the *Alton* [Illinois] *Telegraph*. "They know they can charge whatever they want, so they're just ripping you off. Definite price-gouging." There's no evidence that the gun companies were creating the rumors; it's just that they weren't exactly racing out to knock them down, not with millions of dollars flowing their way, money for nothing. They were profiting from the fear and paranoia of misinformed citizens—and they would not be the only ones to do so in the Age of Obama. Indeed, far from it.

By October 2009 in Knob Creek, prices for ammo were actually easing somewhat from the highs of spring but were still above normal. The paranoia remained near record levels, though. The apparent bullet shortage had taken its toll, adding fuel to the fire for a conspiracy-minded group. Despite all evidence to the contrary, everyone you talked to at Knob Creek still believed that the Obama administration and congressional Democrats were plotting against gun ownership, that they were just waiting until after the 2010 elections (although no one ever explained why they wouldn't be worried about the 2012 elections at that time) or perhaps some Reichstag-like event, in which case there wouldn't be more elections—just like what happened with Hitler.

Indeed, the kind of gun buffs that patronize an event like this are also military history fanatics, and so after a while it's not even that alarming to round a corner and hear the voice of the Führer booming from a DVD player, in a documentary being sold at one of the stands. The fascination with the history of war was the gateway drug for comparing Obama to Hitler, as did the Minnesota merchant at a Knob Creek booth—a Republican committeeman in Michele Bachmann's congressional district, it turned out—who was briskly selling a T-shirt that read "The Fourth Reich: Obama/Biden 2012."

It was a weird thing—all the Hitler references. It seemed to harken back to Richard Hofstadter and his paranoid style, this idea that the radical fringe wasn't just expressing a simple political disagreement but that "[t]he paranoid spokesman sees the fate of conspiracy in apocalyptic terms—he traffics in the birth and death of whole worlds." There was no easier shorthand to provide that sense of purpose and urgency than comparing the modern-day situation in America to the things that happened in Nazi Germany, events not too long ago but just distant enough that few who are alive remember them. Glenn Beck remains the master of this genre, although over time he blurted out so many comparisons to the Third Reich and its key players that the comedian Lewis Black famously, and hilariously, wondered whether the Fox News host suffered from what he called "Hitler Tourette's."

A voice of machine-gun reason—in a relative sense—seems to be a guy named Howard Block, who normally peddles belted machine guns from a small store in Upper Darby, Pennsylvania, just a stone's throw west of some of Philadelphia's most bullet-pocked neighborhoods. He's been coming to Knob Creek for nearly fifteen years now, and he's watched the array of federal laws regulating machine guns and other assault rifles make his business more complicated but arguably more lucrative. "My first one was an MG–5," he tells you. "I built the whole gun for three thousand dollars, but it would be eighteen thousand today." Block adds, "Now, I don't buy anything to collect. I buy to sell."

The gray-haired Block speaks of the gun debate in a slight Philly accent tinged with the exhaustion of a political argument that never seems to go away. "A lot of people think the Second Amendment is crap, and the First Amendment is so important. Well, the Second Amendment protects the First," he says, ignoring the fact that dozens of Philadelphians just a short SEPTA bus ride from his blue-collar-suburban shop have been gunned down in recent years so they wouldn't

testify in criminal cases, an extreme termination of their First Amendment rights. Block insists that the reason for the widespread distrust of
government at Knob Creek is intuitive. Ever since 1968, he says, when
Congress passed the gun control law that required registration of dealers and banned the importation of military assault rifles in the wake
of the assassinations of Robert F. Kennedy and Martin Luther King,
the federal government has been regularly adding restrictions on guns
that are never repealed. "The '94 law—it didn't change anything," he
says of the Brady Bill, which required background checks and five-day
waiting periods for handgun purchases. "New Jersey"—just across the
Delaware River from Block's stomping grounds—"is very restrictive—
you can't even own a machine gun there—but the crime rate isn't lower.
. . . Nobody goes out with a five-thousand-dollar machine gun and
commits a crime."

Block's history lesson isn't 100 percent correct, since that ten-year
ban on semiautomatic assault rifles—a law the weapons industry had
largely ignored anyway by making very minor cosmetic changes to the
heavier guns it churned out—was allowed to expire in 2004. In fact,
for all the alarmist talk, the trend as the first decade of the twenty-first
century came to a close was in the direction of making it easier to own
guns in America, and then to let folks carry them into more places.
Some of that was taking place in the legislatures of the red states that
had voted for John McCain in 2008 and were now taking proactive
pro-gun measures. That was the case in 2009 in Kentucky's southern
neighbor of Tennessee, where lawmakers voted to allow licensed gun
owners to carry their piece into bars and restaurants (although they
wouldn't be allowed to drink alcohol), overriding not only a veto from
the governor of the Volunteer State but also the vow by many restaurant
owners to opt out, fearing for the safety of customers.

By 2010, lawmakers in Virginia had upped the stakes even further, not only voting to okay concealed guns in bars and restaurants
but also seeking to rescind a law that allows only one gun purchase a
month—even though experts had long fingered Virginia as a leading

source of weapons used in crimes up and down the East Coast. The response from the supposedly anti-gun Obama administration to this flurry of action on the state level was silence. In fact, in 2010 the leading gun control group in America—the Brady Campaign to End Gun Violence—issued a report card for the Obama administration with seven grades, all of them failing.

It would be easy to write off all the gun paranoia that you witnessed at Knob Creek as harmless delusion in these remote woodlands so far—both literally and figuratively—from Washington and the other places where decisions are made. But there were growing signs that Second Amendment paranoia was driving lawmakers to take actions that would make it harder for authorities to keep tabs on guns and possibly increase the supply even further—largely to head off the rumored federal crackdown. Montana, for example, home to right-wing populist movements like Celebrating Conservatism, became one of the first states to enact a law barring any federal regulations on guns manufactured and sold within state lines, while Arizona made it legal for its residents to carry concealed weapons without a permit—a law passed months after an armed man showed up in the crowd outside a venue where President Obama was giving a speech.

The power of paranoia is what really undercut the message from gun merchant Howard Block, and the message of all the gun traders and enthusiasts you spoke with over a couple of days in Kentucky's gentle foothills: their words about the rising tide of anti-gun totalitarianism were often shouted over the blam-blam-blam-blam throbbing that echoed off the Appalachian oak like a chorus line of jackhammers, the pinging of the skeleton frames of burned-out Chevrolets. The murmurs about the looming Great Obama Gun Confiscation of 2011 sank into a football-field-sized Persian bazaar of black-barreled machine guns punctuated by the occasional bazooka, stretching as far as the eye could see. This is the biggest disconnect that ricocheted off the hillsides of Knob Creek, the gun-happiest place on earth.

It didn't take more than a few minutes here to begin to see how wide the gulf was between gun talk and gun reality. The advocates of stricter gun laws in the United States are driven by cold facts; studies have shown that the murder rate in this country is about six times higher than those of comparable westernized nations, and that a big chunk of that disparity is attributable to the availability of guns, estimated at about one for every U.S. adult. Yet the Howard Blocks of this world are also right in that actual gun laws that have passed over four decades have done next to nothing either toward reducing crime rates—which seem to ebb and flow more on the availability of jobs than of AK–47s—or toward reducing the kind of heavy firepower now ripping up the hillside at Knob Creek. It's a troubling paradox: after more than forty years of debating gun control in America, the only thing with any power or meaning is the debate itself. The only result we can truly point to since 1968 is an increase in paranoia—and paranoia is a precursor of violence.

Late on the first day of the gun spectacle, you stumble across a small booth in the back corner, farthest from the firing range, manned by a soft-featured and soft-spoken fifty-something gentleman, kind of Wilford Brimley-ish, with a light beard that curves around his face. Unlike all the booths around him with their bazookas or rapid-fire weaponry, the man sells only what you might call machine-gun-shoot accessories—flares and key chains and whatnot. But his main product is a large stand filled with DVDs with titles you'd not seen before—fiery pictures of an exploding World Trade Center and the most menacing public snapshots of the normally-not-very-menacing Barack Obama. The man tells you in the gentle, "you betcha" tones of central Wisconsin that he is Joe Gayan from the once-industrial town of West Bend, and he wants you to know about everything that he has done personally to try to get the Obama birther theory into the mainstream.

Gayan says it all started for him in September of 2008 when he heard the Pennsylvania lawyer Phil Berg—whom the Wisconsin man had already been following because of his theories about government involvement in the 9/11 attacks—give a radio interview about his belief that the future president had been born in Kenya. The idea resonated with Gayan the second that he heard it.

"And right away I just thought it was true," says Gayan, who tells you with enthusiasm about comments from Obama's grandmother and a Kenyan ambassador suggesting the forty-fourth president was born in Africa—all ideas that have been completely debunked by mainstream reports. But Gayan burned eighty CD copies of the Berg interview and several weeks later, at the October 2008 shoot at Knob Creek, he was selling them for three dollars apiece. One of his customers was a woman who—at least according to Gayan's account—was also taken up by the issue and began searching the country for a lawyer who would take the case, and that lawyer was Orly Taitz—which is how Taitz ended up at Knob Creek in April 2009.

Gayan's connection to the spread of the birther theory (which, a Google search shows, Gayan comments about with considerable gusto on newspaper Web sites from coast to coast) sounds plausible—more plausible than most of Gayan's other ideas about topics such as 9/11 and theories that the Twin Towers were brought down by explosives and that a plane did not hit the Pentagon. ("There was nothing there— no luggage, no landing gear, no heads rolling around—no nothing," he says of Flight 77 striking the Pentagon.) And as for Obama, Gayan wants you to know that he is not a racist—he would gladly vote for the black conservative Alan Keyes—but adds that "the people that in-stalled this guy knew that it [his race] would freeze most people, that they would be afraid of being called a racist. If it were a white guy, they'd be all over him."

As a baby boomer who grew up in the 1960s, Gayan—who is mar-ried and a father of four successful children—says the events of his youth caused him to distrust the government. He was an only child whose father had died when John F. Kennedy was assassinated in 1963. "I was ten years old and I saw the shot that they said Oswald had to take to be the lone assassin, and I said there is no way on earth that anybody could make that shot," he recalls. "That's how I got started—now anytime something big comes out, I look at it with a jaundiced eye. That's just me."

You ask Gayan what he does when he's not selling DVDs and other knickknacks at gun shows, and he tells you that he's "retired." You ask what he used to do, and it turns out he'd worked for some thirty-two years at his hometown's West Bend Industries, producing plastic parts for coffeemakers and other small appliances. In 2001, when Gayan was only in his late forties, his position vanished as the small appliance makers of central Wisconsin moved most of their jobs to the cheap labor markets of China. "I lost my job, so I kind of ended up retiring," he says. Does he harbor any resentment? "Yeah, that kind of grates on you. I've said that the next time that corporate America wants to go to war, maybe they should go hire a bunch of Chinese and Mexicans to fight it."

Before you leave, Gayan wants to make sure you see his favorite sale item, a T-shirt with a quote attributed to Thomas Jefferson: "The beauty of the 2nd Amendment is that you will not need it until they try to take it."

"I looked for two years for that quote because I wanted to get it right," Gayan says. "I found it on Fightthebias.com." Actually, there's a reason that it took Gayan so long to find the quote that he's now selling: there's no evidence that Jefferson ever said it—although it now circulates widely on the Internet, one of a number of bogus quotes attributed to the Founding Fathers that fuel the Obama backlash.

The real war in America—the dismantling of the nation's heartland economy—didn't have the same emotional pull for Gayan. Yet for all the folks milling around Knob Creek with a hot dog in one hand and an assault rifle in the other as the fabled Night Shoot approaches, the machine gun extravaganza isn't the largest gathering within range of Louisville this weekend. Back up the Dixie Highway, more than ten thousand people are lining up for something about as rare as a machine gun shoot: the General Electric factory in Appliance Park is adding ninety union workers at newly reduced salaries of $27,000 a year but with considerable benefits, including health insurance. More than half the people on the long job lines lack a high school diploma, according to the *Louisville Courier-Journal*; with unemployment in Louisville at 10.8 percent that month, many of them were clinging to a spouse's income or working part-time gigs, such as laying down home flooring.

A man named Shane Hopkins who'd recently lost his job at a plastics factory told the newspaper that he and his wife—on the books as "an independent contractor" at an auto parts plant—were now paying $300 a month out of their depleted checking account to get health coverage. The forty-eight-year-old man added, "I am thinking seriously about going to McDonald's, just for the benefits if nothing else."

And so now the good people of Kentucky and neighboring states who weren't on the job line at GE were down here in the hollow, ripping apart old refrigerators that might just as well have come from Appliance Park with .50-caliber machine-gun fire that left a Frigidaire looking like a moldy piece of weeks-old Swiss cheese. You didn't need to be Sigmund Freud or even to have taken Psychology 101 to realize there was something more primal going on here. The forces that took away all those jobs in the paper mills and the auto plants and the plastics factory—from globalization to automation—were powerful yet unseen, anonymous, and now, blowing up these relics from the glory days of American industry was oddly cathartic in a way that didn't need to be put into words. Meanwhile, in their huddled conversations underneath hanging bazookas, these folks had finally found the perfect foil in a president who not only was (somewhat) liberal but—in the pitch-perfect description of the Wisconsin Vietnam vet John Grant—was "blaaaaack," with air quotes.

Barack Obama was the inevitable boogeyman that two generations of resentment politics in America had been leading up to, combining the notions that blacks benefitting from affirmative action were squeezing the white working class on one end and that elitists—like Obama the Harvard-trained law professor—were now looking down on their plight. On a gut level, it just made more sense to people at Knob Creek that Obama was going to take away their guns—despite the lack of evidence—than the far-less-sinister idea that his policies were trying to keep a middle-aged guy like Shane Hopkins from having to flip burgers at McDonald's just to get health insurance.

GIVEN THE TENOR of the conversations at Knob Creek and the way the tension slowly mounts toward the big shoot-out, it should come as no surprise that as night descends, the militia types begin to suddenly pop up from nowhere, like stink bugs on window screens.

Late on Saturday afternoon, a man appears handing out small, crudely produced flyers for an Internet radio show. He is in his early fifties, a tad chubby, with a thick mustache, wire-rimmed glasses, and a Nixonian receding hairline. Far from threatening, the man with his postcard-sized flyers for Liberty Tree Radio on the Internet ("Support the militia. Unlike Washington we work to protect American sovereignty.") looks like a Midwestern accountant out for some weekend thrills, perhaps an older version of the weird, geeky, corporate character that Matt Damon portrayed in *The Informant*.

It takes you a few minutes to realize that this is "Mark from Michigan"—Mark Koernke, who gained a smidgeon of national notoriety as a leader of the first militia movement that popped up during the Clinton years of the 1990s. In fact, it was Koernke who—during a stint with the conspiracy-minded shortwave radio station WWCR out of Nashville—not only theorized that the 1995 Oklahoma City bombing was an inside job but first popularized the idea of "black helicopters" that would be the vanguard of UN troops taking away American sovereignty. That decade did not end well for Mark from Michigan, who spent most of the Bush 43 years in a state penitentiary on charges of leading cops on a dangerous high-speed chase, one of several run-ins with the law. But now he was back in business and Knob Creek was a bit of a reunion for him as he greeted old acquaintances, promising to talk to you when he was done handing out his flyers—an interview that never took place, as he seemed to shift his location every time you approached.

Then, while you are waiting in vain for Koernke, you look up and realize you are surrounded by a small cluster of men, no more than a half dozen—several of them in full camouflage-fatigue regalia with Castro-style caps and with long pointed beards, as if the members of ZZ Top had decided to abandon the whole Texas boogie thing and form a militia instead. They tell you they are members of the Ohio Valley Freedom Fighters, a group that—you later learn—holds its meetings in a rural church basement in a nearby Kentucky county and is learning about wearing gas masks and how to fire weapons to disable an assault vehicle. "We've tripled in size since last September [2008]," the apparent leader, who tells you that he is "Colonel Kevin Terrell," says, adding quickly, "it has nothing to do with the president being black," muttering something about anger at the global bankers instead. He apologizes for not being able to talk now but gives you a phone number and hands you a DVD showing an armed infantryman with the message "What will you do?. . . . *when* they come for your guns."

The fatigue-wearing militiamen melt into the growing crowd, but a Patriot-movement wannabe is eager to stay behind and talk. He is a young man, clean cut, and says he is Darren, a software engineer who'd grown up in the prosperous suburbs of Philadelphia, earned a theater degree at Widener University, and then moved to Florida, where he adopted a worldview that was increasingly paranoid. He tells you he's a fan of "Mark from Michigan" and his Liberty Tree Radio; then he prattles on about the eight hundred FEMA camps and the Russian soldiers already on American soil until at some point you stop jotting it all down, except his enthusiastic observation that whenever law enforcement pulls over the wrong militia guy, "It's popcorn time."

At first, all this black-helicopter talk of Russian troops eating McDonald's under the mountains of Colorado and "East German" armored vehicles rumbling through almost-abandoned towns in central Wisconsin is half-alarming and half-amusing, but after two days it just grows tiresome. Darkness seems to take forever to come, as you stake out a low bleacher seat for the long-awaited Night Shoot. The crowd grows giddier as the sun drops—young teen boys with their girlfriends stage a chicken fight to burn off the anticipation; a solitary bonfire appears, and then suddenly streams of white tracer bullets illuminate the shadowy tree line of a Kentucky jungle. Orange explosions shaped like miniature hydrogen bombs rise from the great gully, leaving behind a red, hellish ring of flames, and there is a ton of Rebel whooping barely audible over this nonstop thundercrack. Gleeful faces appear in a split-second flash of pale phosphorous red and vanish back into the anonymity of the night.

The apocalyptic pseudo-carnage is the last flaming brushstroke in a picture that has become clear over two days here, beginning to take shape on Saturday afternoon when the blades of a military helicopter circled over the thick woodlands amid the barrage of bullets ripping into the tree line. There is a generation of working-class Americans desperate to refight the Vietnam War—but on its own terms. Over this fateful first Obama autumn and into the thick snowpack of the 2009–10 winter, you will meet many Vietnam vets knee-deep into the muck of the backlash, some cynical like John Grant and others resentful like the spit-upon Russ Murphy back in Delaware and still others just deeply suspicious of the serious men in suits who sent them—or their loved ones—to Southeast Asia. If it took a whole century for America to get the Civil War out of its system—and even then not all the way—how many more years will we continue to fight the culture wars and other grievances, some petty and some not, that were laid bare by the napalm, real and metaphorical, of the 1960s?

Tonight, the role of Hamburger Hill is being performed by Knob Creek, as it probably would be every six months for decades to come.

Also just like the 1960s, there is music at Knob Creek—performed by a band called Pokerface out of Allentown, Pennsylvania, playing near the snack bar just behind the shooting range. They had started riffing right before the Night Shoot, drawing a small crowd in front of musty lockers and a corrugated shed, and they gave off a mellow, jam-band vibe, except the lyrics dwell heavily on inciting a revolution, and definitely not the kind that they sang about at Woodstock. At the break, you approach the lead singer, Paul Topete, and he hands you their CD called *Peace or War*—inside, there is an elaborate diagram of the U.S. and Israeli culprits he believes were covertly behind the 9/11 attacks—and launches into an Indy-paced monologue on his political beliefs: "I think the way that globalists are trying to plan the demise of the United States with the Obaminator in office that they'd pull off a fait accompli that we become a socialist Communist nation that can be part of the united, you know, global system that they want to have and I look at myself as an American not a globalist and I know my Mexican cousins don't want to become part of the North American Union and I know my Canadian friends don't want to become part of the North American Union. We want to stay Americans—we're sick and tired of this globalist bullshit basically the Zionist bankers and all the groups that they fund are trying to destroy what's left of this nation. . . ."

There is much more, about how "9/11 is a fantasy just like Oklahoma City is a fantasy," and you wonder whether Topete will ever stop talking or even pause to take a breath, until another massive fusillade of artillery from the Night Shoot pounds the hillside and mercifully forces him to be quiet. When the smoke settles about a half-hour later, the band begins again to strike up its unique Dave-Matthews-meets-John-Birch brand of music.

You decide that you've heard enough and take a walk back under the pole tent, to see what Joe Gayan is up to. When you reach his stall, a few customers are milling around, fondling Gayan's birther-porn DVDs and then putting them back in the rack. But the proprietor and mild-mannered conspiracy theorist is nowhere to be found. You glance back at his empty metal stool and notice there is something taped to the counter right behind his seat that was not there the day before.

It is the picture of Obama and Hitler, of course.

CHAPTER FIVE

A Revolution of No

"The Alabama-based Southern Poverty Law Center singles out Oath Keepers as a particularly worrisome example of the Patriot revival." Boy, what would our founding fathers say based on just that one sentence—"a particularly worrisome example of the Patriot revival"? The people saying the government is getting too big and too out of control. All they want to do is make sure you keep your oath to the Constitution of the United States.

Glenn Beck, October 17, 2009

"We don't want to overthrow the government."

Celia Hyde is answering a question that no one has asked her. Hyde is a woman of about sixty, sturdy, with ramrod-straight auburn hair, a bit of a tomboy, which isn't all that surprising considering she joined her hometown police force after her four brothers, the Smith boys, all demurred. She is wearing blue jeans and a soft tan sweater, and as she sits on a high stool across a butcher-block kitchen table, hands curved around a steaming cup of coffee, she could easily be auditioning for a part in a homey commercial for Maxwell House.

Except that Hyde's not talking about the latest Colombian roast. In a husky police-scanner tone with a Red Sox Nation accent, this ex–police chief is explaining that her cause is not really a new American Revolution, not exactly anyway, but that she simply wants the nation's men and women in uniform—all the police officers and soldiers and sailors and sheriff's deputies—to "stand down" at the moment they get their inevitable orders that will shatter the U.S. Constitution.

"We simply want our government staying out of our business as Americans," Hyde is now explaining. "They don't have any business telling us what doctors we can see." But for that not to happen, she believes, there is going to have to come a day of widespread resistance by U.S. troops and even the cops on the local beat, the people who normally are tasked with taking their orders from the gray suits in elected office and carrying them out. "We want them to put their arms down, stand down. Our main target is our active military and our law enforcement. Because they are the ones who are going to be given that issue—'Go into that house, and if they haven't gotten that vaccine, arrest them, transport them, take them out, seize whatever you need to seize, computers, et cetera.'"

Celia Hyde is a founding member and a national leader of the Oath Keepers, an alliance of some current but mostly former soldiers and cops that is equally noteworthy for its rapid growth in the Age of Obama and its jarring worldview. Just as the 9-12 Project and the Tea Parties represent the effort to wrap an organizational framework and put a human face on the disconnected angry voices of talk radio and the spontaneous rants of Glenn Beck and Co., the Oath Keepers are what the rat-a-tat-tat of the firing range at Knob Creek and its underlying conspiracy cauldron look like when some semirespectable people try to capture that barrel of unopened American gunpowder and give it a name and a mission.

It is as if the backlash against the Obama presidency is moving forward on two parallel tracks. One is the Beck Express, which chugs along the route of conservative big media like Fox and Clear Channel radio and has some big-name politicians along for the ride; the other one, leaving the station on the farthest-right platform, is engineered by the likes of Alex Jones and Representative Ron Paul and is now blowing the shrill whistle of these newfangled Oath Keepers, a train with a cargo of conspiracy that could jump the rails at any moment.

But the weirdest thing about your conversation with Celia Hyde—spanning the globe of the modern-day American Apocalypto, from the notion of a military "stand-down" to the more paranoid of the worries about the ramifications of a swine-flu epidemic, with a detour into talk about American "internment camps" just around the corner—is the scenery. Hyde is sitting in the corner of the airy great room on the first floor of a New England bed-and-breakfast in a leafy-to-the-point-of-claustrophobia exurb about three-quarters of the way from Boston out to Worcester. The inn—which Hyde and her husband, Doug, who was a longtime selectman in Stow, have run for more than two decades—is a white slice of Thoreau-era gingerbread, lit by electric candlelight in the second-story windows that beckon the Hydes' best customers, the "leaf peepers" who jam Highway 117 every October.

It is November now, unseasonably balmy, with just a few cars whizzing by, which means there is little to distract Hyde as she explains how she fell into her new role as Massachusetts state director of the Oath Keepers as its membership skyrocketed in the months following Barack Obama's inauguration. The rather enigmatic founder of the Oath Keepers, Stewart Rhodes—a former U.S. Army paratrooper who was injured, earned a law degree from Yale, and helped run the 2008 presidential campaign of quirky libertarian Republican Ron Paul—has just received national exposure on MSNBC's *Hardball*, and a Tennessee Oath Keeper had gotten a mostly favorable write-up in the *Los Angeles Times*. This, even as officials with the hate-fighting Southern Poverty Law Center and the Human Rights Network in Rhodes's home state of Montana debated whether to add the Oath Keepers—with their talk that veered into creepy areas of internment camps, gun confiscation, and dictatorship—to their short list of dangerous groups. Former president Bill Clinton even called out the Oath Keepers by name as a "hatriot" group in a speech to mark the fifteenth anniversary of the Oklahoma City bombing.

The plain-talking Hyde seems to embody all the contradictions that had quickly come to define the Oath Keepers. After all, you don't expect to find the seeds of a modern American Revolution planted right here, in a quaint, white clapboard B&B in the leafy heart of New England, not to mention what is—pre–Scott Brown, at least—presumed to be the bastion of Kennedy-flavored liberalism. And then there is the matter of Hyde's solid-citizen résumé, as a career police officer who spent the first half of the 2000s as the chief of the small force in the neighboring exurb of Bolton, Massachusetts. Indeed, the leadership of the Oath Keepers is peppered with individuals such as this, people who might not be candidates for the Joint Chiefs of Staff but weren't camouflage-wearing militia wannabes living in their mother's basement, either. In addition to its Ivy League–pedigreed leader Rhodes and the ex–police chief Hyde, the roster of Oath Keepers has even included an active-duty commander in the U.S. Navy reserves, David Gillie. But the real enigma of the Oath Keepers isn't so much the messengers as the message.

What Stewart Rhodes and his band of constitutional resistors have accomplished is, in essence, to find the sweet spot between the conventional, election-focused right-wing rage of the Tea Party protestors and the bat-guano craziness of the extremists who showed up at a place like Knob Creek in full militia garb to fire off their MG–50s while recruiting new members. They do this by cloaking their mission in Founding Fathers feel-good boilerplate—"Don't trample the Constitution" is the Oath Keepers' mantra that Hyde repeated over the course of a couple of hours. But rather than advocating—at least officially—for overthrowing the American government or any other aggressive acts, the Oath Keepers avoid that trap by cleverly focusing on what they *won't* do—promising that men and women in uniform will never do things that for the most part no one has really asked them to, anyway.

New members of the Oath Keepers sign on to a list of the "10 Orders We Will Not Obey." The pledge builds in paranoia like a classic Hitchcock thriller, beginning with mild dystopia—"We will NOT obey orders to conduct warrantless searches of the American people," a notion that many liberals would have applauded, circa 2004—and moving up to uncontrolled delusion, such as Order #6, "We will NOT obey any order to blockade American cities, thus turning them into giant concentration camps," followed by Order #7, "We will NOT obey any order to force American citizens into any form of detention camps under any pretext." Does Hyde, the cop-turned-Massachusetts-innkeeper, really buy into all this? Does she think the American government could be rounding up law-abiding citizens in the near future?

"Yes," she answers, her tone growing both softer and more serious. Really? "The internment camps, you mean?"

Hyde pauses. "Well, you know, I'm not a fearmonger at all . . . at least I don't think I am. But you can't help but acknowledge some of these things that you see. Now, I just saw an ad on Monster.com—they're taking résumés for internment specialists. I can show it to you. You got a second?" She gets up and walks across the airy main room of the inn, past all the homey bric-a-brac, picks up a small laptop computer, and walks it back. "Have you done any research on FEMA camps, internment camps?"

She fumbles through a couple of Web sites, trying to find the ad while again bringing up her worries about forced swine-flu vaccinations. "Could it happen again?" Again? Was she referring to the internment of roughly 120,000 Japanese-Americans during World War II? She nods. "Probably, I think it could." On the computer screen, there is a reference to a position for an internment/resettlement specialist, but it is some obscure Internet site, not Monster.com or a National Guard listing. "This is not the one," she says. "It's called 'internment/resettlement specialist,' but there's a better one out there."

In a sense, Hyde was technically correct. You learned later that the National Guard—as well as the U.S. Army—really does advertise for "internment/resettlement specialists," and in fact they've been recruiting for the position for a number of years, long before Barack Obama even started running for the presidency. Indeed, the need for the position soared under President George W. Bush, because of the surge in foreign detainees as a result of the wars in Iraq and Afghanistan. Those facts did not prevent some of the more paranoid explanations of the need for internment specialists from cascading around right-wing Web sites in the summer of 2009, not long after Glenn Beck and Alex Jones had aired programs broaching the notion that FEMA—the Federal Emergency Management Agency—was preparing internment camps right here on U.S. soil. The claim that there was something extraordinary about the National Guard job posting was debunked in a matter of days, even on conservative sites such as Hot Air, where Ed Morrissey patiently explained that "[w]hatever and wherever Guard units get deployed, some of them have to be trained in handling prisoners. It's not really a great mystery, nor is it a conspiracy to set up camps for political dissenters."

The notion that the federal government has its own gulag archipelago of concentration camps—already built or near completion and ready to accept tens of thousands of American citizens at a stroke of the presidential pen—is more than a generation old; it flourished along with antigovernment militias during the Clinton administration in the 1990s, and then the far left fretted it would be the logical extension of the Patriot Act under George W. Bush and Dick Cheney. But it took on its most powerful life ever almost immediately following Obama's swearing-in—fueled by the steady rise in conspiracy-minded Web sites and underground radio and even the occasional validation on Fox News Channel. That meant that even debunking in the mainstream media didn't dissuade true believers—perhaps because it was spread widely only through the so-called liberal media, specifically MSNBC's *Countdown with Keith Olbermann*. Indeed, the only time that Hyde's voice turns harsh is when she is asked where she gets her information about what's going on in America. "Not from the mainstream media, okay!"

For most of her life, Hyde didn't pay too much attention to the headlines at all, except maybe the local news. "The radio that I was listening to was the police radio," she says. She hadn't pursued a career in law enforcement; instead it pursued her as a twenty-something in the early 1970s, when she was a bit of a nomad and a free spirit. One day, the police chief in Bolton—the town where young Celia Smith had grown up—called up Celia's dad, who ran the local construction company, and asked if any of his four sons wanted to become a cop. He offered up his rootless daughter instead. "He was just the kind of man you couldn't say 'no' to," Hyde recalls of the former chief, "and so I said I'll try it for a while until I think I can find an excuse to get out of it—and that was thirty years I was in it. It was a great job. And for thirty years, I practiced preserving and defending people's rights."

It was small-town police work in a fairly affluent suburb—there was not a single murder during those thirty years, and a typical case as reported in the local paper involved golfers at the local country club getting lost and driving their carts onto someone else's lawn. Hyde became a sergeant while she was getting married, buying the inn, and raising a son, and in 1999 she even landed the job as chief. Except nothing is permanent in small-town politics. Despite the dearth of crime, Hyde quickly found herself under fire as top cop for her management skills; a self-proclaimed defender of people's rights, she was reportedly considered an autocrat by some of the police union members who worked under her. There was a barrage of articles in the local *Worcester Telegram & Gazette* about how the union cops had voted "no confidence" in their chief in 2003—accusing her of what the newspaper called "a tyrannical management style"—and how finally in 2005 Hyde agreed to take an early retirement. Suddenly she was in her fifties, out of the career that had been her life for three decades, and her son had grown up and moved to Wyoming. With that extra time, she started paying attention to national issues.

Hyde's quick, unplanned departure from the Bolton station house was just another variation on the same theme that was becoming so familiar from coast to coast as the decade drew to a close—middle-aged Americans, unexpectedly unemployed or underemployed in a nation where everything suddenly seemed to be changing so rapidly, and the only folks who tried to offer any kind of explanation for what the hell just hit them like a ton of bricks were the disembodied voices that came into their car as they ran their errands and the talking heads who arrived in their living room at 5 o'clock.

"As I retired, I got to really sit back and watch what was going on in this country more and more," she says of her four years since she's been off the job. "When you're a police officer and you're in a little town, your world is your town, okay? But I was able to step back and look at . . . the bigger spectrum, let's say."

But where did she get her information, if she came to distrust the mainstream media so much? "I hate to say the Internet . . . ," she says, pausing, "but, yes, I watch a lot of TV shows, a lot of TV. Fox 25"— the digital channel number for the national, conservative Fox News Channel—"gives us lots of ideas—Hannity, Beck, and so forth. Now, I don't take everything they say as gospel . . ."

Still, like many Americans, Hyde had no ready outlet to act on her now smoldering anger over what she saw as the growing threats to the political order. At least not until the spring of 2009, when fate arrived—seeking shelter at the Stowaway Inn. It turned out that Stewart Rhodes's closest ally in creating the Oath Keepers—a retired Las Vegas cop named David Freeman, who like Rhodes had worked on the Ron Paul presidential campaign—is also Celia Hyde's uncle. And there's more: their new Oath Keepers group had come up with the perfect time and place to introduce itself to America, at a big rally at the Lexington Green on April 19, on the 234th anniversary of the shots that launched the American Revolution, at a venue that was only a few miles from Hyde's rambling B&B. And so Freeman, her uncle, called Hyde about renting out a bunch of rooms.

"Then he said you might want to go on our Web site—we're brand new, two or three weeks old—and see what you think," Hyde recalls. "I did, and my first reaction was, 'Oh my Lord, I don't know about this group.'" At the time, the group was involved with little more then the now-infamous 10 Orders, the stuff about not blockading American cities or herding U.S. citizens into concentration camps, so her reaction was understandable. She then mentioned these new Oath Keepers to an old friend named Chauncey Normandin, a former police captain and Army vet from not far away in Lowell, Massachusetts, who had retired and moved to Florida. "And he said, 'They're really cool, I've been following them . . . Save me a room—I'm coming up!' "

Normandin had said the magic words, apparently, to his fellow ex-cop. Recalls Hyde: "He said they were like-minded people."

And so the 234th anniversary of the American Revolution—the first one, that is—came around, and all these like-minded ex-cops and military grunts from all over the country came back to the quaint little Stowaway Inn for what Hyde describes as more like a slumber party than the seeds of a resistance movement to the federal government. They were sleeping on top of colonial four-poster beds and on large, comfy sofas and in sleeping bags under the canopy of maple and oak trees out back, these self-appointed twenty-first-century heirs to Samuel Adams, John Hancock, and Paul Revere, presumably discussing President Obama's gun confiscation plans over fluffed-up French toast.

Hyde describes her subsequent decision to become the Massachusetts state director of the Oath Keepers with all the drama of signing up for the local Rotary. "I liked several aspects of it—that they are not partisan, that they are good people, that they believe in the Constitution," she says. "I saw that they have the American people in their heart and they were sound people—and then there was the fact that they were military and police, which is my background."

Meanwhile, the Montana Human Rights Network—a group that formed in response to the rise of right-wing militias in that state during the 1980s and '90s—was busy adding the Oath Keepers to its informal list of hate groups doing business in the Treasure State. The group's director tied the formation of an Oath Keepers chapter in Bozeman to what he told the local papers was "a resurgence of those anti-Semitic, anti-government groups." They were reaching the exact same conclusion at the Southern Poverty Law Center, the nation's most respected tracker of right-wing extremism. In a major report entitled "Return of the Militias," the SPLC noted that the April date—the one of the Oath Keeper sleepover party at the Stowaway Inn—was also the anniversary of two seminal events in the history of the first wave of militias in the 1990s: the 1993 lethal fire at the Branch Davidian compound in Waco and the antigovernment Oklahoma City bombing in 1995.

The SPLC backed up its strong words by combing through some of the dozens upon dozens of online postings at the Oath Keepers Web site, many of these by ex–military officers announcing that they were joining the group. It's hard to verify these online claims, but some of them seem to be quite extreme indeed. In one, according to the report by longtime militia trackers, a man claiming to be a former U.S. Army paratrooper who fought in both Afghanistan and Iraq alleged that President Obama is "an enemy of the state," adding, "I would rather die than be a slave to my government."

At least a few of the new Oath Keepers were active-duty members of the U.S. military (and thus presumably in more of a position to disobey orders from the commander-in-chief); the hate-tracking groups noted a picture that appeared on the Oath Keepers Web site of a man—so it claimed, anyway—who was on active duty in the Iraqi city of Mosul and who had sewn a small Oath Keepers patch on his desert-camouflage uniform. The anonymous soldier also wore a similar patch for the Three Percenters, an informal militia-syle movement launched around the time of Obama's election claiming—dubiously—that only 3 percent of the American populace took up arms during the Revolutionary War.

"The Oath Keepers have this undertone, that the government is look-ing for an excuse to declare martial law and confiscate people's guns and ammunition," says Larry Keller, the author of the SPLC report. At the same time, Keller concedes that he finds the group to be something of a co-nundrum; he notes the articulateness of its Yale-educated leader, Rhodes, a suggestion that this is not your father's militia, if it even is a militia.

That's the warped beauty—looking at it strictly from a tactical point of view—of the Oath Keeepers. They were, crudely speaking, the lap dancers of revolution—flirting and grinding and arousing frustrated folks on the prowl for a cheap antigovernment thrill but never going all the way, making sure that all the proper laws and codes were obeyed while teasing the boundaries of safe rebellion. Rhodes and other Oath Keepers surely remembered the rise of armed militias in the 1990s during the presidency of Bill Clinton, when an estimated two hundred ragtag bands of middle-aged white guys like the Michigan Militia Corps held training exercises off in the woods and plastered bumper stickers with sayings like "I love my country but fear my government" on the back of their trucks; these fringe groups had little real impact and began to fade with the late 1990s economic boom, the election of Republican George W. Bush, and the patriotic fervor after 9/11. Now, under Obama and amid a deep recession, the militias were making something of a comeback, with the SPLC reporting a 244 percent rise in "Patriot" groups, militias, and related extremists in the first year of the new administration.

But the militias now seemed kind of retro. Not only was there something vaguely withering about these relatively tiny regiments with adherents from a small sample of the local population, but being a member was also a risky occupation—militia leaders from the Clinton era like the Knob Creek hanger-on Mark Koernke not only didn't come within a million miles of overthrowing the government but often ended up behind bars.

The Oath Keepers had invented a whole new construct, one that could appeal to those militia-friendly, hard-core few as well as to the general pool of Knob Creek conservatives who had an overriding sense of fear about what the Obama-led government was capable of doing. They were a national organization with a Yale law pedigree that knew how to recruit and how to avoid getting in trouble. After all, there's no law against declaring what you won't do, at least not until you're actually forced to disobey an order coming from your platoon's captain or your chief of police—in fact, the vast majority of Oath Keepers were no longer in uniform and weren't getting any orders to disobey in the first place. With the well-spoken Rhodes at the helm and with pillars of society like Celia Hyde, an ex–police chief, involved, the group was much more socially acceptable, much more aboveground—attracting seemingly solid citizens who sold the group to "like-minded people."

Indeed, Rhodes went to great lengths to position the Oath Keepers as at least the partially thinking man's alternative to militias, especially in the early weeks of the group when a lot of the enthusiastic joiners were calling for things like an armed insurrection against the Obama administration, as observed by the Anti-Defamation League, which also reported on the rise of the Oath Keepers:

> After Oath Keepers first formed, so many posts about resistance and guerrilla war were posted to the official Oath Keepers blog that Rhodes had to step in and rein them in, saying that "we want active duty to visit this site and if you transform it into a hard-core 'how to wage 4th [-generation] guerrilla war' or 'how to fragg' site, many of them will be wary of participating." However, Rhodes did not oppose such discussions; he merely asked that they be carried on somewhere else, so that they would not tar the Oath Keepers' blog.

So why all the fuss about a group whose main thrust was declaring that it wouldn't do these wacked-out things that there was no way in hell the U.S. government was going to be asking them to do, anyway? At a cursory glance, the Oath Keepers seemed largely just a new twist on some kind of online message board for people to rant, vent, commiserate, and root for the Obama administration to fail. But perhaps the Oath Keepers' most dangerous contribution to the archaic model of militias had less to do with rhetoric and more to do with real-world applications. From the outset they utilized the power of the Internet with overwhelming skill, turning an organization that fifteen years ago would have struggled to attract a couple thousand followers (at most) into a national group. And this was the very real threat from the Oath

Keepers: its ability to attract so many people to a group that normalized extreme paranoia about the American government in a remarkably short period of time—all through its savvy use of the Internet.

Less than a year after its creation, the Oath Keepers had created a Facebook group that had at least 15,000 members and continued to grow hourly. A random check of the main page would have appeared remarkably familiar to Richard Hofstadter as the paranoid style of conspiracy that he studied nearly fifty years ago; in fact, there was a link to a video of the speech that Robert Welch gave in founding the John Birch Society all the way back in 1958, centering on traitors inside the U.S. government who would betray the country's sovereignty to the United Nations for a collectivist New World Order, managed by a "one-world socialist government"—one commenter on the video writes, "they said he was nuts . . . little did we know time catches up with the truth." Also on the Facebook page for Oath Keepers is a plea for members to join a group called "Kick Out the United Nations!" with the comment "Support the constitution and get foreign troops off our soil." There's also a news item, "Breaking News—Obama Signs Martial Law Order"; you wonder why you have not heard of this, although a reading of the text suggests that the issue at hand is actually a fairly innocuous measure seeking more cooperation between Washington and the state National Guards. Another posting reads: "Order your Official Glenn Beck 9-12 Project and Sarah Palin 2012 t-shirts!"

What's more, the rise of Twitter and the birth of the Oath Keepers happened at roughly the same time, and so its growth has also been fueled 140 characters at a time, in short blasts that are sent out to its followers, who numbered more than 1,500 by its one-year anniversary—folks with Twitter handles like "Liberty or Death" or "conserva-girl" or, in the changing-times department, "GayPatriot." Many of the tweets that the Oath Keepers send out carry messages like "I will only obey the constitution" or, simply, "We have been ignored and dismissed long enough," each followed by a hyperlink to an online testimonial by the newest member. Much of the Oath Keepers' online mission seems on a similar track to what Glenn Beck and the 9-12 Project does in person: connecting scattered people out there who are worried about a one-world government or the pending imposition of martial law in the United States and telling them that those things you've been worrying about do not mean that you are crazy, that you are not alone.

Even if a lot of it *is* kind of crazy. It is the kind of viral, instant connectivity that a paranoid pamphleteer like Robert Welch and his scattered band of John Birchers could not have dreamed of fifty years ago, and probably would have killed to acquire.

THE SEEDS OF the Oath Keepers seem to have been scattered from the fall of the Ron Paul presidential campaign in 2008. The Paul campaign was a hard thing for anyone to pin down; its leader was an affable-sounding, mild-mannered, white-haired physician turned Texas congressman who tried to find a home within the Republican Party for a libertarian philosophy that wasn't well contained by the partisan boundaries of the 2000s. There were elements of the paranoid style in some of his more populist positions—such as a call to abolish the Federal Reserve, later the basis of a best-selling book by Paul, and his backing for a bill to get the United States out of the United Nations—but throughout the spring of 2008, Paul was able to walk a tightrope that allowed him to share the GOP debate stage with the likes of John McCain and Mitt Romney even as his campaign became popular with those who shared beliefs with the underground radio host Alex Jones that George W. Bush and Dick Cheney had advance knowledge of the 9/11 attacks. Indeed, there were even pockets of support for Paul on the more liberal political Web sites like Daily Kos, inspired in part by the candidate's criticisms of the wars in Iraq and Afghanistan.

But the Ron Paul campaign's permanent contribution to American politics wasn't so much the message as the use of the media, particularly the newfangled ways that people could now rally around a politician even as his candidacy and his ideas were being largely ignored by people inside the Beltway. Paul consistently drew bigger crowds than pundits expected and got more votes in the early GOP primaries than these same experts predicted. That in turn may have been because he had more Web searches for his name and more people watching his YouTube channel than any other 2008 candidate. And then there was "the money bomb." In October 2007, a video called "RonPaulMoney-Bomb," backed by an active-duty soldier named Eric Nordstrom, led to an event held on "Guy Fawkes Day"—which commemorates a 1605 plot to blow up the English Parliament—that raised over $4.2 million from small donors, a figure that was previously unheard of.

One of the advisors to the Ron Paul campaign was the ex–Army paratrooper with a law degree, Stewart Rhodes—who came up with the idea of the Oath Keepers in the dark night for both conservatives and anti-big-government libertarians following Obama's election. The Oath Keepers were born from paranoia on day one. Rhodes—who studied the use of military tribunals and related constitutional issues while he was at Yale—insists that he was concerned about abuses of power while George W. Bush was the president, particularly with some of the measures that were taken to control unrest after Hurricane Katrina devastated New Orleans. That may be true, but the hard trigger for the Oath Keepers came only a month after the Obama inauguration, in a bizarre episode involving the Iowa National Guard and a proposed mock training exercise in urban warfare in the smallish towns of Arcadia—population 443—and Carroll, Iowa.

It was an event that almost completely escaped the attention of the mainstream media, for understandable reasons. The kickoff was a mundane announcement from Guard officials in the Hawkeye State of a drill prompted by the likelihood that the Carroll County unit that fought in Afghanistan in 2004–05 would face a future deployment to the then six-year-old war in Iraq. To prepare, the unit planned to conduct a weekend training operation in the towns that would involve a door-to-door search for a fictional arms dealer. It was a bit of a novel exercise, to be sure, but not nearly as out-there as the reaction the proposal received once it hit the Internet with radio conspiracy-monger Alex Jones fanning the flames. The Iowa National Guard exercise, the chatter on the Internet claimed, was not an innocent urban warfare exercise but a trial run for the government gun confiscation that they'd all feared under Obama, the one they were talking about at gun shows like the shoot-out at Knob Creek, or something far worse.

"This is part of an acclimation for martial law," Jones told his underground legion of listeners as he devoted his entire show to the topic one morning in February, linking the Iowa operation to an international conspiracy of bankers. Jones also posted an article from the local paper, the *Daily Times Herald* of Carroll, Iowa, about the drill but made up his own headline for the article—"Iowa National Guard to train for gun confiscation"—even though the actual piece said no such thing.

"Everything is accelerating so fast," one of Jones's listeners responded on a message board, as later noted by the Anti-Defamation League. "We need to organize now." That day hundreds of people—practically every one of them from outside Iowa—emailed the *Daily Times Herald* or called local officials about the operation. Some of the emailers said they planned to defend their homes with guns or even booby-trap them. The mayor of Arcadia, Oran Kohorst, who like all other local officials had supported the training exercise plan, told the paper that one man from North Dakota had threatened to bring 5,500 militia members to the town.

The outside pressure campaign worked—Guard officials cancelled the operation the day after the Jones show, citing "readiness concern." Some would understandably see this Iowa stand-down as paranoia run amok, but Rhodes—who had just moved from Montana to Las Vegas—saw something else: opportunity. Government operations after 2005's Hurricane Katrina—where there was indeed a controversy over some mandatory evacuations where guns were taken—and now the Iowa incident convinced him of the need for an outfit that would resist such orders.

When Rhodes announced the creation of the Oath Keepers two months later, he had already seen the powerful first-hand evidence of what "like-minded people" had been feeling at places like Knob Creek, the paranoia and the powerlessness. The Oath Keepers were here to provide reassurance in the form of an oath—just by agreeing to the ten points crafted by Rhodes you were taking one small step to prevent tyranny right here in the United States, finding common cause with your fellow patriots from Maine to Hawaii.

And so by October 2009, fueled largely by the power of his Internet recruiting, the Oath Keepers had grown to the point where the previously unknown Rhodes had landed a coveted national interview on *Hardball* with Chris Matthews on MSNBC, where the rather incredulous host pressed the Oath-Keeper-in-chief about statements such as a claim that foreign troops have been enlisted to fight here on domestic soil before. (After sputtering for a moment, Rhodes mentioned the Hessian troops who fought alongside George Washington in the American Revolution—a somewhat odd example, since Washington is also cited as a hero by the fledgling organization.)

"Do you go to bed at night—when you put your head on the pillow at night, are you afraid that at some point in your lifetime, the black helicopters from the UN will arrive in the United States and deny American sovereignty?" the TV talking head asked Rhodes. "Do you think that's probable or possible?"

"I think it's possible."

"Or plausible?"

Responded Rhodes: "I think we're concerned about . . . look at . . . look at . . . look at Germany, an advanced civilization, and they fell into a despotism in a dictatorship, a murderous dictatorship in the span of ten years after an economic collapse. It could happen here. Think it can't happen here? Ask the Japanese-Americans whether it can happen here."

By then, there was a growing debate about the return of right-wing militarism in America. The reports by the Anti-Defamation League and the Southern Poverty Law Center had caused a stir, but not as much as a report by the federal government's own Department of Homeland Security on potential domestic terrorism that had been prepared at the tail end of the Bush administration but leaked to the media—perhaps, some speculated, by an Oath Keeper sympathizer—in the months after Obama took office. The report's main thrust—that the current political climate meant a higher chance of violent incidents involving right-wing extremists—would be borne out in the months ahead. But three words were found particularly grating to conservatives: that some of the risk could come from "disgruntled military veterans" from Iraq and Afghanistan in the same paranoid style of Oklahoma City bomber Timothy McVeigh, who fought in the 1991 Gulf War.

The flap over the report (the new Department of Homeland Security secretary, Janet Napolitano, apologized to veterans) probably fueled a rush of new members to the Oath Keepers, a classic case of unintended consequences. As Rhodes blogged on the Oath Keepers Web site: "The DHS reports are such broad smears that they basically boil down to 'anyone who doesn't agree with us is a potential terrorist.' The final stage of persecution is to actually apply all the powers of the state against anyone who does dare to speak out, arresting them on trumped up charges of terrorism, for example."

Not surprisingly, the Oath Keepers play up their ties with the seemingly most respected leaders of the organization, such as Celia Hyde, the plain-talking career policewoman. One of the most prominent members, the man the Oath Keepers seem quite eager to promote and whom they had for a time called the group's "National Liaison to Current Serving Military Officers," is David Gillie, a current intelligence officer serving as a commander in the U.S. Naval Reserve. Gillie's résumé claims that he earned a graduate degree from the U.S. Naval War College in 2006, and that in addition to his reserve duties he is employed as a Principal Systems Integration Engineer at Concurrent Technologies Corp. Gillie appeared at that initial Oath Keepers gathering on Lexington Green in uniform, wearing his full-dress Navy whites and cap, and gave an interview that has been viewed on YouTube at least 2,600 times. In the six-minute clip, Gillie gives a rambling explanation of the Oath Keepers' core tenet, that a soldier can disobey an unlawful order:

> Because all of our executive power is lodged in one man, the president of the United States, and because I only hold my office by his commission and because my superiors only hold their office by his commission and because all of the orders come down through him, if any of those issues an unlawful order, thankfully we are all bound to a superior power aren't we, the people of the United States, through the oath by condition of which we hold our office. Thankfully, we can just say, I'm sorry, sir—I have no power to do this. You don't have the power to make me do it and don't have the power to (garble) me to do it because we're both serving to the same oath to the Constitution of the United States. Now if my superior persists in lawlessness, either because he's stupid or he's stubborn, you just say sir, I'm sorry, I'm going to have to resign. And isn't that a wonderful thing?

You called Gillie later, hoping to get an elaboration and also to find out why he'd later abruptly disappeared from the Oath Keepers' national board of directors and whether that was a sign of disapproval from higher officers in the Naval Reserves. He insists to you that it was not, that it was simply a matter of too many commitments, although he did voice some embarrassment at filming the Lexington YouTube video in full uniform; he was there for an official reenactment of a 1798 oath ceremony, he says, and should have changed if he was going to be discussing the Oath Keepers. Gillie, who is well-educated and long-winded, insists to you that many of the circumstances in which an order violated the Constitution—confiscating firearms, for example—would be clear-cut, and that "it's a crime to obey an unlawful order."

However, there's something else very important that Gillie, Rhodes, and the other top Oath Keepers tend to omit from their monologues.

What the actual oath of enlistment for the U.S. Army says is this: "that I will support and defend the Constitution of the United States against all enemies, foreign and domestic; that I will bear true faith and allegiance to the same; and that I will obey the orders of the President of the United States and the orders of the officers appointed over me." So in fact, a soldier disobeying an order from President Barack Obama or any other president would not be upholding his oath but violating it. In 2009, officials with the Department of Defense—alerted to that photo of an unidentified soldier on patrol in the Iraq city of Mosul wearing an Oath Keepers' patch—said the new organization wasn't on its current list of extremist groups, which hews more toward groups that preach racial or religious hatred.

The DOD, like everyone else, had no idea what to make of the Oath Keepers, the Revolution of "No."

As the months progressed, the Oath Keepers became increasingly visible at anti-Obama protests. When the president traveled to Elyria, Ohio, in January 2010 to give a speech, protesters were led by an Oath Keeper named Bob Trosper from nearby Vermillion, who gave an interview to a local newspaper reporter and said, "There's a soapbox, a ballot box and God forbid, if it does come to it, we will defend our rights with a cartridge box."

By the spring of 2010, there were increasing signs of support for the Oath Keepers in the active-duty military—drawn using some of the same Web-driven recruiting techniques that had been working so well for Rhodes. An active Marine Corps sergeant and Iraq veteran stationed at Camp Pendleton named Gary Stein quickly attracted four hundred Facebook followers to his Armed Forces Tea Party who apparently agreed with Stein's promise to "preserve common sense conservatism and defend our Constitution that is threatened by a tyrannical government." Stein also posted that "my oath was to the Constitution, not to the politicians," and when asked by the Web site Talking Points Memo if he was mimicking the Oath Keepers, Stein told them, "I think we're very like-minded with the Oath Keepers. I strongly support the Oath Keepers."

Meanwhile, the involvement of solid citizens like David Gillie and Celia Hyde allowed the Oath Keepers brass to disavow the activities of entry-level recruits who were not so guarded in their enthusiasm for taking on the government right now. In the very early days of the Oath Keepers, a fifty-two-year-old Oklahoma man named Daniel Knight Hayden promoted the new group on his MySpace page and as CitizenQuasar on Twitter—where he also sent out a series of increasingly manic updates as he prepared to head to an April 15 anti-tax rally in Oklahoma City, not far from where the domestic terrorist McVeigh had killed 168 Americans in 1995. One of the last ones read: "Locked AND loaded for the Oklahoma State Capitol. Let's see what happens." Hayden was arrested by the FBI that day at his house; the Oath Keepers' Rhodes quickly dismissed him as "a nut" who had nothing to do with the group.

The case of former U.S. Marine Charles Dyer—also known as "July4Patriot"—was a little trickier for Rhodes and the Oath Keepers to explain.

Charles Dyer joined the Marines in the military tradition of the Dyer family, which dates back to the Civil War. In 2007, he chose to reenlist, knowing that he would be sent to Iraq at a time when the conflict there was still in a bloody phase. "I know he was up Euphrates River, north of Baghdad. I asked him what he was doing and he said, 'running with Navy SEALS, a demo crew,' that was enough," his father told the local Duncan *Banner* newspaper in 2008, adding, "Charlie loves weaponry. He started shooting a bb gun when he was 2-years-old and he could shoot a beer can with that bb gun."

But soon, Marine Sergeant Charles Dyer would begin leading a double life. While still serving in the Marines, he began recording inflammatory and antigovernment videos and posting them to YouTube under the screen name "July4Patriot." He joined the site on February

20, 2009—exactly one month to the day after Obama's inauguration—although one of his first videos, posted to the site about five weeks later, was more about George W. Bush, whom he accused of shredding the Constitution, with a reference to soldiers patrolling American streets. The video—"Give me liberty or give me DEATH!!!"—is largely Dyer/July4Patriot speaking over ominous music; to shield his identity he wears the bottom of a cheap Halloween-type skeleton mask over the lower part of his face, although his prematurely bald scalp and sky-blue eyes are clearly visible on top.

"I fear that if we are ever to be free again there will have to be a time when we stand up and fight," Dyer says into the camera, his head sometimes a jerky blur when his voice becomes animated. "They tell us we stand no chance against a powerful government, but when will we fare a better chance." At the end, he shouts the famous Patrick Henry line for which the video is named, and there is a cut to an upside-down American flag. In less than a year, the clip had been watched at least 51,000 times.

A few weeks after that, Dyer came to Lexington Green and was present for the seminal event of the Oath Keepers—where he hobnobbed with the likes of Stewart Rhodes, Celia Hyde, and David Gillie. In fact, the Oath Keepers leadership was so impressed with the soon-to-be-ex-Marine that they recruited Dyer to give a speech on behalf of the Oath Keepers at a July Fourth rally that was to be held at Broken Arrow, Oklahoma.

"I am an Oath Keeper," Dyer said, dressed in a gray T-shirt, speaking to an apparently small crowd on that rainy patriotic day. He talked for fifteen minutes, ranting about the abuses committed in the wake of Hurricane Katrina and then again asserting, ominously, that training exercises are taking place in which American soldiers "and sometimes even foreign troops occupy small U.S. cities" and warning that local police could be replaced by "jack-booted federal thugs." He added: "Are we all sheep to be led silently to the slaughter? Who will defend their oath to the Constitution of the United States?!!!"

Afterward, Dyer's speech won rave reviews from his fellow Oath

Keepers. One of them wrote in the comments on the corresponding blog post: "Charles—you don't need a silver tongue to deliver your message, your passion and dedication is so very obvious—nice job kiddo—keep it up!" The author signed her name as Celia Hyde, the ex–police chief, presumably writing from the cozy confines of her inn in leafy New England.

But in the months after Dyer earned kudos from the respectable wing of the Oath Keepers, and as thousands of new fans became Facebook friends and the Oath Keepers even won radio praise from Glenn Beck, things started taking a turn for the weird for the July4Patriot, who now had his own channel on YouTube and a growing following.

By the fall, a liberal blogger from Oklahoma with the unlikely pseudonym of Gossip Boy (the name of his Web site was later changed to Hate Trackers) took up the case of Sergeant Charles Dyer, now a private citizen who'd moved back to the Sooner State. In August, just a month after his hyped event with the Oath Keepers, Dyer confirmed that he was establishing a paramilitary training camp about eighty miles south of Oklahoma City near Duncan, Oklahoma, and that he occasionally posted items on the neo-Nazi hate site Stormfront.org. In one of his videos, the self-proclaimed patriot said, "Me? I'm going to use my training and become one of those domestic terrorists that you're so afraid of from the DHS reports."

Eventually, "July4Patriot" graduated from long-winded speeches with the half-skeleton mask to posted videos showing him and comrades conducting military training exercises for an outfit called the American Resistance Movement (although the drills, conducted with air-soft rifles at a site in California, come off mainly as glorified paintball); another "July4Patriot" video from that same time frame intersperses more of the militia-style training with news footage of police brutality cases; at one point, as a masked rifle-toting militia member rides to the training site in the back of a Jeep, the voice of Glenn Beck is spliced in. "What is it that the average person can do to wake Washington up?" asks Beck. "What will wake these clowns up?"

On January 5, 2010, Dyer/July4Patriot went on the Web site of the American Resistance Movement and wrote: "My name is Sgt. Dyer, Charles A., of the United States Marine Corps. I am currently living in Duncan, Oklahoma and attempting to form the Oklahoma militia network . . . There are many steps that are needed before we are operational, but this is the beginning . . ."

It wasn't the beginning. Exactly one week later, sheriff's deputies from Stephens County, Oklahoma, came to Dyer's home and arrested him. The charge was that Dyer, in the process of divorcing his wife, had sodomized a seven-year-old girl. The horrific sex charges had no connection to Dyer's activities as a would-be militia leader, but something else the law-enforcement officers uncovered did. They found a Colt M–203 and a 40-millimeter grenade launcher in Dyer's home. Their investigation also uncovered that the latter of the two lethal devices was one of three that were stolen from Fort Irwin in California, just before it was supposed to be shipped out to Iraq. Dyer would be quickly tried and acquitted on a federal charge of knowingly possessing an unregistered grenade launcher—he successfully insisted to jurors that he believed the device was a flare gun. According to news accounts of his acquittal, Dyer told the FBI that the California friend who gave him the stolen grenade launcher was "a militia member who believes the government will raise taxes so high people will begin to riot."

Dyer's activities—although quite public—had bubbled under the surface of the mainstream media, but his arrest did make a mild splash in the local news, the Associated Press wire, and a number of liberal blogs. In the wake of reports that labeled the jailed ex-Marine and militia wannabe an Oath Keeper, Stewart Rhodes backpedaled furiously. He said:

"Charles Dyer never became an actual member of Oath Keepers. I met him when he attended our April 19, 2009 gathering at Lexington, and back then I considered him for a position as our liaison to the Marine Corps, but I decided against that when he made it clear he intended to train and help organize private militias across the country when he got out of the Marines."

But Rhodes's explanation looked pretty silly in the face of the most powerful tracking tool ever invented—not anything that was invented by the Department of Homeland Security, but the indestructible cache of cyber-postings preserved by the search engine Google.

As the online trail clearly revealed, no one had promoted Dyer's July Fourth speech in Oklahoma more enthusiastically than Stewart Rhodes himself. In a Web announcement of the coming rally, Rhodes acknowledged renewing his military oath alongside Dyer on the Lexington Green, and then he told his fellow Oath Keepers that "you can bet that Sgt. Dyer will deliver one fiery speech. Take that to the bank.

"Don't miss it, and bring your friends and family."

CHAPTER SIX

Phoenix in the Ashes

I t's 7:30 on a Sunday morning, and things are pretty quiet on East Thomas Road in Phoenix—too quiet, if you ask the gaggle of eight or nine Latino men standing under a small, lonely stand of palm trees. They are mostly Mexican men in their twenties and thirties, straddling the curbside of a small strip of asphalt that divides the Home Depot from the Wal-Mart, hands thrust deep into windbreakers as the nippy March winds whipping down off Camelback Mountain refuse to yield to the rising desert sun.

The small huddled mass of men are day laborers—primarily undocumented Mexicans, willing to hang drywall or paint a house for any employer who is willing to show up here at the Wal-Mart parking lot and pay them for their low-wage toil. For weeks, this location across from budget-minded day-care centers and pawn shops has been the unlikely front line of a war that's being waged here in Arizona over what America will look like in a generation's time, a war that is now providing both energy and new recruits to the backlash against the presidency of Barack Obama. But now the SUVs and cargo vans with hiring men and their pockets filled with cash are in short supply—and the rowdy protestors who used to harass the Mexican wannabe workers have melted away, too.

It's reportedly been at least several weeks now since anyone at the

Wal-Mart hiring scrum has seen Lynne Stevens, the notorious sixty-five-year-old lesbian anti-immigrant zealot who wields a video camera in her arm—her popular handle on YouTube is "Jackie40D"—and who always has a Smith and Wesson at her side, which she notoriously brandished during a dispute in early 2010. Ditto for the man they call "Angry Jim" Markins with his array of hateful signs, like the one that claims (with no evidence to back it up) that some 143,000 Americans have been killed by illegal immigrants since 9/11, or their wheelchair-bound sidekick, a Native American known only to their chronicler—the *Phoenix New Times* investigative reporter Stephen Lemons—as Nelson. The unremarkable big-box-store parking lot was once their small battleground, but those angry anti-immigration protestors, loosely affiliated with a virulent group called United for a Sovereign America, or USA, have dwindled over the last year or so from an initial handful to those hardy three and now to zero. During that decline, the number of would-be Latino day laborers has plunged as well.

But the idea of grabbing off a tiny slice of the American Dream on-the-sly dies hard for the small posse of Hispanic men who are out here on a slow-starting Sunday morning in East Phoenix—even as the time line of a punishing recession here in the formerly real-estate-crazed Arizona, and of the angry protests and law-enforcement crackdowns that followed, is no longer marked in months but in years. Some of the men have been through a variant of hell—a long walk across miles of barren Arizona desert—just to make it to this forlorn slab of asphalt.

When an Anglo with a button-down shirt and a notebook walks over, several of the day laborers surge forward at this vaguest hint of work, only to hang back—understandably a tad suspicious, given everything that happens here in Phoenix—when you explain you aren't offering a day's pay, merely seeking a little information.

"No English . . . *Poquito* English," a man who looks to be in his late forties mutters. His light-brown face is weathered from sunny days and wind-driven nights, a black woolen cap with the incongruous New York Mets insignia pulled down tight over his ears. But as he realizes you are neither an anti-immigrant zealot nor an undercover agent, just a guy with a pen and a couple of questions, he agrees to tell you his name, Roberto Valdez, and his age, which is thirty-nine, or about ten years younger than he looks. How long, you ask, has he been coming to the Wal-Mart looking for work?

"I came in yesterday from Mexico—it was one week walking over the desert. Right now, my stomach is sick, because I drank the water from a creek. Right now, I'm sick." But he is here now and eager to do whatever work is available—"everything . . . construction, landscaping, painting, drywall." He pauses for a second. "Plumbing . . . everything." Valdez says he's been doing this now for fourteen years, traveling back and forth between Mexico City, where his family is, and Phoenix, where he has usually been able to find work.

Until now.

"Yeah, it's hard for everybody because everybody needs money," Valdez says. "Everybody no food, you know, everybody no shoes, no clothes, everybody cold." It's not just the winter that turned unseasonably cold in early 2010. In the middle of the first decade of the millennium, the housing market went crazy here in Phoenix, creating an insatiable demand for low-cost labor. But now the average price of a home in the Valley of the Sun has crashed 50 percent from the peak, with thousands of homeowners in this desert considered "under water"—that is, with homes worth less than the dollar value of their mortgage. Several SUVs whiz by toward the front of the Wal-Mart as you speak, but there are no foremen, only early-bird shoppers. Valdez turns to a couple of the men on the curbside, banters some in Spanish, and turns back to you.

"We're looking for work, not looking for trouble . . ."

But trouble has had a way of finding this place. The exact sequence of events is unclear, but several accounts concur that a few months back, Stevens—the armed anti-immigrant crusader, who once boasted to the *New Times*'s Lemons that she'd spent time near the U.S.-Mexico border firing potshots at migrants just like Roberto Valdez—took her

gun out of her holster, causing several police cars to race to the parking lot and restore order. Stevens claimed someone threw a rock at her;
other witnesses say she just got mad at a shopper who'd told her to get
lost. Whatever happened, Stevens wasn't arrested—but she is no longer
coming back here to East Thomas Road.

Now, at least on her YouTube channel, Stevens, a.k.a. "Jackie40D,"
has taken up a brand-new crusade. That would be politics, Tea Party
style. Instead of harassing day laborers, she is now dogging the Arizona
man who tried but badly failed in keeping Barack Obama out of the
White House in 2008. That man is Senator John McCain, the ex-POW
and 2008 GOP standard-bearer who as of winter 2010 has suddenly
found himself embroiled in the political fight of his seventy-four-year
lifetime. Stevens and her band of rabble-rousers follow him to places
like the local American Legion hall—bringing signs with sayings like
"NO AMNESTY FOR ILLEGAL ALIEN INVADERS—SUPPORT
SHERIFF JOE," a reference to the tough-as-cactus county sheriff Joe
Arpaio, and trying to make the reelection-seeking McCain as miserable
as possible.

The new celebrity for the anti-immigrant warriors is J. D. Hayworth, who has risen from the political ashes here in greater Phoenix
after losing his congressional seat in embarrassing fashion in 2006.
Today, Hayworth is capitalizing on conservative Arizona fury against
McCain for at one time supporting an immigration bill that includes a
path to citizenship for undocumented people. And so when Hayworth
announced his candidacy not long after the Morning of the Gun in
front of the Wal-Mart, Stevens, her Smith and Wesson, and her video
camera were there in the back of the crowd, uploading the event to her
channel on YouTube. The biggest whoop she captures on film is when
Hayworth calls McCain's immigration policy "an illegal alien bailout!"

Stevens may be standing at the back of the Hayworth announcement, but other extreme nativists take center stage. One of them is
Chris Simcox, who founded a border anti-immigration vigilante group
called the Minutemen Project after arriving in the Arizona town of

Tombstone in 2002 and deciding to launch a newspaper warning its readers that "a swarm of uncontrolled refugees" is "fleeing a Marxist structured government" and overrunning Arizona. The Southern Poverty Law Center later reported that Simcox himself was fleeing two bad marriages tagged by disturbing personal allegations as well as talk of increasing paranoia stemming from the September 11, 2001 attacks, after which Simcox "talked endlessly about stockpiling firearms and apocalyptic premonitions." But neither Simcox's history of extreme statements nor the other touchstones of his troubled past had stopped him from announcing that he would run for the Senate against McCain. Though that bid proved to be short-lived, Simcox found a candidate of like mind in Hayworth, and at the kickoff for Hayworth's campaign against McCain, he joined Hayworth onstage, throwing his support to the new challenger.

"From New York to New Jersey, Virginia to Massachusetts, and Florida to Texas, conservative Republicans and their brothers and sisters in the Tea Parties have united to say 'No More!' to the liberals who run our nation," Simcox declared, adding, "So it is with great pleasure that I stand with J. D. Hayworth and endorse his campaign!"

As the upstart Hayworth—who'd been reconnecting with conservative Arizonans as a talk-radio host since his political humiliation in 2006—lurched from nowhere in the polls to within striking distance of the four-term incumbent McCain, other elements of the paranoid far-right fringe raced to endorse Hayworth. In addition to Simcox, there was ALI-PAC, the Americans for Legal Immigration, which has been targeted by the SPLC for tolerating racist talk on its Web site and for other offenses. ALI-PAC—which had been touting the anti-immigration crusader and former CNN host Lou Dobbs for president until Dobbs made the mistake, in their eyes, of moderating some of his caustic comments on the topic—had no such qualms about backing Hayworth.

The SPLC highlighted a comment that founder William Gheen had posted on the ALI-PAC site that just as easily could have been a verbal dart hurled at Roberto Valdez and his fellow day laborers: "Call me old fashioned, but people should be able to shop at Wal-Mart without worrying about catching [t]uberculosis."

FOR ALL THE people who wonder whether this increasingly not-so-pent-up rage in America could make an impact on actual government policy or question how the coiled energy of the Tea Parties and the 9-12ers and the Oath Keepers and the gun freaks and those militias out in the wilderness might shape the lives of us all, there is one thing you can say to any of the remaining skeptics:

Let them come to Arizona.

It is here—in a land of luscious painted deserts bisected by blue highways, in the forty-eighth state, in practically the farthest corner of the United States from the temperate, coastal habitat of the Founding Fathers—where the rubber finally met the road for the backlash against the presidency of Barack Obama. It is as if the rising mercury in these arid badlands was symbolic of the skyrocketing political temperatures, where the promise of an American melting pot gave way to the realities of immigration and fears over our national identity in the twenty-first century.

Arizona had it all. The loose strands of unrest that you witnessed in other corners of the United States—the gun worship of Knob Creek, the strange notion that Barack Obama was "not American," all the paranoia about Washington and "socialists" and big government—were all wrapped together there with a big xenophobic bow. Geographically, this might be the extreme lower-left corner of America, but it was increasingly clear that the Grand Canyon State was the center of a great divide cleaving the nation in two.

The rest of the nation probably should have seen it coming. Political rage had been simmering here for years—even when economic good times and a real-estate boom tamped down the natural tensions between a mostly white, older, transient citizenry and a blue-collar workforce heavily comprised of undocumented Hispanics. The angry background noise was also submerged in the 2008 elections when the moderate and—at the time, anyway—self-proclaimed maverick Republican John McCain became the political face that Arizona was proud to show the rest of the nation. In particular, the middle-of-the-road albeit occasionally mixed signals that the longtime GOP senator sent out on immigration meant that most outsiders weren't aware of just how angry the talk had become on the radio down in McCain's hometown, and many didn't know about the armed Arizonans patrolling the barren border regions or harassing the day laborers.

Just a few short weeks after your visit to the Phoenix area, the passion of the anti-Obama uprising swept like a flash flood into the very corridors of the statehouse there, in a flurry of some of the most powerful anti-Washington legislation enacted since the day 150 years ago that South Carolina had actually seceded from the union in a similar jumble of concerns over states' rights—and skin color. In a remarkable two-week stretch, the Arizona legislature enacted a law that made it easier for rank-and-file citizens to carry guns in public, nearly added an arcane ballot rule for presidential candidates aimed to sow uncertainty about Obama's citizenship, and allowed law-enforcement officers to use racial profiling to make arrests and create a climate of fear among Latinos. The three bills may have seemed quite different from each other, but they collectively demonstrated the head start Arizona had when it came to the backlash. Together these pieces of legislation contained all the seeds that had been planted by the far-right radicals ever since Obama's election, and they all addressed the same problem in the eyes of white conservatives wielding political power, "manning the barricades of civilization," in the historian Hofstadter's famous phrase, against the invasion of the dark-skinned Others.

Thus, it is Arizona where the world is seeing the dire consequences of this whole backlash movement—the most alarming rips in the very fabric of national unity in a century and a half, a nation that appears to be coming apart at the seams for the second time in its young history.

The nativist streak in America is a very deep one, actually predating the Civil War of the 1860s, going back to the Know-Nothing Party, whose origins were in fear of immigration from Ireland. In modern times, the leaders of the movement that culminated in Arizona's strict immigration laws have been very explicit in wanting to forestall a day when whites are no longer the dominant culture; the founder of the Federation for American Immigration Reform (FAIR), which drafted Arizona's newly draconian anti-immigration law, once asked whether "the present majority [should] peaceably hand over its political power to a group that is simply more fertile."

Arizona's journey to becoming a hotbed of right-wing reactionaries began in the mid-2000s with a surge in illegal immigration for a variety of reasons, including instability in Mexico and elsewhere in Central and South America and the home-building boom in the Sun Belt. Their arrival sparked a debate over whether these newcomers were taking on low-income jobs for which there was a lack of interest among white American citizens, or whether they were helping business owners drive down wages. But there were other factors to stir up unrest in the middle of the decade. The growing blast furnace of conservative talk radio needed constant fuel, and the embers of passion over 9/11 were dying down. What's more, a conservative president in George W. Bush was becoming increasingly unpopular even within his own party, thanks to the twin fiascos of Katrina and Iraq. By 2006 and 2007, on the eve of a lengthy race for the White House, the immigration issue took over talk radio, along with cable TV shows like that of the nativist-minded Lou Dobbs on CNN. The jingoistic appeal of the topic allowed right-wingers to draw a line not just against liberals but against Bush, who along with many business interests favored immigration reform. It was a national conversation that was based on a contradiction, since there was little evidence that the undocumented migrants were "taking away jobs from Americans"—the battle cry of thousands of radio callers—amid a reality that they were holding up the low-wage bottom of the economic pyramid.

In addition to kowtowing to his big-business donors, Bush and his advisors such as Karl Rove had another reason for supporting a plan that would provide the undocumented a better path to citizenship: they knew that the GOP could cling to power in the years ahead only by appealing to the new Latino voters who were becoming a bigger share of the electorate every two years—not exactly the message that white-oriented Talk Radio World tuned in to hear. In the years leading up to the 2008 campaign, an anti-immigration frenzy exploded both in places where you wouldn't expect it—including your own Philadelphia, where a popular cheese-steak entrepreneur stoked controversy with a sign commanding patrons to speak English—and in places where you would, such as the increasingly militarized border region on the boundary of Mexico and Arizona.

Here in the desert, Karl Rove's political worries about the elections in 2008, 2010, and 2012 just weren't the main focus of people—because the year that had everyone so terrified was 2050. In that year, according to the U.S. Census Bureau, the U.S. population would grow to some 399 million people—but only 49.8 percent of them would be white, while the majority of citizens would include a huge slice of Latinos as well as growing populations of blacks, Asians, and other non-Caucasians. In Arizona, it wasn't just the issue of adults like Roberto Valdez crossing the desert; the Brookings Institution found that the desert state, as a magnet for affluent retirees, had a senior citizen population that is 83 percent white, while children in Arizona were only 43 percent white. That kind of gap exists all across America, but nowhere else is it so pronounced.

And so for callers to Arizona's white-oriented talk radio, the year 2050 was synonymous with Armageddon, the year that "The Other" would inherit political and cultural control of the United States through sheer numbers. At first, there had been studies pegging the year of this cultural Armageddon as 2037; one reason that the date had been moved back thirteen years was aggressive anti-immigration tactics like those undertaken by Sheriff Arpaio, who was moving Mexicans back across the border by the busload. In Arizona, state lawmakers and elected officials worked overtime—their efforts culminating in that legislation in spring 2010—to capitalize upon and codify the fury of talk radio land, passing laws that made it easier to arrest Latinos here than anywhere else in America, and that made it harder for them to find work.

The crisis in Arizona accelerated after two very hot matches were tossed into this pooled gasoline: the global economic crisis, which landed on Arizona's overextended and overmortgaged housing market harder than just about anywhere else, and—arguably more importantly—the election of Barack Obama. The Democratic upstart—and his legion of supporters among the nonwhite as well as the young— was a 9/11-sized jolt to the white masses already so worried about the cultural implications of immigration. The year 2050 suddenly wasn't two generations away but right here knocking on the front door, with a dark face and with that scary name: Barack Hussein Obama. Like a fire spreading across dry sagebrush, it took no effort for fear of The Other to leap from the Mexicans in front of the Wal-Mart to the man now inside the Oval Office.

The irony was overwhelming—after years of arguing over who was an American and whether some arrivals to Arizona deserved a "path to citizenship," conservatives here and elsewhere were now in essence questioning the path to citizenship taken by Obama. In 2010, Arizona Republicans were asking the forty-fourth president of the United States the same question they were asking Mexicans with a busted taillight: "Your papers, please."

It should come as no surprise that it was Arizona where the Tea Parties blossomed early. The ideas of the Tea Party "like minds," which included Beck's 9-12ers, gun aficionados, and the militia-friendly, spread quickly among voters here, proceeding rapidly up the political totem poll, where career-driven politicians were eager to translate the most extreme of these into law. Under the sun-soaked sheen of red-tile roofs, this was a state of paranoia, a place where men now brandished their legal weapons at the edge of speeches by Obama and where a pastor openly prayed for the president's death. But the significance of Arizona's daring moves on immigration extended beyond the state's borders; they rocked any hopes for a realistic federal immigration policy, as some moderate Republicans fled the issue to adopt the Tea Party positions and even top Democrats cowered in fear, as they often do.

So powerful were these forces that they threatened the previously unthinkable: the possible end of Senator John McCain's political career. Despite being the modern politician most closely identified with Arizona, the erstwhile 2008 Republican presidential standard-bearer sought another term in the Senate in 2010 with two massive strikes against him. For one thing, his desperate attempts to renounce his mid-2000s advocacy of a moderate path toward amnesty for undocumented immigrants did little to mollify the furious conservatives who tend to vote in a GOP primary. But on a more psychic level, McCain was the man who failed to save America from Barack Obama, which for some was a political capital offense.

McCain's history with immigration had not been clear cut. In 2006, McCain unsuccessfully carried Bush's water on the "path to citizenship" in the Senate, but by 2008 he'd renounced that position when he was wooing Republican primary voters. He then skated back to the middle for the general election, leaving his plan for the undocumented immigrants at a vague "they are also God's children, and we have to do it in a humane and compassionate fashion." However, there was no more of that pretty talk as the GOP lurched even farther to the right and Hayworth waited in the wings. Many political observers, still thinking of the McCain of years past, foolishly thought he would denounce the racial-profiling measure that was becoming Arizona law that springtime; instead he offered his support, along with the bizarre claim that drivers carrying the undocumented "are intentionally causing accidents on the freeway." His reelection platform consisted of begging the Obama administration to send troops to the border to forcibly prevent any more of "God's children" from surging north.

In fairness, McCain wasn't the only major American politician to go south on the immigration problem as the political zeitgeist shifted to the right, egged on by the collapsing U.S. economy, which caused middle-class voters to look for scapegoats. McCain's election rival Obama had been an unabashed backer of the pathway to citizenship for an estimated 10.8 million immigrants now in the country without documents—en route to winning the vast majority of Latino votes in 2008. But Obama then did essentially nothing on immigration during his first year in the Oval Office, gave the issue just one line in his 2010 State of the Union address, and finally came out behind a Senate-led reform effort that was probably too late, given the nation's exhaustion over the bruising battle over a health-care reform bill. While Washington dithered on a new immigration policy, the Obama administration embraced the old one with surprising zeal, shipping back 400,000 Mexicans in its first year, far more than were deported in the final year of the Bush administration.

But that wasn't the worst of it. The old policy also involved hundreds of millions of dollars to build new border fences in California and Texas—but not in Arizona, where it was assumed that the harsh desert (and, who knows, maybe vigilantes like Stevens and Simcox) would be enough to dissuade migrants. Yet here is Roberto Valdez in the Wal-Mart parking lot to prove in the battered flesh that no such thing happened, not in a brutal economy where people will risk their lives just to hang drywall for a day's paltry pay. And not everyone was as lucky—if that's the right word—as Valdez. From October 2009 through March 2010, some eighty-five migrants were found dead in isolated pockets of desert in southern Arizona—some corpses too decomposed to even identify the gender of the deceased. The pace of the dying was 60 percent higher than in the previous fiscal year that began when Bush was president—not exactly a change that we can believe in.

And so into this volatile and long-festering conflict stepped J. D. Hayworth and his newfound nativist friends. He was backed by many of the Tea Party activists of Arizona, but he stood for something far greater, demonstrating the speed with which the fringe right wing had hijacked the old guard of the Republican Party in Arizona, the danger that lurked in having a United States senator support such racially motivated laws, and the fear of The Other—be it in the White House or the house next door—that seemed to be pushing the whole thing forward in Arizona and around the country.

THE SCENT OF chlorine lingers in the air at the Scottsdale Plaza Resort, about ten miles up Scottsdale Road and a world apart from the down-to-earth Western Union shops and fast-taco joints of East Thomas Road. It is not the glitziest resort in the valley, with its stylish-for-the-1970s low-rise tan stucco and rust-red tile roofs, but it is an oasis nonetheless, the kind of Arizona that most upscale out-of-state vacationers experience for a few days—dominated by the endless flapping of the waterfall in the main swimming pool, punctuated by the occasional spike of a tennis ball.

Back in Phoenix, sheriff deputies from Maricopa County are busy rounding up 111 people—about half of them undocumented migrants—in the latest of a series of crime-suppression sweeps undertaken by Arpaio that have aroused the concern of the Obama administration. Apparently things with the raids were going just swimmingly, because Arpaio is here in the flesh in this large white tent behind the ever-gurgling pool on a Saturday morning, helping J. D. Hayworth raise the cash he'll need to defeat John McCain. Later, Hayworth will make the obligatory joke about the Republicans being the "big tent" party—here inside this tent at a hotel with $299-a-night patio suites, in front of a sheriff who's notorious for keeping his predominantly Mexican jail inmates in a different kind of "Tent City" where top bunk temperatures have been measured at 150 degrees.

"My goodness gracious! What's going on?!"

J. D. Hayworth has just entered the tent, bemused that a writer has traveled from Philadelphia to watch him in action. He is a big man with outsized features, jutting brow on a sloped forehead, attired in a funeral-director kind of navy-blue suit and well-knotted tie even on this sun-soaked Saturday morning. The affected "goodness gracious" is a proper prelude to his overly melodramatic speaking style, introduced in his initial career as a TV sports anchor and later honed in his stint on right-wing talk radio. There is one adjective that sticks in your head as you watch Hayworth work the room, and that is "unctuous."

He seems unfazed by the soft turnout for this event, at which diehard Hayworth supporters are expected to dial up potential donors across the country and beg them to give up to $2,400—the legal limit—to his campaign. Aides said there were two hundred RSVPs and some one hundred were expected to come, but there are only about fifty or sixty volunteers in the noticeably underfilled tent. The volunteers struggle to make up for their numbers in enthusiasm—several race to put Hayworth or the arguably more famous Arpaio on their cell phone to seal a donation, and one lucky woman garners a special prize for snagging a $500 contribution: a pair of pink underwear—just like the ones that the Mexicans are forced to wear back in Arpaio's Tent City detention camp, except this pair is autographed by Arpaio himself. Hayworth moves around trading political gossip with the rank-and-file, grumbling that 2008 and likely 2012 presidential hopeful Mitt Romney told Hayworth he wanted to back him over McCain but couldn't, saying "forgive me but I have to do it [endorse McCain] because of the money."

In an interview, Hayworth softens his rhetoric on the immigration issue, but the consequences of his energetic right-flank challenge—let alone his potential election—for any possibility of real reform are clear. He asserts, "Obama's latest effort for amnesty will have one less major supporter—Mr. McCain will be gone and I guess Mr. Graham"— Republican senator Lindsey Graham of South Carolina, one of the few remaining Republicans at that time still willing to consider a deal on real immigration reform—"will be moved up from understudy" to McCain. In 2006, when McCain was on board with serious immigration reform, Hayworth was publishing a book called *Whatever It Takes*—to stop illegal immigration, that is—featuring the now slightly dated tie-in to the post–9/11 "war on terror." The book obsesses about the idea that illegal alien murderers and rapists are walking the streets of America, despite several studies showing that crime rates among these economic refugees are actually quite low. Hayworth also voices strong support for the "Americanization" of immigrants in the same manner first championed in the early twentieth century by Henry Ford, who said that "[t]hese men of many nations must be taught American ways, the English language, and the right way to live."

Hayworth says that he had a term for the Tea Partiers that support him—"awakening Americans"—and that the immigration issue was the start of the waking-up process. "For some of them, the wakeup call came with amnesty, with McCain's amnesty bill in 2007," he says, "but for others it was the leftward lurch of the Obama administration," brought to a head by the health-care reform bill the new president was pushing. But what about Hayworth's prominent support from the far-right paranoid fringe—the folks like Chris Simcox and ALI-PAC? The candidate replies that McCain "has tried to make some linkages that are absurd. It would be as absurd as saying to Senator McCain that because some elements of the KKK are saying that I'm going to endorse you for president in 2008 that I'm going to hold you to that association." It's true that there's not much Hayworth can do if a radical from United for a Sovereign America like Lynne Stevens decides to show up at his rally, but the endorsements from Simcox and ALI-PAC were welcomed with open arms.

But Hayworth is also proving the lessons of Sarah Palin, not to mention Glenn Beck, that the best path to idolization if not leadership in today's conservative movement is not through the hallways of government but behind a microphone. In his twelve years in Congress, the desert pol developed a reputation not just for overheated rhetoric but for hot blasts of air in general; *Washingtonian* magazine twice named Hayworth the second-biggest "windbag" inside the Beltway. He lost his congressional reelection bid to Democrat Harry Mitchell in 2006 in part because of Hayworth's ties to the scandal surrounding the lobbyist-turned-convicted-felon Jack Abramoff, in whose football luxury suite Hayworth used to hold fundraisers. After the loss, all of that windbagging managed to come in handy, as two things revived Hayworth—anger over McCain on immigration, and his newfound platform as a local conservative talk-radio host at KFYI in Phoenix, which also broadcasts Rush Limbaugh and Michael Savage, and where Hayworth enthusiastically pandered to the extremist views of listeners even on the touchy subject of Obama's birth certificate. Hayworth had at one point told MSNBC's *Hardball* that "the president should come forward with the information, that's all. Why must we depend on the governor of Hawaii?" Later on, the candidate told FNC's Bill O'Reilly that he believed Obama was born in the fiftieth state and that "those comments were taken from a radio program where I was a catalyst for conversation," adding, "That's what happens in broadcasting." By the time Hayworth issued that clarification, a proposal requiring future presidential candidates, including Obama in 2012, to provide a birth certificate was making its way through the Arizona legislature—one more powerful example of how things that radio and TV personalities were saying to be provocative and entertaining were not only shaping opinions but also policy in the real world, sometimes to dangerous effect.

Now Hayworth hopes to also ride the support of "Sheriff Joe," clearly the real rock star at this small resort gathering. The eighteen-year sheriff of Phoenix-centered Maricopa County, Arpaio is reviled by as much as 45 percent of the local electorate and often blasted by human rights groups such as Amnesty International, but is also an American idol for the not-so-silent-but-shrinking majority here. He is Strother Martin from *Cool Hand Luke* except clinging to the dour accent of his youth in the Northeast, a crusader whose pink-underwear-and-hot-sun treatment for his predominantly Mexican inmates is nothing short of cathartic for angry white voters.

"I'm afraid of what would happen without 'Sheriff Joe' around here," one of the female volunteers says to fellow Hayworth backer

Marilyn Anderson, who like many Arizonans hasn't even been here that long, just three years. Her husband, Chuck Anderson, is employed by the software giant Oracle and can work anywhere, and so he has chosen the exurb of Waddell, where the Phoenix sprawl collides with the desert and he was able to get more house for his money. The couple, both senior citizens, wear similar American-flag shirts and are highly conversant in the latest talk-radio talking points. "ACORN is going to be all over the state, no doubt about it," Marilyn Anderson says in explaining why she feels it's important to make fundraising calls for Hayworth. "They've got billions of dollars!" In reality, the front page of the *New York Times* on sale in the resort lobby shop that very morning is reporting that the poverty-fighting group is actually filing for bankruptcy and going out of business, the victim of a smear campaign cheered on by Fox News and Glenn Beck.

Yet for all the fuss, Arpaio doesn't exude much charisma as he works the tent. A gruff man with wire-rimmed glasses, dressed in an understated, well-worn corduroy jacket, the then nearly seventy-eight-year-old sheriff looks more like a retiree you might see in a diner back in South Philly—Frank Rizzo with a desert tan. While Hayworth is a slick, overproduced radio baritone, Arpaio—who spent the 1960s as a federal drug-enforcement agent—is a low-tech reincarnation of Nixon-era resentments. He tells you that the common people love him but the elites hate him.

"I believe in the people—the Tea Party is the people," Arpaio says. On immigration, he tells you, the Tea Party "is speaking out on what the people feel, which confuses me. We just locked up 111 people last night in a big crime suppression, made national news. What surprises me is that if eighty percent of the people want something done? . . . let's localize it; how come all of the politicians aren't standing next to me and kissing my ring? Well, they're all kissing my ring for endorsements—don't say that! But why aren't they standing next to me and saying we support the sheriff, if the people want it. That confuses me." He tells you that maybe those other politicians are afraid of losing

Hispanic voters. There may be something to that since despite his wild popularity among white conservative Phoenicians, Arpaio has actually seen his percentage of votes shrink in every election.

Arpaio's new tougher stance on finding undocumented immigrants and shipping them back across the border—an astonishing 37,000 immigrants were processed in his jails and sent home in 2009, one of the reasons that the overall national figure was so high—is making friends but also a boatload of enemies, some in high places. Local pols—as well as Arpaio—are arguably squandering millions of taxpayer dollars in an array of complicated and messy legal battles involving "the world's toughest sheriff," while the Obama administration has sought to strip federal funding from Arpaio's office and launched a probe of his arrest policies, and a powerful Latino protest movement called Puente has now risen in defiance of the controversial lawman. On this morning, "the world's toughest sheriff" lingers in the big tent behind the babbling waterfall for two hours, in no hurry to leave. He seems to feel safe here, surrounded by a handful of adoring fans.

Not all of Arpaio's admirers are as well behaved as the polo-shirted retirees or self-employed contractors here at the Scottsdale resort. In the early months of the Obama administration, a videotape taken—by Lynne Stevens, of course—at a large march by Puente and other pro-immigration advocates shows Arpaio having a friendly chat with right-wing protestors including a man from the neo-Nazi National Socialist Party who calls himself "Vito Lombardi." Other protestors are living symbols of how extremists can glide in and out of more mainstream Republican circles here in Arizona; one of them, the notorious J. T. Ready, a former Republican precinct captain in Mesa also known for his anti-Semitic rants, waved a Confederate flag at the Latino marchers. On the video, "Lombardi" yells at Arpaio, "We've got your back." In late April 2010, a news conference where Arpaio endorsed a local Republican candidate was attended by five men in neo-Nazi uniforms who were brandishing rifles.

Now, Arpaio bristles when you ask about his extremist pals: "I don't approve it but I said what do you want me to do, lock them all up? They got the freedom of speech, too—right? If I went around and locked them all up, then the sheriff is locking up neo-Nazis and everything else. I gotta get this, okay," he says, and he moves away.

There is a weariness about the sheriff—a weariness that doesn't reflect the raw anger felt by many Arizona conservatives who worship him and who have flocked to Tea Parties here. You wonder where that anger lurks—and then it fills the streets like a spring flash flood barreling down the once-parched terrain. You are headed down Scottsdale Road back to Phoenix when you stumble into an honest-to-God Brooks Brothers riot—right there on the ritziest main corner of this sun-soaked suburb resort, in front of the Sprinkles Cupcakes and the P.F. Chang's Asian Bistro and the massive American Apparel store with its giant round turret filled with self-described "disco fashions." There are two hundred people in the street—ringing a cowbell and carrying signs, mostly saying hurray-for-our-side slogans like "Stop This Madness" or "Simple Math: More Government—Less Freedom."

The dry desert air is filled with the nonstop roar of car horns bleating out their approval, blending with the anti-Obama and anti-healthcare chants in what sounds like a European soccer match of political rage. You'd seen other Tea Party protests over the course of a year but none with quite this intensity or spontaneity, directed at a government nearly three thousand miles away that is now seen not as their representatives but as a kind of evil empire. It is one more screen shot of how Arizona and its overheated political climate has made it the poster child for a nation's anger.

One of the leaders of the rally is a blond, thirty-something woman named Judy Hoelscher, a member of the Mesa Red Mountain Tea Party activists. She has staked out a prime spot, right there in front of the P.F. Chang's, and has a small video camera in one hand and a sign blasting the Scottsdale area's Democrat congressman Harry Mitchell—the man who'd ousted J. D. Hayworth four years earlier—in the other, as she shouts back her approval at this nonstop cacophony of honking SUVs at the top of her lungs. Another nearby placard calls for Mitchell to be tarred and feathered.

Hoelscher tells you the health-care reform that was being debated in Washington is a step toward a single-payer system run by the government, saying, "It's my body, my choice, basically, and they are completely taking that away from me." She adds, "Our most basic rights are the right to make decisions about my own body. . . . And the American people are not going to stand for it."

You note that she sounds exactly like an abortion rights activist, and you ask her if her comments mean she is pro-choice.

"I'm not," she responded, stammering a bit. "But that's not the issue with health care. The issue is they're taking control of my body."

Hoelscher says she was busy raising her three children when she decided shortly after Obama took office to join the Tea Party and also to start a blog called Angry Right-Wing Housewife, which features a rendering of a stern-looking homemaker brandishing her rolling pin. "It was the way . . . the stimulus bill, I felt, was nothing more than a slush fund and they were spending my children's future—and it's not fair." Like the others who've taken to the streets, Hoelscher is steamed this day about health care but isn't happy with illegal immigration, either. "Our state is going broke because of the illegal immigrants," she claims. Behind her, the honking and all the shouting at Harry Mitchell and Barack Obama is reaching a deafening crescendo.

A few days after all the sound and fury, Representative Mitchell reported that other people were calling his office and even his home and making death threats. One recorded message from a woman who called his office said: "I cannot tell you how much I wish a panty bomber would come in and just fucking blow your place up." The death threats against Mitchell would be alarming even if they were just isolated incidents, but they were both a foreshadowing of the violent talk that was farther on down the road and an echo of some Arizona hate speech that had already come from a most unlikely setting.

. . . .

THE REVEREND STEVEN Anderson is pounding a driftwood pulpit, a Baptist fundamentalist minister getting worked up over one of his favorite subjects—the power of prayer to make big things happen.

"We need to pray!" Anderson says, again smacking the pulpit here at his tiny Living Word Baptist Church in suburban Tempe. He is young—just twenty-nine years old, in fact—and more boyish than you'd expected, high-pitched, and nattily attired in a blue suit and tie. "Don't go through life without praying! We need to be praying and asking God to help us and a lot of the reason we don't have the things we need is we're not praying for them!"

Despite his young age and the fact that he preaches from a tiny storefront in this strip mall across the street from the Wendy's, Steve Anderson is already famous for praying. Actually, for one prayer in particular—the one he told his congregation about in which he prays for the death of President Barack Obama. His revelation came in August 2009, the night before Obama came to the Phoenix area to deliver a speech, in a sermon that Anderson had videotaped and—as he does with all his sermons—posted to the Internet on YouTube.com. In it, he'd said:

Now, turn back to Psalm 58 and let me ask you this question. Why should Barack Obama melt like a snail? Why should Barack Obama die like the untimely birth of a woman? Why should his children be fatherless and his wife a widow, as we read in this passage? Well, I will tell you why. Because, since Barack Obama thinks it is okay to use a salty solution, right, to abort the unborn, because that's how abortions are done, my friend, using salt—and I would like to see Barack Obama melt like a snail tonight.

The very next day, Obama came to speak to the VFW convention in Phoenix and one of the congregants who'd heard Anderson's sermon, a man named Christopher Broughton, was spotted outside the hall with a loaded AR–15 rifle and a handgun—all legal under Arizona law, despite the proximity of the president. The Secret Service reportedly talked to Anderson—the pastor claims they merely called him on the phone after CNN had been pounding the story for several days—but there was really nothing else to be done.

The only thing that's indisputably clear about the boyish Anderson is that he is a man whose craving for attention knows no bounds. The services at Living Word Baptist Church are fairly short, just barely an hour, and consist almost entirely of Anderson preaching, thumping his Bible at the barren pulpit. About thirty people sit on stark blue armless chairs, in a jumble of attire from sneakers to seersucker suits; several are young men with severe buzz cuts, an unusual sight at any church these days. The walls are a plain white with no pictures of Jesus or anything else, and there is no organ playing, as the closing hymn is sung *a cappella*. A miniature video camera is propped up and record-ing the minister the whole time. The storefront is next to a pawn shop and beaconed with the kind of red electric sign you might see above a Chinese lunch buffet, and its foyer is almost completely barren except for an incongruous foosball table that a couple of kids race to play as the service ends.

Anderson is glib, friendly even, and happy to talk to a writer—and talk and talk. He answers the question that everyone must ask him, saying that of course he still prays for Barack Obama to die and to leave his wife, Michelle, a widow and his young daughters, Sasha and Malia, without a father.

"I made it clear in the sermon that I wasn't advocating any kind of vi-olence and that I was praying that God would deliver us from Obama," Anderson says. About Obama's family, the minister adds, "Well, that's his fault because he deserves to die . . . It's not that I don't like his presi-dency—it's that he's taking my money and using it to kill human beings."

Anderson is not exactly what you might expect in an Obama-death-wishing pastor. Like many people on the fringes, his political hero is

Ron Paul, and he claims that there's no difference between Obama and George W. Bush, even though he never made national headlines by praying for Bush's death. And on the hot-button issue that lured you all the way to Arizona in the first place, which is immigration, Anderson is a square peg not neatly fitting into any of the available holes. In fact, the young preacher harbors intense anger not toward incoming Mexicans but toward the other side—the U.S. Border Patrol, whom Anderson accuses of setting up checkpoints "like it was Nazi Germany or something."

As a result, Anderson took to not answering questions at these checkpoints, and one day shortly after Obama took office in early 2009, there was an encounter that did not turn out well for Anderson at all. "This one time I went through and they just won't take no for an answer," he says. "And basically they're demanding to search my trunk, saying their drug dogs want to search my trunk so I just refused, and so I sat there for an hour and a half and . . . to make a long story short, they bust out my windows, slam my face into broken glass, step on my head, Taser me for eighteen seconds straight, according to their own records, and I'm not doing anything to fight back."

He may not have fought back, but when the police beat-down started, Anderson's first instinct was what it always is, which was to turn his video camera on himself and later post it to YouTube. He tells you the war on immigration is just an excuse for national ID cards "and all this stuff like a police state." Anderson may be fairly neutral on the issue of Mexicans, but when your state is an immigration battle zone, the psyche is often collateral damage anyway. Still, ugly as Anderson's 2009 encounter with the border cops was, he is still here in Tempe, still preaching his "Living Word."

Others in Arizona have not fared as well with law enforcement.

IT WAS EERILY quiet on the streets of Phoenix one night back in January 2009—only the harsh winds of a midwinter's night in the desert can be heard as a video camera captures a young Mexican boy, about eight or nine, and his slightly older sister peering from the window of an eerily illuminated sedan where a sheriff's deputy is questioning their mom, Ciria.

"The lights were off—that's why they stopped her," the forlorn boy says to a cameraman in Spanish.

What did the officer say?

"To be quiet, but I couldn't because I wanted to go with my mommy," the girl says, a long strand of hair over her misty right eye, as she clutches a rabbit doll close against her chest for dear life. The mother is arrested because of an unpaid ticket and eventually deported to Mexico without her children. In Maricopa County, there are hundreds of kids like these two, American citizens unlike their parents, needing to find a new home for months before they can hopefully be reunited with a mother or father, most likely in Mexico.

The arrest was captured on videotape by activists working with the protest group Puente and is posted on its Web site, evidence of some of the fear on the streets of Greater Phoenix that existed even before the enactment of its newer draconian immigration law in 2010. Indeed, the law that provoked such a national uproar and talk of boycotts is really the culmination of a crackdown on undocumented Latinos that began around 2006. That was the year J. D. Hayworth published *Whatever It Takes* and Arizona lived up to that dictum by passing a law that banned human smuggling—the real-world effect of which was to give Arpaio and other law-enforcement officers a new reason to arrest and then ship migrants back to Mexico without the traditional trigger of some underlying crime, clearing the path for the wholesale deportations that continue to this day. At the same time, the state also moved to slash the economic oxygen lines to Mexican migrants when—at a time when the real-estate prices were still rising in the Valley of the Sun at an astronomical rate—it enacted a law barring cities like Phoenix from funding day labor centers, which had been created to keep men like Roberto Valdez from loitering for hours in a Wal-Mart parking lot with no restrooms. Another subsequent Arizona law went even farther, imposing strict sanctions on employers who knowingly hire undocumented immigrants.

But the surprising thing about Phoenix is that unlike what you see in other parts of the country or with other controversial issues such as gun control or health care, the anti-immigration fervor here in Arizona eventually sparked a counterreaction—a backlash to the backlash, reflecting the life-and-death issues at stake. The Puente movement has been able to turn out as many as twenty thousand people—local Latinos and their allies, and even celebrities like Phoenix-born Linda Ronstadt—at a time to march in protest against Arpaio's harsh tactics. Carlos Garcia, a young activist who is one of the top leaders of Puente, tells you that without comprehensive immigration reform in Washington, the main argument of the Hayworth supporters—that undocumented Mexicans need to "stand in line" like their ancestors did when they came to America—doesn't hold any water.

"Their first argument—'Why don't they wait on line like everybody else did or like my parents did' . . . so when they refer to this 'line,' there's no line, okay. It doesn't exist, in which folks can get into line to come here," Garcia tells you. "A lot of these folks have been here fifteen or twenty years. There's no line. It's an imaginary line."

Overhead, the steady stream of big planes en route to Sky Harbor descend past this nondescript parking-lot view from a Starbucks, where Garcia takes a short break to meet you as he races around the valley to deal with the fallout from the latest Arpaio crime sweep. Meanwhile, other Puente leaders are nearly three thousand miles away marching on the U.S. Capitol, trying to keep a focus on immigration reform in an early springtime when the political chattering classes are still fixated instead on health-care legislation and the angry reaction from the Tea Parties.

Barrel-chested and energetic, a rebel in a polo shirt with a goatee and a long black ponytail down to the small of his back, Garcia came here to Arizona as an undocumented immigrant as a child, but he gained legal U.S. status at fourteen when his mother remarried and he was adopted by his new stepfather. Almost immediately, he began crusading for other Mexican immigrants, venturing out into the desert in an effort to maintain water stations for those traveling on foot. This was where he learned all about right-wing vigilantism.

"We would fill these large plastic tanks, and we had to take a little fire"—a welding flame, that is—"in order to weld the plastic back on—because what the Minutemen would do is shoot the tanks so that all the water would come out, and we had to fix them," Garcia recalls. There would be angry encounters between the pro-immigration volunteers and the Minutemen, which inspired Garcia to become a student activist at Arizona State University, and now an organizer with Puente, focused on helping the day laborers.

Over the first year of the Obama administration, Garcia says he has watched the hard-core extremists from groups like United for a Sovereign America that have clashed with Puente now melt into the more respectable Tea Parties and provide a base of support for that political movement. "They're just changing shirts—it's nothing different," he says. The Tea Party lingo, he adds, "is just the same rhetoric as J. D. Hayworth or Sheriff Arpaio have been using for the last five years."

But as we spoke that spring afternoon, the highly flammable combination of the Tea Party momentum in Arizona and the smoldering anger over high unemployment and foreclosures was on the brink of a combustion that would bring the ongoing civil war here to the attention of the entire nation. The catalyst was a piece of legislation with an innocuous-sounding name, the "Support Our Law Enforcement and Safe Neighborhoods Act." The sponsor, a state senator named Russell Pearce, is a nexus of old-school far-right extremism, the up-and-coming Tea Party movement, and Republican politics. Pearce is a longtime ally of the Confederate-flag-waving right-wing radical J. T. Ready, and he now regularly speaks at Tea Party rallies in the Phoenix area. His new measure—which passed in the face of growing local protests and a coast-to-coast outcry and was signed into law by Republican governor Jan Brewer in April 2010—gives law-enforcement officers like Arpaio sweeping new powers to arrest citizens merely on "reasonable suspicion" that they might be here illegally.

Critics immediately branded the law as a racial-profiling measure that would create a climate of fear for all brown-skinned people in Arizona, regardless of their legal status, and even bring about the "papers, please" paranoia of Nazi Germany. Indeed, that kind of hostile climate was exactly what the bill's supporters wanted. A chief sponsor, GOP state representative John Kavanagh, told the *Arizona Republic* that "our intention is to make Arizona a very uncomfortable place for them to be so they leave or never come here in the first place." At the same time, liberal opponents of the law were building support for a nationwide economic boycott of Arizona, ensuring that the uproar would drag deep into the 2010 election season and possibly beyond.

The right's ever-expanding crackdown on immigrants continued full bore despite growing evidence that even the earlier, not-as-stringent measures are already doing more harm than good to the Arizona economy—that the nativists are, in essence, cutting off their nose to spite their face. Garcia and pro-immigrant forces argue that the Tea Partiers have it exactly backwards—that undocumented workers aren't soaking up services at the expense of middle-class taxpaying citizens but are actually a net source of government revenue.

"Every tax that a documented person pays, an undocumented person pays as well," Garcia patiently explains. "Most undocumented folks work a low-level job where they would get a refund at the end of the year—but because they fail to have these documents they never get a refund. In Arizona, they're so afraid that they'll get deported." The argument from Garcia and Puente is backed up by the numbers; a study in 2007 by the immigration policy manager for the University of Arizona, Judith Gans, found that an estimated 280,000 undocumented workers brought in nearly $2.4 billion in tax revenue for Arizona but used just $1.4 billion in government services, for a net gain for the state of $940 million.

Gans told a panel that year that an Arizona crackdown on undocumented workers would mean that "we're deciding as a matter of policy to shrink the economy." And that is exactly what has happened—amplified, of course, by the global economic meltdown. When the state pols and Arpaio's deputies launched their jihad against the undocumented, Arizona was at nearly full employment, with 4 percent joblessness; by 2010 that number had soared to 9 percent, and the state trailed only Nevada and its overheated Las Vegas market in the rate of home foreclosures. One part of the backstory that has been lost in translation, as Garcia has pointed out, is that an unknown number of the Phoenix-area foreclosures involve undocumented workers who lost their jobs thanks to Arizona's tougher laws. From the peak of the housing boom in 2007 until Obama's inauguration in 2009, the undocumented population of Arizona dropped by an estimated 13 percent, but none of the supposed benefits of this immigration crackdown—the end of the in-reality-nonexistent drain on government services, or more job opportunities for documented workers and native citizens—had materialized. Instead, the state of Arizona was now so broke it was closing its rest stops on the interstate.

The state government's response to the crisis was not so much to focus on practical measures for creating jobs as to seemingly give in to impulsive acts of rage with the imprimatur of law. While the Pearce-sponsored immigration measure garnered most of the attention, within the space of a few weeks lawmakers also made Arizona just the third state in the country to allow citizens to carry concealed weapons without a permit, and the state House even passed what became known as a "birther bill" that would have required the Arizona secretary of state to verify the citizenship of presidential candidates before they could appear on the ballot there—although the measure eventually died in the Arizona Senate amid the national outcry. Indeed, this trio of legislative acts reflected the talking points of everyone from Russ Murphy to Crazy Eileen. Only now, instead of being the ramblings of online message boards and talk radio, some of these ideas had actually become state law.

Clearly, the state's downward economic spiral was creating anger, frustration—and more cactus juice for the Arizona Tea Party movement. While at first glance they might seem disconnected, the state's "birther bill" and the racial-profiling crackdown on Mexican immigrants sprung from exactly the same impulse: lashing out and blaming The Other.

"Historically, that's been the case—finding a scapegoat," says young Carlos Garcia with a shrug. "That's how the Tea Party people see the undocumented."

You had already seen in other sections of the country how unemployment and economic anxiety was driving folks in new directions, whether it was Al Whayland's Navy Jack–waving, Glenn Beck–fueled seventy-something brand of activism or fired police chief Celia Hyde's adoption of the Oath Keepers. The roots were the same here in the arid soil, but what came out of the ground looked and felt different here, nurtured by the soaring temperatures of the U.S.-Mexico border. Elsewhere, The Other was more likely the uncomfortable feeling of watching Barack Obama on a thirty-two-inch screen, but here it was waiting in the parking lot at the Wal-Mart. And the fact that undocumented immigration was such a powder keg for the Tea Party movement was powerful evidence of what some critics have been saying from day one: that a primary motivator of the angry backlash across America is race.

Specifically, it is unknown how much of this fury directed toward Washington was really concern over big government or federal deficits or the specifics of health-care legislation and how much was just simply discomfort or even raw hatred that a black man was in the White House, coupled with anxiety over the economy that translated into rage against the powerless who were even lower down the ladder, illegal immigrants supposedly sopping up the legal residents' tax dollars or—up North—the "handout people" in black neighborhoods.

It's certainly reasonable to ask how come massive protests suddenly targeted federal debt one month into Obama's presidency, after the debt increased by an astronomical $5 trillion on George W. Bush's watch, and why it was motivated by an $800 billion drive for public works projects backed by Obama when unrest over $700 billion to bail out banks and their millionaire execs under Bush drew such a muted initial response. As the months passed and as talk grew of a segregation-era revival of states'-rights planks, and as Virginia's governor even signed an ill-timed resolution honoring Confederate History Month with nary a mention of slavery, the notion that racism lurked just under the surface became harder to shake. It was hard for pundits and political bloggers not to see an aha moment when an attendee at an April 2010 Tea Party on the National Mall told a journalist that opposition to Obama was *"not just* because he's black."

Over time, polling data emerged to confirm that many participants in the backlash against Obama had views on racial issues that were troubling. The April 2010 *New York Times*/CBS News poll of both Tea Party supporters—which it pegged at 18 percent of Americans—and the general public found that just over half (52 percent) of the self-identified Tea Partiers believed that too much has been made of the problems facing black people in America, while just 19 percent of Americans who are not Tea Partiers felt that way. Likewise, the poll found that a majority of the Tea Party people thought the Obama administration favored the poor and 25 percent said explicitly that it favors blacks over whites (just 11 percent of all Americans said that). Three out of every four Tea Partiers told the pollsters that Obama did not share the values of most Americans.

It took different forms depending on where you lived—black residents of crime-ridden Wilmington, Delaware, or Latino men looking for work in a Phoenix parking lot—but the face that animated the passion of the backlash was clearly not a white one.

To many Americans, Roberto Valdez and Barack Obama looked exactly alike.

OF COURSE, THE Tea Party served other purposes as well. Just as you found elsewhere in America, a brand-new political movement was also a drive-off-the-lot vehicle for personal reinvention. The day after the Hayworth-Arpaio fundraising event, you met for lunch with three leaders of the Arizona Tea Party movement who were backing the anti-McCain insurgency. Soaking up large bowls of pasta and garlic bread on the outdoor parking-lot-engulfed patio of a popular Tempe restaurant, the men shared similar ultraconservative outlooks but had little else in common.

Jeff Greenspan, youthful and energetic, had honed his ideas in the far-right incubator of Utah and served as a top regional coordinator for Ron Paul's 2008 presidential bid; he had just moved to Arizona and quickly won election as the second vice chairman of the Maricopa County Republican Party. Ron Ludders, a portly and affable older gentleman, was still resentful over the treatment of his 1980s boss, the disgraced former governor Evan Mecham, who became a national pariah by blocking the Martin Luther King holiday for a time and was then impeached over a local scandal. The third leader, Doug Ardt, takes off the tie he was wearing on a warm Sunday afternoon and hands you a card for Send Out Cards, a firm that helps businesses mail out greeting cards. A few months ago, these men were nowhere on the political radar, but thanks to the instant explosion of the Tea Party they are suddenly players. In addition to Greenspan's role in the Tea Party coup taking over the GOP in greater Phoenix, Ludders is now running a group called AZ Project 2010 that is targeting insufficiently conservative Republicans, with McCain atop the hit list.

"We need to get back to the Founding Fathers and listen to George Washington—they never intended for anyone to become a professional politician," Ludders says. This is a diatribe about McCain—whom he also describes as an "East Coast liberal"—but he could be talking about the threesome around the pasta table here. Their once-barren schedules have suddenly booked up with a slew of Tea Party rallies and strategy sessions—and unlike the pistol-packers of East Thomas Road, the immigration crisis is only one of the many articles in their bill of impeachment against Washington insiders and against big government.

Yet for all their newfound energy, you can't help but think that in energizing the mostly white conservative base of Arizona, the Tea Partiers might win a few short-sighted battles but stand on the brink of losing the long war. There was a sound reason that George W. Bush, his "brain" Karl Rove, and John McCain all wanted to make peace with Latino-Americans in the mid-2000s and bring the more socially conservative ones into the GOP fold. The pro-immigrant America's Voice Immigration Fund found that Latino voter turnout across the United States rose by a whopping 64 percent from 2000 to 2008, and that four key states that flipped from the Bush-GOP column in 2004 to Obama in 2008—Nevada, New Mexico, Florida, and Colorado—did so with a huge assist from Hispanics. Arizona did not join them only because Obama was facing McCain, a favorite son. Or so he used to be, anyway.

This is the political paradox of Arizona. Was the anti-Latino jihad really keeping Arizona safe for white conservatives—or were people like J. D. Hayworth and Jeff Greenspan leading a political suicide mission? The only thing that seems certain here is that paranoia is now embedded in the sandstone like a twisted vein of quartz crystal.

Indeed, you are pondering the seemingly low priority that the Tea Party trio is placing on immigration when Ardt says he wants to explain something about the subject—that there was a time in the nineteenth century when the border of Mexico extended right up to Sixteenth Street in downtown Phoenix, and that this mapped out the real goal of the pro-immigrant groups like Puente.

The *reconquista.*

"They have people openly calling for invasion and to kill all the white people," Ardt calmly tells you, as kids at the surrounding tables are busy twirling their spaghetti-and-meatballs, "and they're teaching it in the universities. We've got a mini-war going on down here that the Eastern Establishment can't appreciate, that they don't understand in New York City."

The other heads at the table nod in approval.

Still, Greenspan, Ludders, and Ardt were the respectable face of a Tea Party movement in Arizona that masked a regiment of unrespectable types—many of whom flooded the state's first major Tea Party on April 15, 2009, on the steps of the state capitol in Phoenix, where the omnipresent *New Times*'s Lemons noted scattered extremists such as neo-Nazis and members of the anti-immigrant United for a Sovereign America. Also in attendance was a controversial border-patrolling member of one of the Minutemen groups, a woman named Shawna Forde. Forde, age forty-one, had worked with Chris Simcox and his group for a time and blogged about her first Tea Party.

"This is the time for all Americans to join organizations and REVOLT!!!," she wrote in a blog post that was retrieved from the Google cache by Lemons. "Refuse to be part of a system only designed to enslave you and you children. Times will get worse before they get worse, *Say no to illegal immigration* Lock and Load, Shawna Forde."

But Forde's first Tea Party was also her last. By that summer, the anti-immigration activist was sitting in the Pima County Jail down in Tucson, awaiting a capital murder trial on charges that she, along with two men, staged the home invasion of a family of Mexican heritage, near the border in Arivaca, Arizona, in which a nine-year-old girl and her father were murdered and the man's wife was wounded. Prosecutors believed the motive was money and possibly drugs—in part to finance their anti-immigrant crusade. Members of Minutemen groups rushed to disassociate themselves from Forde, whom they portrayed as mentally unstable for some time. But as 2010 arrived, a growing pattern of violence and paranoia was heating up along the border.

As the Border Report Web site noted in the spring: "Federal agents have received complaints from hunters in Southern Arizona of being accosted by armed white men in camouflage who told the hunters they are with the Department of Homeland Security, sources say. They weren't affiliated with the Minuteman Civil Defense Corps, but law enforcement doesn't know yet who is driving this group, what their members are like, and what their motives are."

As Arizona's spring madness continued, there were indications that even the strict new laws and the economic meltdown that was leading to a net loss of undocumented immigrants were not enough for a radicalized right wing determined to take matters into its own hands, to fight a border war with Mexico beyond where even the politicians were quite ready to take things. It was as if Arizona was firing a warning shot across the bow of the greater United States, that rapid societal change could start breaking down the established order of things long before 2050 arrives.

In late April 2010, a man named Bill Davis—who heads a militia group in Cochise County, Arizona, on the border to the east of Tucson—told the *Arizona Daily Star* that he was forming a new paramilitary group to patrol the border for unlawful crossings, and that he was hoping government officials would support him in that effort. Davis said that private landholders had asked him to start the effort after the murder of a local rancher, and that "we're not about to step aside anymore and let them through. We're going to turn them around and send them back scared."

In a sense, Bill Davis was just one more example of a slew of Americans seeking rebirth from the raw energy of the Tea Parties—a group that included not just activists like himself but also slick politicians and fast-talking hucksters of various stripes. As the political situation across America and in places like Arizona spiraled down, here were people like Davis who were standing up. But for now, Davis wanted to assure the authorities and readers of the Arizona paper that he knew exactly what he was doing, that his outfit would be no bunch of amateurs but skilled combat veterans.

"They all have confirmed kills, from Vietnam or later on," Davis said. "They're not wannabes who go out and buy a set of camos and go out in the woods with a rifle."

CHAPTER SEVEN

The Broun Identity

On October 17, 2009, there was a black-tie gala dinner at a luxury hotel in Atlanta, Georgia, where guests dined on balsamic-laced flank steak and mango coulis. After dessert was served, the ballroom full of mostly men in black ties and dinner jackets, and a few women in their Saturday-night best, leaned back in their seats to hear the night's main event—a speech by a member of the United States Congress. Nothing remarkable about that . . . in theory.

Except that the gala was held to celebrate the notorious, conspiracy-minded right-wing political group the John Birch Society, the band of Commie hunters made famous in the early 1960s, who'd seemingly vanished—only to burst back into the newly mainstreamed paranoid fringe within months after the election of Barack Obama as president. Rather than back away from its divisive views—most notably that popular U.S. president and World War II hero Dwight Eisenhower was somehow an agent of international communism—the Birchers were doubling down in the age of Obama, still maintaining that a planet-wide conspiracy hatched some two hundred years ago by the ultra-secret Illuminati in search of a "New World Order" continues to flourish today.

The congressman addressing the John Birch Society get-together was a relatively obscure Georgian in his first full term in office—Paul Broun Jr. of the state's Tenth Congressional District, which starts out in the liberal-for-the-Deep-South bastion of Athens, Broun's hometown, but fans out into northeast Georgia across rolling red Appalachian foothills over some of the most conservative real estate in the United States. Amid the thundering hooves of a 24/7 news cycle, Broun has achieved about forty-five minutes' worth of fame here and there, especially when amid the mostly raised hopes in the days following Obama's election he stunned some people—even in his Georgia district—by remarking that the president-elect's ideas for a national service corps smacked of Adolf Hitler. But with much less fanfare, Broun has been working quietly with a coalition of extreme right-wing outfits—not just the Tea Parties but even with groups on the more out-there fringe like the John Birch Society and members of the Oath Keepers. In doing so, Broun is now in a race with the libertarian Ron Paul of Texas to be the most extreme member of the 111th Congress. And in 2009–10, that is quite an achievement.

For Broun and the Birchers, it was apparently love at first sight—at least as described by Jim Capo, the national director of trade policy for the John Birch Society, who also posted the video of Broun addressing the Atlanta gala on the organization's Web site. Capo related in a Web posting that he was walking into a congressional office building in Washington in 2007 when he happened upon Broun, who'd just won his seat in a special election to replace the late Representative Charlie Norwood. The Birchers were carrying copies of the society's *New American* magazine, and on the cover was a picture of "the North American Union flag." According to Capo, Broun stopped the magazine-toting lobbyists, said that he knew all about the North American Union— the same conspiracy theory that the Zionist-plot-seeking rock musician Paul Topete had been babbling about at Knob Creek—and added that he was against it. Never mind that there is no such thing as the North American Union. A theoretical clone of the European Union with a joint currency between the United States, Mexico, and Canada, the North American Union exists only in minds infused by the paranoid style, and there's certainly no such thing as the North American Union flag. Nonetheless, in that chance encounter, a friendship was born.

In fact, the John Birch Society grew so fond of Broun that there was even talk of paying him to speak at its 2009 gala. In an online announcement of the event, a Birch Society activist named Jim Sandman from Tennessee asked attendees to consider an additional donation of $100, $250, or $500 for the event, in part because it "will help with the honorarium for Dr. Broun." Congress had in fact moved to ban such honoraria during its ethics reforms of the 1990s. When contacted by telephone, Sandman confirmed there was an initial understanding that he was raising money for such a payment, but after checking with Birch higher-ups he called back to report that no payment was offered or made.

Meanwhile, Broun's fall 2009 speech to the Birch gala is a pretty good overview of where the congressman's head was at in the first year of the Obama administration. What was happening in the nation—the government bailout of banks and efforts to save the auto industry and create jobs through an $800 billion spending plan—was not a response to the worst economic crisis in eighty years, Broun said, but rather "the steamroll of socialism that's being driven by Nancy Pelosi and Harry Reid and that is fueled by Barack Obama." Larded with quotes from and references to the Founding Fathers—especially George Washington—Broun's speech to the John Birch Society argues that the system of taxation that the American government uses to raise revenue is socialist to the core. Our government, he argued, "is taxing those it believes make too much money, and redistributing it to other people. We must stop that trend."

The way to do that, according to Broun, is to enact policies that would make George W. Bush's tax cuts for the rich look like chump change. "It is not the government's place to redistribute wealth," he told the men in their tuxedos and women in evening gowns. "I believe that death taxes should be zero, I believe that corporate taxes should be zero, that dividend taxes should be zero, and that all taxes should be very low."

Broun's economic theory—which would destroy government as, for better or worse, we have come to know it in twenty-first-century

America—is kind of like the *National Review* on steroids, a brand of antitax talk that has lost its ability to shock in an era of Reagan revisionism. But it is nothing compared to Broun's embrace of conspiracy mumbo jumbo—implying that even a former Republican president, George H. W. Bush, was part of a plot to destroy America from within. Broun started with an indictment of man-made climate change theory, adding:

> They used to talk about global warming—y'all might remember a few years ago they were talking about an ice age was coming. It's the same folks, the folks who want to change America, want to rule America. They want to change us to a New World Order. President George Herbert Walker Bush, remember, very openly said he wanted to have a New World Order. And all of these things are a progression of their outward efforts to destroy America, to destroy our freedom. . . . The John Birch Society is trying very hard to get the right people elected to Congress. There are very few of us—very few.

Broun—who when he's not hobnobbing with Birchers is just as likely to be speaking at a Tea Party rally or talking to members of far-right fringe groups as doing the traditional meet-and-greet grunt work of the representative of a congressional district—may be an extreme case, but he's also very much part of a rhetorical three-step to the far right among many Republicans in Congress in the Obama era. This can be seen in the willingness of so many elected officials to go on national TV and move the boundaries of political dialogue—to the point where a year into Obama's presidency, the term "socialist" now seemed tame compared to the other things that were being said or implied about the commander-in-chief or some of his Democratic allies. In 2008, before Obama's election, Minnesota representative Michele Bachmann—en route not just to reelection but to status as a heroine of the soon-to-arise Tea Party movement—caused a stir when she said on MSNBC's

Hardball that Obama "may have anti-American views" and even called upon journalists to investigate whether or not members of Congress were "pro-American."

Bachmann—an attractive woman in her early fifties, brown-haired, blue-eyed, and clear-skinned, with a glazed expression as if she represented the town of Stepford and not the exurbs of Minneapolis—had arguably a better knack than Broun for getting attention for her out-there comments that Americans should be "armed and dangerous" to prevent higher taxes on energy, or her paranoid fears of an intrusive 2010 Census, or that the United States was looking to move toward a global currency. But in the months that followed her *Hardball* firestorm, those once-controversial comments were eclipsed by the extreme rhetoric of some of her GOP colleagues. That was driven home in February 2010 when a narcissistic and clearly on some never-to-be-diagnosed-level deranged software engineer who had some federal tax grievances—a man by the prosaic name of Joe Stack—took his private plane in Austin, Texas, and flew it full throttle into the local IRS office. Stack killed himself, of course, but also murdered an innocent federal employee named Vernon Hunter, a sixty-eight-year-old Vietnam vet on the brink of a retirement day that never came.

Now, the same right-wing pols who insisted on a fiery kind of angry "political correctness" when talking about Islamic terrorism in the 2000s were suddenly loath to label Joe Stack a "murderer"; instead, they viewed his insane actions as somehow an extreme version of a legitimate antigovernment Tea Party movement they hoped to channel and lead. Thus, Senator Scott Brown—who in the early weeks of 2010 became a hero of the Tea Partiers by winning the late Ted Kennedy's former seat in left-leaning Massachusetts—insisted that Stack's suicide attack was a function of the same anger that got him elected, saying that "people are frustrated. They want transparency. They want their elected officials to be accountable and open and, you know, talk about the things that are affecting their daily lives."

But Brown's tone-deafness was quickly subsumed by the words of a congressman who at times has rivaled Georgia's Broun in his extremism. Representative Steve King of Iowa showed up at the annual conservative confab in Washington known as CPAC and used the airplane attack as an excuse to assail the very concept of the IRS, saying "it's an agency that is unnecessary and when the day comes when that is over and we abolish the IRS, it's going to be a happy day for America." In words that were not recorded but noted by one observer, King was reported to have said he'd like to see followers "implode" IRS offices.

The remarks by the likes of King and Brown were extreme examples of top Republicans both raising the stakes and shifting the parameters on what is acceptable political speech in America—but it was also emblematic of a much more serious problem. After the GOP lost control of the government over the second half of the 2000s, the party's direction and indeed its very life force has been seized by a new breed of political huckster—who saw that the paranoia and anger of the extreme political right was the only thing resembling a pulse in the modern conservative movement. This cynical ambition of high-ranking elected officials not to tamp down the paranoid style but to adopt its latest fashions became a successful strategy for the politicians who might have been unknown back-benchers if they had acted more responsibly. Their mainstreaming of the political fringes made them into darlings of cable television and helped ensure reelection within their deep-red conservative districts.

However, the paranoid style simply did not fit when it came to actually governing; it led to sound-bite proposals that would never become law—such as Broun's notion of zeroing corporate taxes, for example—and a lack of focus on concrete solutions to the problems of constituents. In the meantime, the willingness of leaders like Broun or a Michele Bachmann to speak at so many Tea Parties or to validate questions about Obama's citizenship or the idea that the 2010 Census was a big-government intrusion (Broun revealed that he didn't even answer most of the Census questions) offered a powerful token of legitimacy to the right-wing radicals. The anger and doubts that these Republicans fueled were critical in driving distrust of government to its highest level in more than a generation, and in granting a self-fulfilling prophecy of an America where nothing gets done.

This was dangerous new territory for our national politics; for many decades there were grown-ups involved in the conservative movement who tamped down the flames of extremism rather than fanning them. Ironically, the main reason that the John Birch Society failed to gain much traction in the early 1960s was because mainstream Republican politicians turned against them, even though the party was at a low ebb in the Kennedy-Johnson years. Barry Goldwater, the leader of the so-called New Right movement who won the GOP presidential nomination in 1964, did have considerable support from the Birchers, yet not only did he not embrace them but secretly authorized the intellectual leader of 1960s conservatism, William F. Buckley Jr., and his *National Review* to go after the organization, successfully marginalizing it and helping to keep its Richard Hofstadter–described paranoid style in the shadows, even as that decade grew more tumultuous.

What changed in the years between Goldwater and Broun? One factor was the great political reshuffling that started with that 1964 presidential election—when the South voted Republican for the first time because of opposition to Democratic-led moves on civil rights—and continued through the Reagan Revolution of the 1980s, when the GOP began to win many local races across the Sun Belt, especially in the former Confederacy. For every reaction there is a counterreaction, and by the 2000s the born-again, Southern-fried, strident conservatism of the GOP—epitomized by the likes of Georgia's Newt Gingrich, Tom DeLay of Texas, and finally the unpopular presidency of George W. Bush, also from the Lone Star State—had caused voters in the Northeast to rebel against the last diehard Republican moderates. Politicians seeking to represent these heavily polarized deep-red or solid-blue congressional districts were frequently candidates of the extremes within both parties. They were often aided by the incumbent-protection system of drawing district maps, called gerrymandering.

In the wake of the election debacles for Republicans in 2006 and

2008 that put Obama in the White House and created large majorities of Democrats in Congress, there was a GOP leadership vacuum, and talk radio—with its message of no compromise, as celebrated in Rush Limbaugh's famed pre-inaugural wish for Obama that "I hope he fails"—raced to fill it. Republican back-benchers who felt that Limbaugh and his colleagues like the up-and-coming Glenn Beck were moving their party too far to the right, too fast, found themselves flattened in the stampede. When one of Broun's Republican colleagues in the Georgia delegation, Representative Phil Gingrey, made the mistake in the first week of Obama's presidency of saying that entertainers like Limbaugh weren't real leaders and that "it's easy if you're Sean Hannity or Rush Limbaugh or even sometimes Newt Gingrich to stand back and throw bricks," he soon found himself backpedaling faster than an NFL cornerback. The very next day, Gingrey called Limbaugh's show to grovel on live radio, pledging to the audience that he "actively opposed every bailout, every rebate check, every so-called stimulus. And on so many of these things, I see eye-to-eye with Rush Limbaugh."

Indeed, within a few weeks House Republicans staged a remarkable show of unity, voting unanimously in futile opposition to the $800 million stimulus package—even though not only was it a measure hailed by Nobel laureates, among others, as the only surefire way to create jobs in a deep recession, but it would mean large federal checks for projects in their home districts. It was slightly different in the Senate, where three Republicans actually negotiated changes and broke a potential filibuster (although one of them, Pennsylvania senator Arlen Specter, ended up jumping to the Democratic Party in the messy aftermath). When the dust settled, Republicans who'd shown tentative signs of moderation raced to take it back. Case in point is the moderate Delaware representative Mike Castle, who promised to work on a bipartisan health-care plan but gave that up to join his party's obstructionists after his encounter with the birth-certificate-brandishing Eileen M. and the rest of the town-hall rebels. As the backlash spread, that was just one congressional retreat of many.

Nowhere was the political muscle-flexing more evident than on the issue of climate change, where nonstop ridiculing of global-warming supporter Al Gore and then a series of East Coast snowstorms in 2009–10 led to entrenched conservative groupthink that climate change was not real. South Carolina senator Lindsey Graham, that close ally of Senator John McCain and a fixture on political talk shows, had supported the controversial greenhouse-gas reduction plan known as cap-and-trade throughout the first year of the Obama presidency, stating in November 2009 that "I am no scientist, but I've . . . seen the effects of a warming planet." However, despite his initial support, he eventually withdrew from cosponsoring a climate change bill, bowing to the new political realities. Meanwhile, McCain, reeling from J. D. Hayworth's aggressive primary challenge, was backpedaling, too—not just on global warming but in breaking a promise to support the end of the "don't ask, don't tell" policies restricting gays in the military if he was asked to do so by the top commanders in the Pentagon.

Career politicians like McCain, Graham, and the party-flipping Specter were powerless in the face of the radical right-wing tsunami hitting Washington, D.C. The tail was now wagging the dog; the new Republican direction was driven by radio hosts and—in the case of Beck—a TV personality who could espouse extreme views without ever having to cross the partisan aisle to fashion a workable deal, and whose ultimate success was determined not by tangible results but by Arbitron and Nielsen ratings that typically went to the most outrageous among them. Perhaps the clearest embodiment of this power shift came on July Fourth weekend in 2009 when the glamorous and divisive superstar of the new right-wing politics, Alaska governor Sarah Palin, abruptly resigned her governorship, deciding that her path to success—certainly financially, and perhaps in presidential politics as well—was not in the mundane compromises and numbing schedule of the statehouse but under the bright lights of Fox News, which she had joined as a commentator by the end of the year.

The new pecking order in conservative politics was critical to understanding how the rising tide of the backlash led to the breakdown of the political process during the first year of Obama's presidency. Left with the flaming wreckage of the irresponsible Bush-era policies and devoid of both interesting new political policies and bold leadership, what rushed to fill the vacuum were what you might call political hucksters—looking to stay alive and in the headlines no matter what they had to resort to. Suddenly, there was no incentive to get things done for their constituents—instead, the only thing that made sense for right-wingers like Georgia's Paul Broun was to just say "no" to everything Barack Obama ever proposed, raise their media profile on Fox News and talk radio, and hopefully ride the backlash to reelection. In this new topsy-turvy environment, the members of Congress or governors who sounded the most like talk-radio personalities were no longer fringe players but the new stars, in constant demand on cable TV and celebrated in speaking gigs to the fired-up crowds of the Tea Party.

Ironically, the advent of the anti-Obama movement provided seemingly powerful pols like Broun, Bachmann, or Steve King the same opportunity that it gave to regular citizens like Russ Murphy of the Delaware 9-12 Patriots or the pro-Hayworth activists down in Mesa: the chance to completely reinvent themselves. That said, the reinvention was a little different for the politicians than it was for the rank-and-file activists, who were largely motivated by either anger over their circumstances or fear of a changing America. The Republican members of Congress who might have been demoralized after the election defeats of 2006 and 2008 instead saw a new opportunity to be a different kind of leader, the leader of a movement. They saw a future in all this raw energy against Barack Obama.

So it was that Broun—gala celebrator of the John Birch Society and high-wattage basher of the forty-fourth president of the United States—came to find himself not on the rough fringes of our political life but straight down the fairway of this new backlash. Increasingly, the Georgian's schedule filled up with speeches to Tea Parties or attending a closed-door gathering of the Oath Keeper–sponsored National Liberty

Unity Summit, after which he introduced legislation that sounded as if it was hatched in a talk radio studio, pushing corporate tax cuts so extreme Broun failed to round up a single co-sponsor. Broun's sound-bite brand of politics worked well on his Twitter feed, which he updated frequently (even during presidential speeches to Congress), and certainly got him on the radio. But what, if anything, was Broun's radical brand of politics—his media profile and his bills that weren't going anywhere—getting his constituents atop the fire-truck-red soil of the north Georgia hills?

THE FIRST THING that you learn about Homer, Georgia, is not to go there hungry at dinner time. The county seat of Banks County, population 950, was—for many years, anyway—home to the world's largest Easter Egg hunt, but it's difficult now to find a place to get so much as an egg-salad sandwich. The Tiny Town Restaurant with its twin Coca-Cola signs and its faded white coat of paint is shuttered tight at 5:30 p.m., the gravel parking lot empty, its rusted sign—"Open 2 Chicken"—looking out on both an auto-salvage graveyard and the town cemetery for humans. A Sherman tank proudly guards the American Legion post on the bend in Highway 51, but several run-down strip malls are comprised mostly of vacant shells interspersed with a doctor's office or a "Sleep Center." Junk foodstuffs are available at the busy Golden Pantry gas station—"Always Convenient Always"—where a group of about twenty hawks is circling ominously overhead.

You pick up the local newspapers inside the Golden Pantry and it confirms what you are seeing with your own eyes: that Banks County is roughly the epicenter of a region that is faring the Great Recession even worse than most. The *Athens Banner-Herald*—Representative Paul Broun's hometown paper, printed about twenty miles south of Homer—is reporting on this day that Metro Athens lost two thousand more jobs in the last three months of 2009, a time in which the government claimed the economy was recovering. In fact, in Athens, government was the only sector that added jobs in late 2009. Below that is a feature about a "job fair" for schoolteachers at the University of Georgia at which teachers who showed up were told there were virtually no jobs. The banner headline the next day would be that a copper wire manufacturer in Watkinsville, Georgia, was cutting its workforce in half because of the slump in construction, and the day after that was a report that the university itself—the largest employer in Broun's Tenth Congressional District—was "facing 'extreme' cuts" because the state of Georgia was virtually broke. In late 2007, the largest private employer near Homer, a massive garden store and warehouse called The Pottery, abruptly closed because of changing consumer habits, a reflection of working-class jobs that did not come back.

"It's terrifying at some points to see all the people coming in for benefits," says Debbie Paulk of the Georgia Department of Family and Children's Services, which deals with unemployed people from Banks County as well as surrounding areas. She adds that requests for food stamps and temporary public assistance have risen by 30 to 50 percent in various Georgia offices over the prior year—in part because the state agency has made it easier to apply online instead of making a potentially embarrassing visit to a welfare office. "It's not as much of a stigma," she says. The newly unemployed in northeastern Georgia are much more likely than in the past to have college degrees and to come from better-paying jobs; Paulk says she and her co-workers advise them to take anything they can get. "A few people are getting jobs—they may not be the jobs they wanted, but any job is a good job in this economy." If openings exist, they tend to be in fast-food restaurants or in retail in places like Gainesville, some forty minutes away on back roads.

But increasingly, Paulk says, the state is steering people into a state labor program called Good Works that is barely a notch above volunteering—taking on an internship where the only pay is a state stipend on the order of $300 a month, not enough to live on. "It's an opportunity for people who don't just want to sit at home," Paulk explains.

"They want to hone their skills." The question of what they are honing their skills for hangs in the air.

Paulk, a large woman whose voice carries the stressed tones of manufactured bureaucratic optimism, is addressing a gathering of about twenty-five residents of Banks County and surrounding areas. They've come out on a chilly February weeknight mostly to voice their frustrations with government, and particularly with Representative Paul Broun. A University of Georgia law student named Russell Edwards—who'd spent a good chunk of 2008 volunteering on behalf of Obama in this Southern state where the politics now runs as red as the soil and the Georgia Bulldogs' helmets—became so fed up with GOP obstructionism of the new president's proposals that he'd launched a political effort called Pull the Plug, which he hoped would generate enthusiasm for voting the right-wing Broun out of office, even as no serious candidates to challenge Broun in 2010 were emerging. (By mid-spring, Edwards declared that he would challenge Broun himself since no one else would.)

The folks who'd turned out for the group's meeting on economic development were the ones who were frustrated by two years of throbbing economic misery—but not too beaten down to care. Some were active Democrats, but others were independents like Joe and Diane Cook, who came down from Illinois a few years ago to open a shipping and packing store near the I-85 exit in Commerce, Georgia, only to see the promised arrival of Atlanta's once ever-growing exurban sprawl grind to a halt before it ever stretched that far east.

Greg Mann was another new arrival to Georgia in attendance at the meeting. A former political aide turned real-estate appraiser back in Michigan, Mann and his wife had moved to Virginia in early 2009 because she'd been offered a job training nursing supervisors, but within weeks her new employer had changed management—and laid her off. The couple then arrived in Georgia where they had some family members, only to find the economy here even worse. Mann—bearded, stocky, and surprisingly chipper—quickly ascertained there was little real estate for him to appraise here, as he drove around and looked at new three-home subdivisions that sat completely empty. So he began looking for other work, perhaps as a security guard or at the local Publix or Trader Joe's supermarkets. "I'm fifty-six years old and a college graduate," he says. "My degree is in history." He chuckles. "Everybody tells me, 'You have an impressive résumé and you should be able to readily find a job—but we don't have anything for you.'"

In his short time here, Mann has contacted Broun's office about his problems in obtaining health insurance beyond high-cost catastrophic coverage that doesn't pay for doctor's visits or routine care but only aims to forestall bankruptcy in the event of a major illness. "He sent back a letter saying that if they adopted his plan, he was sure that would save us money—that wasn't what I was asking him."

That was the theme throughout the two-hour Pull the Plug discussion in Homer—that Broun seemed too busy politicking with the likes of the John Birch Society or posturing with simplistic and mostly symbolic pieces of conservative legislation that had no chance of becoming law and would help mostly millionaires if by some miracle they were actually enacted. The attendees scratched their heads over Broun's "JOBS Bill—HR 4100," which had no co-sponsors—and which among other things sought a two-year experiment with his stated goal of eliminating dividend and capital gains taxes. Several attendees connected with the University of Georgia said officials have taken to asking alumni representing other congressional districts to lobby for federal dollars because they can't depend on Broun for help. People here said Broun wasn't addressing their practical concerns about the lack of jobs—but then again, neither was anyone else in Washington.

"I have lost faith in my government, and I think there's a lot of people in here who feel the same way," says Joe Cook, the packing store owner. His complaint sounds much like those of the people you'd been meeting at Tea Parties, but whereas so many of those individuals were either retired or laid off, Cook is far too busy to get involved in attending lots of protests. In the last eighteen months he's been forced to go from eleven employees to two part-timers, and his grown daughter has been working at his store since she lost her job at a nearby FedEx Kinko's. Besides, Cook says he wouldn't know whom to trust. "I feel like we've been lied to for so long and I don't believe anything—and that's what the problem is. They're fighting among themselves for power or for the White House while we're the ones that are suffering."

There is a lot of talk about just how a right-wing ideologue had come to be their congressman in the first place—and why no one was even making a serious bid to challenge him in 2010. Finally, the lone African-American attendee (the rolling hills of northern Georgia are predominantly white) speaks up; her name is Mary Dixon and she'd left the area to work in Florida in law enforcement for thirty-six years—and now she'd moved back here to retire and was appalled at how little had changed since the early 1970s. "It's all because Obama is the president," says Dixon, a diminutive woman in a purple head scarf, of all the opposition she sees around here. The problem, in other words, wasn't with the specifics of the White House's ideas on creating jobs or overhauling health care, but quite simply that some of her neighbors won't consider his ideas because "it's who's proposing it"—the nation's first black president. A roomful of white heads nod up and down.

PRACTICALLY NO ONE outside the winding, tin-roof-rusted highways east of Athens had even heard of Paul Broun Jr. until the days that immediately followed the election of that first African-American commander-in-chief. In early November 2008, Broun—who'd been in office for only about eighteen months—told a reporter for the Associated Press that he was worried that President-elect Obama had the potential to put America on the path to a dictatorship in the style of Marxist Russia or Nazi Germany.

"It may sound a bit crazy and off base . . ." Those are nine words that a congressman should never say to a journalist, but now Broun was rolling. He insisted he was alarmed by a suggestion that then candidate

Obama had uttered that summer for a national service corps, and that he was worried that such a corps could be used to take guns away from citizens. "You have to remember that Adolf Hitler was elected in a democratic Germany," he said. "I'm not comparing him to Adolf Hitler. What I'm saying is there is the potential of going down that road." The comments created a minor, brief firestorm with all the usual hallmarks—liberal blog outrage, and Broun's statement that he apologized "to anyone who has taken offense at that," quickly followed by his insistence that his apology wasn't really an apology. In fact, Broun may have achieved the greatest accomplishment of his congressional career, which was shifting the so-called Overton window—a political theory on how extreme statements can shift the boundaries of what becomes acceptable speech (adopted by Beck as the title of his 2010 novel)—on what could be openly said about the new president. Ironically, this may have been one case where politician Broun was actually ahead of the right-wing media pack with his demagoguery; as late as December 2008 even Glenn Beck was saying things about Obama like this: "I didn't vote for you but you are now going to be my president." Within months of the flap, commentators calling Obama "a socialist" was such a routine event that it was greeted with a yawn.

Meanwhile, some people around the country—joined by some voters in Broun's own Tenth District—were starting to ask, just who is this guy, anyway? There was a time when Paul Broun Jr. asked the same question of himself. It happened in 1986, when the forty-year-old baby boomer was into booze and into his fourth marriage already—and having problems with both. Broun was at an NFL football game and drinking heavily when he noticed the fan who was a quasi-celebrity back during the Reagan years, the guy with the crazy rainbow-haired wig who stood in the end-zone seats with the sign "John 3:16." Broun said in a speech on the floor of Congress after his election to Congress two decades later that he was captivated by this "gentleman with this big-type hair wig on" A few weeks later, after another fight with his new wife, he took out a Bible, read the verse, and decided to dedicate his life to Christ. (Interestingly, it was the exact same year and at the same age that George W. Bush quit drinking.) Broun now considers his odyssey to the corridors of power the result of Jesus's calling. He fails to add the kicker to the story: that the wig-wearing fan, a fellow named Rollen Stewart, is currently serving three life sentences for kidnapping.

But the creation story of Paul Broun Jr. is also a powerful illustration of the political evolution that has taken place in the Deep South. His father, Paul Broun Sr., who died in 2005, was a Democrat who served in the Georgia Senate for thirty-eight years, arriving in Atlanta in 1962 as a moderate from the university town, in the era of segregation and Lester Maddox. Broun Sr. was a Southern populist who fought to have government dollars spent inside his district to build up the infrastructure for a booming economy. As chairman of the state senate's appropriations committee, he steered big bucks not only to the University of Georgia but also to expand Athens Technical College and to build a gleaming convention center, the Georgia World Congress, in the state capital. One of his greatest bricks-and-mortar achievements is the perimeter highway that now circles the congested downtown of Athens—today that road is named the Paul Broun Sr. Highway. The father's success and those road signs provided priceless name recognition and a kind of free advertising for Paul Broun Jr.—even though the son is an ultraconservative Republican who is dedicated to fighting to kill the types of government projects that his father had championed.

Today, Paul Broun Jr. talks of his dad as someone with whom he differed politically at times but for whom he had enormous respect. The favor wasn't always returned. "His father denied him," a Democratic state lawmaker from the junior Broun's congressional district—Alan Powell of Hartwell, Georgia—tells you. Powell was a close friend of the father who initially doubted the two men could even be related to each other when he heard of the Republican Broun's extremist views in the 1990s. "That's my crazy-ass son," Powell says his colleague sighed after he asked Broun Sr. about it at lunch one day.

It's not surprising that Paul Broun Sr. would view his own son as a ne'er-do-well. Even Broun himself characterizes his misspent young adult years, before he found Jesus, in that way. Born in the very first year of the baby boom after World War II, he managed to avoid Vietnam with a stint in the Marine Reserves—something he obfuscated in his 2007 congressional campaign when he called his 1964–67 service "pre-Vietnam." When that was completed, he earned his medical degree on the Athens campus and launched a family-practice career in south Georgia. Working out of Americus in the 1970s and 1980s, Broun even achieved a modicum of fame as the physician for the nearby relatives of Jimmy Carter, presiding over mother Lillian's death and—ironically— brother Billy's referrals for alcoholism treatment. The latter is ironic because Broun had drinking problems, too, not to mention his women problems and—finally, related to all this, no doubt—money problems.

After Broun declared bankruptcy in the early 1980s, a federal judge ruled—according to news accounts in Athens—that he "falsified financial documents in an effort to obtain a loan and misrepresented his assets and debts during bankruptcy proceedings," and ordered him to pay nearly $70,000 to an Americus bank. According to a bankruptcy complaint, the young family doctor "has a reputation of having an extravagant lifestyle evidenced by the acquisition of a number of expensive rare hunting books, expensive rare ceramic items related to hunting, safari to Africa, expensive gun collection and the acquisition of the very best in everything purchased." Broun had to pay more than $61,000 in back taxes to the IRS, and one of his ex-wives even took him to court for alimony and child support. There was a time when that kind of résumé would have sunk a would-be politician, but the twenty-first century has proved to be remarkably kind to past sinners who adopt the language of twelve-step recovery—just ask Glenn Beck how that works—and even awards bonus points when Christianity is involved.

By all accounts, Broun did successfully clean up his personal life after joining the Baptist church and marrying his fourth wife, Niki, but sobriety was no guarantee of political success when the physician, who for the last few years has continued to see patients but only on house calls, switched to the GOP and eyed elected office. He lost badly in two runs for Congress in south Georgia, which didn't deter him from a disastrous primary race for the U.S. Senate in 1996, when Broun said Democratic candidate and eventual winner Max Cleland, who lost three limbs from a grenade explosion in Vietnam, was "play[ing] that wheelchair to the nth degree" to get sympathy and votes. Broun got just 3 percent of the primary vote and eventually moved back north to his native Athens, his political ambitions seemingly crushed.

Still, Broun entered a ten-candidate special election when that district's longtime Republican congressman, Charlie Norwood, died of cancer in 2007. He gained the runoff with a surprising second-place finish but was universally predicted to face crushing defeat by the Republicans' handpicked candidate, a state senator named Jim Whitehead. In fact, Whitehead—from Augusta, at the other end of the district—was so cocky that he didn't campaign in Athens for the runoff, even after it was dredged up that he'd once joked he'd like to see all of the University of Georgia bombed, except for the football team. Broun won a stunning narrow upset thanks to 90 percent of the vote from Athens. The most liberal city in Georgia had just unwittingly elected the most conservative congressman in America. Conservative-watching journalist David Weigel, then with *Reason* magazine, called Broun "the accidental congressman."

But accidents are virtually impossible to undo in modern American politics, especially in districts gerrymandered to favor one party or the other. Broun turned back a well-funded and well-regarded GOP primary candidate in the 2008 race for a full term, even as voters slowly came to terms—approvingly, for some—with just how conservative Broun really was. That became clear when he was one of only four members of Congress to vote against a $20 million program to help kids in drug-infested neighborhoods and even joined just two other colleagues in opposing money for a registry for Lou Gehrig's disease, or ALS. Asked about that by Weigel, Broun whipped out his pocket

Constitution and insisted there was nowhere that it was written that the federal government could do these things. "I'd say most of the things this Congress does, we don't actually have the authority to do," the freshman insisted.

There was one thing, however, that the born-again congressman did think the government had the authority to do: ban the sale of *Playboy* and other racy magazines on U.S. military bases. Broun's Military Honor and Decency Act—which an aide boosted by touting the congressman's medical qualifications as an "addictionologist"—was the only piece of legislation that he authored in that first term. What's more, it turned out that Broun's aversion to government spending applied to legislation but not to taxpayer dollars that could help out his political career. In 2008, during his tough reelection battle, Broun spent so much on taxpayer-funded mail to his constituents that his office nearly ran out of money to pay staff and maintain district offices.

One could make the case that Obama's election that fall was the best thing that could have happened to Broun politically. While he was still a low-seniority member of the minority party in the House, he was now becoming something else that offered more excitement and even a kind of power—as a leader of the backlash against a new president. Weeks after the Obama-Hitler firestorm, Broun—as reported by Max Blumenthal, author of *Republican Gomorrah*—joined two pastors in praying over the Capitol doorway where the first-ever black president would emerge to take the oath of office. "I hope and pray that as God stirs the heart of our new president that President Obama will listen and will heed God's direction," Broun reportedly uttered.

The fact that health-care reform emerged as a leading issue in Obama's first year was also something of a godsend for Broun, since it gave him a chance to play up his credentials as a medical doctor. In the long, hot summer of angry town hall meetings, the Georgia conservative gave a virtuoso performance before a mostly supportive gathering of four hundred people in the town of Watkinsville. He entered the room with three large binders, announced loudly, "Folks, this is

Obamacare," and then forcefully slammed the binders to the ground. "This is a stinking, rotten fish, and they don't want you to smell it, and they want to shove it down your throat and make you eat it before you smell how rotten and stinky it is," he said. The congressman also suggested that Obama and congressional leaders were "a socialistic elite" who might potentially use a pandemic—swine flu was in the news that September—as an excuse to declare martial law. One woman reportedly stood up to ask Broun a question about covering the uninsured while the congressman was still speaking; sheriff's deputies briefly escorted her out of the room but then she was allowed back inside, as audience members shouted out, "Cut her mike!"

After that, the odds that Broun might have to answer hostile questions shrank, because he was increasingly devoting his time and energy to igniting the Tea Party movement and even indulging its more extreme elements, as evidenced by his appearance at the John Birch Society gala. Two months after the John Birch speech, Broun joined his Georgia congressional colleague Gingrey in attending a closed-door conference supported by some of the most right-wing factions of this "grassroots movement." The National Liberty Unity Summit in Washington was co-sponsored by several groups that have been cited as right-wing extremist groups by the Southern Poverty Law Center. That would include the Oath Keepers, who were quite active in organizing and promoting the December 2009 event, which sought to organize the disparate "Patriot" groups that either were created or were gaining strength in the first year of Obama's presidency.

A photo from the event shows a smiling Broun posing with a key organizer, Georgia conservative activist Nighta Davis, and with Maryland pastor David Whitney, a leading activist in the Constitution Party and a senior instructor for the Institute on the Constitution. The Constitution Party—which the Southern Poverty Law Center has branded "the most extreme right-wing political party in the United States," citing its 2004 platform that called for undoing every amendment since 1913 (that includes women voting and the income tax) and extreme views on immigration and abortion—was also a major co-sponsor of the conference attended by Broun. One of the featured speakers was the leader of the National Center for Constitutional Studies, a group founded by Glenn Beck's favorite extremist author, Cleon Skousen, in 1971 as—in the words of *Salon*'s Alexander Zaitchik—"a research organization devoted to the study of the super-conspiracy directed by the Rockefellers and the Rothschilds." Others on the agenda included Walter Reddy of the Committees of Safety—who produced a 1996 documentary calling the Oklahoma City bombing "an inside job"—as well as Houston Tea Party activist Dale Robertson, later dogged by controversy when a picture surfaced of him bringing to a 2009 rally a sign comparing Congress to the (misspelled) N-word, and the Oath Keepers' David Gillie.

These were the extreme fringes that echoed off the hillsides of Knob Creek, animated the Oath Keepers and their paranoid fantasies about urban concentration camps, and rallied to the support of "Sheriff Joe" with their crude signs. Now these far-right groups that had always been way out there on the edge weren't just growing in size since Obama's inauguration, but here were two members of the United States Congress bestowing a brand of legitimacy on them that was almost priceless. In return, Broun appeared as a leader, albeit not as the representative of the Tenth Congressional District in northeast Georgia but of an amorphous place that you could call Oath Keeper Nation. The risk going forward was that Tea Party anger within the gerrymandered far-right districts of Red America might lead in 2010 and beyond to a much larger political wing of Paul Brouns, and America's paranoia-fueled political gridlock would only get worse.

Organizers of the right-wing summit understood and appreciated the gift that Broun bestowed upon them. "He is a statesman," says Nighta Davis, who planned the event and lives within his Tenth Congressional District in Georgia. He recalls Broun spending time with the summit's Second Amendment Committee, which included the above-mentioned Walter Reddy as well as Larry Pratt, the executive director of the Gun Owners of America, a group frequently described as "the

NRA on steroids"; Pratt himself has been called "a gun rights abso-lutist" by the Southern Poverty Law Center, which also criticized him for playing footsie, in essence, with militia groups during the 1990s. It's not known what Broun and Pratt discussed, but five months later Broun will be the only one of the 435 members of the House to address a heavily publicized Second Amendment March on Washington that was spearheaded by Pratt.

"We had a nice talk, about how the Second Amendment is not really functioning the way the Founders intended it to," recalls the militia enthusiast Reddy of his meeting with Broun, when contacted by phone. Apparently, Reddy didn't get a chance to tell the congressman about his documentary purporting to expose the U.S. government's involve-ment in the Oklahoma City bombing, but he did lobby for his current pet cause of establishing true state militias that would be independent from the National Guard or any federal authority. Still it wasn't clear whether some of Broun's newfound friends were stuck in the 1990s . . . or the 1860s.

IT'S ONLY NINE miles down Interstate 85 from the site of Dr. Martin Luther King's marble crypt to the Atlanta Airport Hilton, but on a bit-terly windswept and unseasonably cold day in February, the psychic distance feels like light-years. King, a national icon honored with his own holiday, should have had the last word on the not-quite-lost cause of extreme states' rights; in his 1963 "I Have a Dream" speech, the civil rights leader said: "I have a dream that one day, down in Alabama, with its vicious racists, with its governor having his lips dripping with the words of 'nullification' and 'interposition'—one day right there in Alabama little black boys and black girls will be able to join hands with little white boys and white girls as sisters and brothers."

Nearly a half-century has passed, and now the parking lot behind this nondescript high-rise hotel is filling up with cars and SUVs with garish bumper stickers reading "Vote the Socialists Out in 2010" or

"Global Warming is a Hoax," the latter plastered on a not-so-carbon-neutral Infiniti G35. Inside, a long line is forming to enter what's being billed as the first annual Tenth Amendment Summit. The event is a joint venture of the Los Angeles–based Tenth Amendment Center—a think tank promoting the idea that most political power is vested not in Washington but in the states—and the most extreme far-right candidate in the 2010 Republican Georgia primary for governor, Ray McBerry. Among the four hundred or so people who fill every seat in the hotel ballroom are a good number of local McBerry supporters but also candidates for Congress and other offices in thirteen states, and a decent smattering of regular folks, even some who flew down from the bluer Obama-friendly states up North. For seven hours, the words "nullification" and "interposition"—the doctrine that holds that states have the power to nullify unwelcome federal legislation or interpose state authority between Washington and their citizens—are dripping from their lips.

Leon Moe, who sometimes calls himself "DynaMoe" on the Internet, is one of these folks. He is sixty-eight—a plain-spoken Minnesotan from outside of St. Paul, wearing a stylish American-flag sweater with a Disabled American Veterans baseball cap that covers his baldness. Moe says he suffers from post-traumatic stress from his service in Vietnam in the late 1960s, although it was worsening diabetes that caused him to retire from his longtime job at a trucking terminal about five years ago.

Since then, however, Moe has put his newfound extra time into working on conservative causes—not unlike other young retirees like Delaware's Russ Murphy and his full-time devotion to the 9-12 Patriots. In Moe's case, he is campaigning tirelessly for his seemingly quirky cause of Minnesota sovereignty—that is, encouraging state officials to ignore or disobey federal laws under the authority that proponents believe they are granted under the Tenth Amendment. Moe says he opposes the growth of big government but also was against the war in Iraq, and based on audience reaction there seems to be growing opposition among these strict Constitution buffs for such once liberal crusades as ending the Bush-launched wars and for undoing government antiterror laws such as the Patriot Act.

"I'm something of a history nut," Moe explains—another common refrain—when asked how he came to view the Tenth Amendment as a solution to the problem of encroaching power. "A lot of the things that take place in government were a little perplexing to me—as a veteran I took an oath to honor the Constitution and I don't expect anything different from our elected officials." You ask Moe if he knows, then, about the Oath Keepers, and he says that he just joined the group six months ago after he heard about it from a fellow veteran—living proof of the ways that interlocking ties between groups were luring new recruits toward the fringes, the once-diverse tentacles of a movement coming together in strange new ways.

In fact, the Tenth Amendment Summit had ties—albeit not overtly— to a group that a decade ago had been labeled by the Southern Poverty Law Center as "a racist hate group," an alarming outfit called the League of the South. The League has strongly denied the racist tag, but there is little doubt that the group both celebrates the Confederacy and advocates secession from the United States, sometimes as a moral cause if not as a practical one—its founding papers from the 1990s argue that the South "must throw off the yoke of imperial [federal, or central government] oppression." Of the five main speakers at the Tenth Amendment Summit (which also included a top official of the suddenly omnipresent John Birch Society), two are current board members of the League of the South: the gubernatorial candidate McBerry and the closing speaker, Franklin Sanders, whom the SPLC has described as "a peculiar mix of neo-Confederate fantasist and seasoned tax protester" as well as a convicted felon for failure to pay taxes on his gold and silver business, the outgrowth of his belief that paper money is worthless.

Race was the eight-hundred-pound gorilla in the ballroom full of $50-a-head attendees—99 percent of them white—who mostly heard a series of repetitive speeches on the Tenth Amendment, which simply states: "The powers not delegated to the United States by the

Constitution, nor prohibited by it to the States, are reserved to the States respectively, or to the people." To the speakers, these twenty-eight words are a magic bullet that would allow states to stand up to Obama's health-care plan or federal efforts to regulate climate change or anything that was politically unpopular. There was only passing reference to the fact that the Supreme Court has consistently blocked Tenth Amendment–inspired efforts to deny Washington's authority, frequently by citing federal powers to regulate interstate commerce. And there was no mention of the next logical step, which would be secession—even though McBerry has previously endorsed secession as "a last resort." McBerry, a youthful ex–history teacher with a close-cropped beard, walked the audience through early Tenth Amendment cases such as Virginia's challenge to John Adams and the Alien and Sedition Acts of 1798, but there was no mention of the Civil War, or slavery, or the later battles over states' rights when George Wallace stood in a schoolhouse door in the 1960s, the causes that states' rights is closely associated with. (Afterward, McBerry told an *Atlanta Journal-Constitution* columnist that the racial issues were, in essence, water under the bridge—before reverting to League of the South mode and adding that "when the South lost the war, it totally transformed the American republic into basically a federal empire.")

But while these were the things that McBerry left out, the things he did say to rile up the attendees were scary enough. The gubernatorial candidate told the receptive audience, which interrupted him with cheers about a half-dozen times, that since federal dollars funded only about 3 percent of Georgia's schools—suffering at that moment from extreme budget cuts—the state could ignore federal mandates by returning the cash, asking, "Would it not be a small price to pay to restore our liberties by throwing off the yoke of federal tyranny?" He also said that he's pushing for Georgia to adopt a system from the nineteenth century in which the state would collect federal tax revenues on behalf of Washington—and then decide which federal programs passed constitutional muster and could be funded with the cash. He brought up the ever-present bugaboo of the impending Obama gun confiscation, claiming that if governor he would arrest any federal agent attempting to disarm citizens in Georgia.

But there was one thing that was even more disturbing.

In discussing the history of states' rights, McBerry mentioned the case of *Chisholm v. Georgia*, the first major case to go before the U.S. Supreme Court in 1793. The issue was whether Georgia could be sued by a citizen who claimed the state owed him money in federal courts— Georgia lost (a key fact that McBerry fails to mention) after taking a defiant antifederal stand.

Said McBerry: "You're really going to like this part—and the state of Georgia went on to say that any federal agent caught within the boundaries of the sovereign state of Georgia attempting to enforce these unconstitutional measures would be, and I quote, 'arrested and hanged by the neck until dead.'" At the mention of the hypothetical killing of federal agents, the crowd let out its most thunderous rebel yell of the day, and about half the room even stood up to prolong the cheering and hollering. It had been only eight days since a federal employee—Vernon Hunter of the IRS—had been murdered by the rambling tax protestor Joe Stack.

The thing is, Ray McBerry's campaign wasn't going anywhere; most polls showed him in the single digits, in fact, with a U.S. congressman and the state insurance commissioner, among others, well ahead of him in the Georgia governor's race. But McBerry and his mad-dog supporters were having an impact. In a survey of Georgia Republicans taken three months after Obama took office, 43 percent said their state would be better off as "an independent nation" than as part of the United States. The Georgia Senate voted 43–1 to pass a state sovereignty resolution that was endorsed by the front-running GOP gubernatorial candidate, the insurance commissioner John Oxendine, who said "our federal government has become oppressive in its size . . . and its interference into the affairs of the states." A similar stance arguably saved the governor of the nation's second largest state, Texas Republican

Rick Perry, whose reelection prospects were dim before he attended the first round of Tea Parties on April 15, 2009; when reporters asked him about Texas secession, he stunned many with his response: "There's a lot of different scenarios. We've got a great union. There's absolutely no reason to dissolve it. But if Washington continues to thumb their nose at the American people, you know, who knows what might come out of that?"

Much of this was political hucksterism, pandering to an increasingly irrational hard-core base for votes—and it worked; in Perry's case he came from behind and won his March 2010 primary against Senator Kay Bailey Hutchison, now suddenly seen as "a Washington insider," and Tea Party upstart Debra Medina (who campaigned with Oath Keepers and others on the extreme right). Just a few years earlier, the governor of a large state talking about secession or a U.S. congressman comparing the president to Hitler would have been killing his career, but suddenly politicking like a talk-radio host—taking what radio's Bill Colley might call the "hang 'em" approach to undocumented immigrants or to gun issues—was the pathway to fame, and maybe even to higher office.

But there were also increasing signs as the 2010 fall elections approached that those buzzwords of "nullification" and "interposition" once condemned by Martin Luther King were actually being put to use to thwart federal efforts and create misguided state policies. In the days leading up to his primary, Perry announced he would sue the U.S. Environmental Protection Agency over its greenhouse gas regulations, saying he would "defend Texas's environmental successes against federal overreach." In Montana, the state government was attempting a scheme to lift regulations on guns that were made and sold within its borders, and other conservative states were looking to copy Montana.

Representative Paul Broun was not at the Tenth Amendment Summit—not because he didn't support it, but because Congress was still in session. In fact, a Broun congressional staffer, Jessica Morris, was the emcee of the event, providing gushing introductions for the likes of McBerry and president John McManus of the John Birch Society as "statesmen." Morris—a stylish young former Tennessee TV anchorwoman in a white pants suit who at times was the only African-American in the room—said that the congressman supported the goals of the summit. "He would prefer to call himself a constitutionalist more than a conservative," she tells you, although she notes that her boss wasn't supporting McBerry in the governor's race but was behind U.S. Representative Nathan Deal, one of a handful of members of Congress who has questioned Obama's birth certificate. But she's quick to add, "I love Ray McBerry," as the rocking strains of "Sweet Home Alabama" begin to fade from the big speakers.

THERE'S USUALLY NOT much going on at 8 a.m. on a Saturday in Hartwell, Georgia, a half-asleep town at the South Carolina border where a good many folks are retirees who moved here to live and motorboat on the banks of the large man-made lake, created when the U.S. Army Corp of Engineers built a large dam in the early 1960s—before such large federal projects were an object of local scorn. But today is the annual Eggs and Issues Breakfast by the Hart County Chamber of Commerce, and so about eighty small-business types and local pols are here in the basement learning center of the public library, piling cheesy scrambled eggs and biscuits onto plastic plates and gulping down coffee from Styrofoam cups before the politicking begins in earnest.

Representative Paul Broun Jr. ambles down the steps a few minutes after 8 o'clock, making sure that everyone knows he was on a very late flight back from Washington. Broun is more casual than many of the chamber-of-commerce people, wearing an aviator-style coat with a big collar, a white T-shirt barely peeping from behind the top button of his dress shirt. Nonetheless, Broun gives off the aura that politics—despite all his early failures—was his life's calling. He eschews breakfast to work the room, one by one. "May I say hello to you, sir—Congressman Paul Broun!" Reaching out for the hand of a senior citizen who appears to be wrist-deep in the cheesy eggs, Broun clamps the man's non-eating left wrist, smiles, and moves on.

The breakfast event in Hartwell feels routine, yet for the congressman it is rare. It took several weeks to find an event where Broun would answer questions from his constituents, which was not helped by the failure of his staff to return emails or calls. One of the attendees at the Hartwell breakfast tells you he regularly stays in touch with Broun through a monthly "telephone town hall" meeting, but he suggests the phone number for this event is given out only to supporters who already agree with the Republican congressman. This morning's Eggs and Issues event is actually a panel discussion of many politicians—mostly state and local—but Broun approaches the moderators and tells them he needs to dash off to other events, so it's agreed that the congressman can give a quick spiel and answer a few questions before he must go. Before anyone can ask a question, Broun wants Georgians to know that he knows that they're hurting. He relates that an official in Lincoln, Georgia, told him that unemployment dropped there from 14 percent to 10 percent but when he asked what jobs had been created, he learned the answer was none. "People have just stopped looking because there aren't any jobs," Broun says.

For about fifteen minutes, Broun stands in front of this breakfast club while he verbally dances in circles—zigzagging back and forth between touting his bill that he believes would create jobs by the two-year elimination of capital gains and dividend taxes and deep cuts in payroll taxes and his sponsoring of a balanced budget amendment. "We've got to stop the outrageous spending," he says. He attacks Obama and Democratic leaders for putting the focus onto health care and away from jobs—but then he keeps doing the exact same thing. He also seeks to reconcile his Bircher-inspired views on the Constitution with his own lifelong struggle against addiction and for control that he finally answered for himself with Jesus Christ. "Liberty is freedom bridled by morality," he explains, adding that "we have to have something to control our freedom—which is morality."

Who defines what is moral was not clear.

A man in the back of the room shouts out a question about jobs, complaining that he can't buy a toaster that isn't made in China and that doesn't break down after a few months. "We need to start producing things," the man says, and Broun agrees—launching into a long rap about how things like agriculture and manufacturing bring wealth into society without really suggesting how that could happen again here in America. Then he abruptly veers off: "The House just passed a health-care bill that the president's own economic advisor said will cost five million jobs if passed," he says, adding that the motivation was "they want to do socialism." Broun's statement was a lie; the objective Pulitzer Prize–winning PolitiFact.com had written earlier that Obama aide Christina Romer had said no such thing, that the "five million jobs" number was an unfair extrapolation of fuzzy math performed by the Republicans themselves. Meanwhile, the path to job creation, beyond vague talk of further tax cuts and fewer regulations, was left hanging there in the Dixie dew.

"I apologize—I have to run, I have to go to Atlanta," Broun says, but then he talks to you and another reporter outside the rear entrance. He makes it sound as though what is happening in the Tea Parties is a lot more energizing than his duties in Congress: "The sleeping giant is rising up and I'm excited because freedom-loving Americans all across this country are saying no to this huge growth of government," says Broun, who speaks repeatedly of the backlash movement as "lighting grassfires" and calls himself at one point "a freedom fighter."

He acknowledges that he's certainly aware of the Oath Keepers but is unable to elaborate much—"I look more across the board and not at specific groups." He is more explicit in his defense of the John Birch Society: "The thing about the John Birch Society is they've been promoting constitutional government for a long, long time—so yes, I think they have a very strong place to play to try to educate the American people."

And how does he view Obama now? He seeks to explain away the

Hitler controversy but also insists that the president has changed little from his college days, when Obama had written in his autobiography that he was drawn to Marxist professors. He also cites Obama's mention in speeches of basic Marxist doctrine—" 'from each to his own ability to each according to his need'—which came right out of Karl Marx's writing," although there is in fact no evidence that Obama has ever cited that passage. You ask if Obama is an authoritarian, and Broun launches into a monologue about the auto takeovers, his aide who's been described as a "car czar," and health care. "So, yes, I see that he wants to set up authoritarian rule. Whether it's based on Marxism or purely socialistic, I don't know." He goes on to add his displeasure that the president (in Broun's worldview, anyway) seems to believe that America is part of a family of nations, that it is not special. "We're the only superpower in the world—we're the only exceptional country."

Back inside, the citizens of "the only superpower in the world" are still beseeching their local elected officials for help, trying to figure out how Georgia would cope with the looming massive cuts in higher education, or whether any local companies might be expanding instead of laying people off for a change, or why their state spends more money on incarcerating citizens than other states. When the meeting finally breaks up, you talk to a newly elected Hartwell city councilman, Arthur Craft, who campaigned and won on a jobs platform after retiring from a large fiberglass factory over the South Carolina line that went from 1,100 workers to little more than one hundred during his nearly four decades there. Like Mary Dixon back in Homer, Craft, who is also black, tells you he believes a lot of the opposition to the president that is so exciting to Broun ultimately comes back to the simple issue of race.

"To be perfectly honest, I don't think he [Obama] could do anything right for a lot of people—if he gave them a million dollars they wouldn't want to [take it]," says Craft, a very soft-spoken man. He said the president's experiences remind him of some of his problems when he supervised eleven engineers at the mostly white fiberglass plant. Says Craft: "It's just some people resent who tells them things, you understand what I'm saying?"

Meanwhile, Congressman Broun had missed most of his constituents' economic complaints by heading off—even though you find out that his event in Atlanta actually isn't until 3 o'clock that afternoon. It's a Tea Party rally organized by the pro-business Freedomworks on the steps of the state capitol—ninety minutes removed from where the economically battered constituents of Broun's Tenth Congressional District live and look for work.

CHAPTER EIGHT

The Nashville Predators

Tea Party Emporium spotlights a product, this finely crafted piece of jewelry, which we believe to be the single unifying symbol of the Tea Party movement, a TEA BAG®. Worn not just for its beauty, this TEA BAG® identifies your support for conservative/libertarian beliefs, which in our country is in such dire need. The tiniest of symbols can be *a catalyst for change.* Let your voice be heard by proudly wearing this most unique *icon of Freedom.* A portion of proceeds will be donated to the Heritage Foundation, an institute committed to building an America where freedom, opportunity, prosperity and civil society flourish.

Sign above the Tea Party Emporium table at the first-ever
National Tea Party Convention in Nashville, Tennessee

By the time that Sarah Palin bounced up the podium for the long-awaited climax to the first-ever national convention of Tea Party activists, most of the more than one thousand people in the giant banquet room were far too engorged from large plates of prime beef or shrimp to leave any room for dessert. Dessert plates with half-eaten remnants of mousse were scattered everywhere, as if a giant gourmet chocolate bomb had been set off, when Palin finally delivered the TV

sound bite of the event: "I think America is ready for another revolution, and you are a part of it!"

Shopping is a part of it, too. A few hours earlier, Melissa Carbone
and her teenage daughter pulled into the parking lot at the Gaylord Opryland Hotel ($18 plus tax) in their car with the New York "TPRTY"
plates and now find themselves looking at jewelry at the Tea Party Emporium stand—this before they even have a chance to be exposed to
any of the weekend's political messages. A registered nurse from Rock-
land County, New York, Carbone is a stylish woman wearing mod eye-
glasses with tinted frames, and she is already considering adding some
Tea Bag jewelry to her ensemble.

"There's a tenderness about it," she says, looking over the table of
tiny bejeweled tea baggery. Carbone laments that her mom is no longer
alive to receive a piece, but she is planning on purchasing one for each
of her three sisters. She says it appeals to her love of American history.
"It just struck me that it's something they'll say one hundred years from
now—'Remember that?'"

Carbone says she's been to every big Tea Party event—the first ones
on April 15, 2009, and then of course the big 9-12 rally in Washington,
D.C. But on this day she is part of the ultimate captive audience—one
thousand of the most hard-core Tea Party activists in America, rounded
up from coast to coast and then herded into a relatively tiny corner of
the Gaylord Opryland Hotel, a seemingly alternate, infinite universe of
real palm trees, fake rivers, and Greek statues plunked down willy-nilly
on the other side of a Tennessee freeway from the Waffle House, inside
this massive humid-in-February domed place, where bombastic conservative journalist Andrew Breitbart was actually being understated
for once when he called it "The Biosphere." Even with a locked-in customer base, and with mania over the Tea Party and its star speaker,
Sarah Palin, rivaling that weekend's Super Bowl for hype, owner Jeffrey
Link has made sure that everything at his Tea Party Emporium was
priced for a quick sale.

In fact, the regular price for his signature item, the jewelry that replicates a tea bag (or, more accurately, a TEA BAG®)—made from sterling silver, quartz crystal, and semiprecious gemstones such as onyx, mother of pearl, tigereye, and bloodstone—was crossed out at $89.99; for the Nashville confab he was offering a deal with a second piece, which can be worn as a pendant or a pin ("Flaunt your patriotism in fashion!" notes his Web site), for just $49.99. And that wasn't all: the Tea Party Emporium was throwing in a free baseball hat with the purchase. Everything else was also marked down—a bag of Freedom Brewing coffee ("guaranteed to get your American spirit moving!") that normally went for $12 was selling for only $9. Business at Link's two perpendicular tables could best be described as a steady trickle; it was hard for customers to make it across the plush carpet of the grand-ballroom foyer without first getting buttonholed by a reporter for CNN or the *New York Times*, eager to explain this grassroots populist uprising to the puzzled masses outside "the Biosphere."

The jewelry entrepreneur Link didn't look or talk much like his Tea Party customer base that was milling about—soft retirees in cashmere and loafers, interspersed with the random curly-haired rabble-rousing housewife. Link's angular face was framed by his curved and stylish hair, a bit wild yet carefully moussed, and he was a tad overdressed for the convention in a navy-blue wool suit and sheen-y tie. He looked as if he were waiting for the 5:15 from Grand Central to Irvington—his posh suburban hometown back in New York—and he talked in the rapid-fire cadence of Jeweler's Row. In fact, he was an heir to an upscale family jewelry business—A. Link & Co., founded in 1904 by Viennese immigrant Adolph Link and located now at the tony address of 444 Madison Avenue.

Link tells you that he came to the Tea Party movement by way of the 1960s. In fact, his only protest prior to this was marching against Richard Nixon's bombing of Cambodia in 1970. "I grew up with liberal, hippie sensibilities," he says, inspired at first by the Camelot days of JFK. "I lived with my sensibilities until I realized that Kennedy was fucking everything with a dress, and Nixon was just a little bit too smart for his own good, and after Jimmy Carter I kind of went off the edge . . . and then found the *Mashiach*—Ronald Reagan."

Mashiach?

Link throws you a mildly disgusted look. "The Messiah."

He tells you that he started the Tea Party Emporium in the early days of this new movement, back in the summer of 2009 or so, and that business has been okay, that "when ladies touch it, when they get really close to it, they like it." Still, it's nothing like his normal business with A. Link, which he acknowledges catered heavily to the $10-million-bonus set on Wall Street that was thrown—at least for a short time, anyway—for a loop by the 2008 crisis. The economic end-of-the-world-as-we-know-it meltdown in his Midtown Manhattan core had driven him toward the Tea Party movement as a place where all the action had moved, and it was also a place that he felt reflected his freedom-loving political views. But Link does not speak the lingo of an ideologue; politics for him is personal, in stark black and white. Kennedy the philanderer. Reagan the Messiah. And Barack Obama?

Link pauses for a long time, debating how to respond to a journalist that he's just met. Finally. . .

"I think he's the Antichrist."

Sometimes, however, the Antichrist can be very good for business. In a broad sense, Jeffrey Link was drawn from New York to Nashville by the same basic instinct that lured so many paying customers from the ranks of everyday folks and arguably caused Palin to board a private jet in Wasilla and hustle her way down here: the great American promise of reinvention and renewal. During the first year of the Age of Obama, you had seen how the anxieties of the economic crisis and fears, especially among older whites, of fast-moving demographic changes had caused people to do unexpected things—from Russ Murphy launching a new political coalition in his trailer to seventy-four-year-old Al Whayland waving his flag at Glenn Beck book signings. They were people whose need for rebirth through politics was, in some cases, a matter of dire necessity.

Nashville felt different from that. New players were entering the game. Most of them clearly shared the same worldview as the initial grassroots phase of the Tea Party movement—such as Jeffrey Link and his innate disapproval of Obama—with conservative ideals, oriented toward traditional values and religion. But the second wave of the Tea Party, which had its coming-out amid the central Tennessee woodlands, was chock full of opportunists, especially of the capitalist variety. People like Link and some of the other merchants, as well as the profit-minded organizers of the Nashville confab—along with old-school political consultants and even televangelists—were savvy operators. And in the burst of energy that was the anti-Obama backlash they saw a different kind of rebirth, which was career reinvention powered by a large new pool of potential customers. It was actually quite similar to what politicians like Paul Broun or Michele Bachmann saw, but it mostly involved the one form of currency that was harder than votes: cash.

It was an easier sell than some audiences, because most Tea Party activists—swayed by their gurus like Glenn Beck and Rush Limbaugh—all but worshipped at the altar of capitalism, which meant there was no inherent conflict between supporting the movement and making a buck off of it. In fact, what was celebrated here in Nashville wasn't so much the coming-out of the conservative movement as the commoditization of it, in a kind of political trade show that brought merchants of different stripes together with people willing to spend good money to find different ways to show their solidarity, even with a baseball hat or a piece of jewelry. Some revolutions may take aim at materialism, but this one lauded it—and there were plenty of merchants eager to slap this rebellion with a trademarked Tea Party brand.

Truth be told, every revolution has had its share of hucksters, including the left-wing counterculture of the 1960s—patronized by record execs who told kids they could "stick it to the man" by shelling out four bucks for their label's LP. But the zeitgeist is different when it's a right-wing counterrevolution on behalf of the free-enterprise system.

In this political arena, anyone who begrudges the right of a guy making a dollar must be some kind of socialist, or worse. Yet in a world of newfound paranoia and fear, this right-wing movement in America was becoming an unabashedly for-profit venture, a RIGHT-WING MOVEMENT®.

Despite the fact that many activists in this new movement were unemployed or hurting economically, many of the middle-aged or retired newcomers to the politics still had money in the bank—indeed, a *New York Times*/CBS News poll of the Tea Party movement released two months later found that one out of five earned more than $100,000, whereas that figure was just 14 percent for the general public. And now here were all these nice people telling them how to spend those dollars in support, however vaguely, of the cause.

Make no mistake, the main course in Nashville arrived wrapped in the same kind of red-meat political rhetoric that was becoming so familiar—immigration bashing, questioning Obama on everything from his policies to his citizenship, always launched with a prayer. There was a steady flow of politicians—many of whom had fallen dismally short in past ventures, like the nearly forgotten 2008 GOP presidential hopeful Tom Tancredo—who had a new opportunity to shine here. But unlike the Russ Murphys of the world, who gave every sense that resentment and combat with big government was now embedded in their souls, much of the right-wing parade through Nashville left behind an impression that at some future date they would be moving on to the Next New Thing.

The potentially great rewards for the quasi-political capitalist like a Palin certainly seemed to outstrip the pedestrian benefits of actual politics. Believe it or not, it used to be that political movements were led by politicians; some of them were born fairly rich, like John F. Kennedy, and some became millionaires doing other things, like actor-turned-governor Ronald Reagan. But in 2010, the conservative cause was spearheaded by two unrestrained and arguably run-amok capitalists: Glenn Beck, who planned to reveal a hundred-year "Plan" for America in a for-profit book, and Sarah Palin, who quit her elected position as governor of Alaska to write a book for a seven-figure advance and to give speeches for $100,000 a pop. Even for the National Tea Party Convention.

But then, truth be told, you could make the case that the National Tea Party Convention was never really the three-day anti-Woodstock of right-wing baby boomers that it came to be portrayed in the mainstream media. (Woodstock inadvertently became a free concert, after all, while here they still checked for people's $549 ticket.) Instead, it was an unorthodox fundraising scheme that took dollars from these retirees and small business owners and housewives and dumped them ultimately into the purse of Sarah Palin, with perhaps some loose change—and a burst of unlikely prestige—for the once-obscure organizer of the Nashville event, a small-time lawyer named Judson Phillips.

Before the Nashville confab, the fifty-one-year-old Phillips—a defense lawyer and former assistant DA with one badly lost primary race for a small-county commission seat in his scanty political past—had come off as kind of a shadowy figure, generally not returning calls (including yours, seeking a press pass) from journalists wanting to ask him about whether his for-profit company that organized the event, Tea Party Nation, was advancing the anti-Obama political uprising or just profiting off of it, and whether it was all part of a broader movement to co-opt the grassroots by the Republican Party establishment. Thus, it was something of a surprise for you and the rest of the journalistic bee swarm to finally meet Phillips—an affable, good-humored soul in a baggy suit, with a soft face behind round, wire-rimmed glasses, as eager to answer any and all questions from reporters as he'd been to avoid them before.

He seemed relieved that his convention took place at all. In the days right before the event, two congresswoman—Michele Bachmann and Marcia Blackburn—had pulled out, citing ethical concerns over addressing the for-profit affair, and onetime allies like the conservative group American Majority had not only withdrawn but lashed out, as that group's president, Ned Ryun, told the media: "Listen, I'm all for people making a buck, but this seems very crass, very opportunistic."

Now, Phillips is working the room to say, in essence, that critics of a for-profit event were socialists, haters of free speech. "In 90 percent of the countries of the world, we could be shot or put in prison" for staging such a convention, he self-servingly told one of many impromptu press conferences.

On the last night of the convention, you approach Phillips while he is holding court and posing for snapshots with a group of attendees from Indiana, and the self-hired Tea Party Nation chief is still steamed that some rival Tea Party activists from Tennessee had punctured the biosphere to hold an angry news conference denouncing the cost of the event. "They're the people who say that it's bad that it's a for-profit group, et cetera, and I want you to know that they're socialists. And . . . and . . . and, I've got some really good news for you! Our profits are in the high two figures. We're going to be able to take our volunteers to the Dollar Menu. All-right!!!"

Phillips then asks you to pull up a chair "We are offering something of value in exchange for their payments. They're coming here, they're getting involved; they're getting training." Phillips says that the National Tea Party Convention is actually a much better deal than the well-established conservative gathering called CPAC, where the food is à la carte. "We did $549 and we're feeding everybody some wonderful meals. I've had a couple of people say to me, 'I hope you make a million dollars off of this!' That's not going to happen."

He probably wishes it would. Most of the mainstream journalists who parachuted into Nashville for the weekend were too busy lining up to interview Phillips or primping for their Sarah Palin stand-ups to notice a devastating profile of the attorney that was published on AOL News by freelance journalist Luke O'Brien, which begins at Phillips's hokey Web site ("Up the Creek?," it asks, showing the suited lawyer at water's edge with a large paddle. "Judson Wheeler Phillips can steer you through rough water . . .") and takes you through a lifetime of failed ventures by this member of the National College for D.U.I. Defense.

An unremarkable prosecutor in Nashville eventually became an unremarkable defense attorney with a world of personal woes, including a divorce in the mid-1990s, a Chapter 7 bankruptcy in 1999, and an IRS tax lien covering the years 2004 through 2008. Phillips was turning fifty just when the Tea Party movement emerged out of nowhere, and in that increasingly familiar saga it offered an opportunity for the attorney to start over. "From the beginning he talked about wanting to make a fortune off the Tea Party movement," former volunteer Tami Kilmarx told O'Brien. Volunteers like Kilmarx raised questions about what happened to money—estimated at $4,000—that was donated to a PayPal account controlled by Phillips's wife Sherry while they were spending hours, free of charge, helping the couple achieve the vision of a Facebook-style social-networking system for Tea Partiers. According to O'Brien, two Tea Party Nation activists who eventually fell out with Phillips claimed that his law firm address was really a construction company and that he was meeting his clients at Starbucks. Weeks after the convention, Phillips would also be sued by the baseball-card dealer who fronted the first $50,000 to get Palin to the show, Bill Hemrick, who accused the Tea Party activist of bad-mouthing him and failing to keep a number of promises.

But Phillips didn't just play the role of a political extremist for the cameras. He increasingly appeared on Facebook in his new right-wing radical role, typing out pronouncements that even some in his highly conservative corner of the Bible Belt might find a little far out. Here, for example, is Phillips's policy on illegal immigration as funneled through Facebook: "Take a plane load of them and dump them in Somalia. Make no secret of it and tell the illegals, every time we catch them, that is where they are going. 99% of them will head back to the border on their own."

And so the National Tea Party Convention was cast in the image of Phillips's midlife-crisis radical makeover. Once Palin's role was secured with the help of that $50,000 loan, ginning up interest from big media and small ticket buyers, the Tea Party Nation went to work selling those tickets at $549 (just $349 for the five hundred or so who opted only to see Palin and skip the rest) and lining up pricey sponsorships, and at the same time recruiting a lineup of events that provided an ugly underbelly to Palin's lipstick-y sheen. The tone was set by the immigrant-bashing, failed presidential candidate Tom Tancredo, who told the Thursday-night dinner crowd that the election of "a socialist" like Obama happened because "we do not have a civics literacy test before people can vote in this country." The next night was turned over to the publisher of the influential-among-right-wingers WorldNetDaily, Joseph Farah, who used the presence of national TV cameras from C-SPAN to promote his theory that Obama is not a U.S. citizen. Farah was "Crazy Eileen" in a nice suit and a thick mustache.

Maybe it is a consequence of Phillips's ridiculous ticket prices, but to say this National Tea Party Convention is not demographically diverse is an immense understatement. Indeed, when at one point Farah asks how many of those attending are baby boomers born between 1946 and 1964, almost every hand shoots into the air, and the few who keep their arms down are mostly older than that. Good thing Farah doesn't ask how many of them are white. Occasionally, the big room seems to have two or three African-American attendees—two of them are congressional hopefuls running as Republicans in black-heavy Southern districts, and a third is the minister who gave the Friday-night invocation. They are vastly outnumbered by the Opryland Hotel's black and Latino waiters and busboys.

The Tea Party convention is an audience susceptible to sales pitches . . . and fear, often closely intertwined. On the middle night, the attendees haven't yet digested dinner when they are shown a manic, loud, quick-cutting documentary called *Generation Zero*, which—under the direction of a former Goldman Sachs employee and the tutelage of the above-mentioned right-wing media figure Breitbart—seeks to blame the 2008 financial meltdown on the permissive parenting of "Woodstock Nation" and a quasi-socialist plot to intentionally topple capitalism. The next morning, a shaken-looking Kimberly Fletcher, the president of Homemakers for America, addresses the big room. "I had a hard time getting to sleep after that movie!" she says. "It was really hard not to have a sense of hopelessness creep in."

Ka-ching! No wonder Breitbart and a few staffers stay in Nashville for the whole weekend, hawking the *Generation Zero* DVD at a table directly across from the Tea Bag Emporium and its TEA BAGS®. Attendees stop there on their way to such events as a forum on "How to Involve the Youth in the Conservative Movement," which, judging from the number of baby-boomer hands that went up the previous day, does in fact seem like an urgent priority. Still, there is one event on the weekend schedule that seems to have no connection to the current political condition, not to Obama's "socialist takeover" or his supposed Kenyan citizenship. And so you wander up a long stairway into the upper reaches of the biosphere into a windowless conference room; here, about one hundred Tea Partiers have gathered to discuss "Emergency Preparedness."

AT "EMERGENCY PREPAREDNESS," there is no socialism in sight— rather, a massive wall of brightly boxed consumer products lines the entire front to the right of the podium. You feel as if you are under a survivalist Christmas tree—there are solar-power radios and water-proofed tents and windbreakers and a giant camp ax, not to mention propane heaters and propane tanks and all manner of stainless-steel cookware, including a big stainless-steel coffeepot. There to explain it all is a young Tennessean named Walter Fitzgerald and the man who'd brought all the goodies, Jarrod Bishop from the Bass Pro Shops, a massive outdoors emporium located at a shopping plaza just one big parking lot down the freeway.

"We call this emergency preparedness and that could be for anything . . . ," Fitzgerald starts out, " . . . earthquakes—of course we don't have any volcanoes close by, but you've seen what that could do if you're ever close to those . . . lots of rain, like you're seeing down in Southern California; forest fires; recently we've had ice that has shut this city down with several surrounding counties. You run out of power and you're on your own. *Strugg*-ling."

The program isn't exactly what you'd expected, and maybe not what some of the Tea Partiers were expecting, either. For much of the next hour, Walter and Jarrod from the Bass Pro Shops come off a little like a propane-powered version of those Blue Collar comedy tours with Larry the Cable Guy and Jeff Foxworthy, jokey chicken-fried survival tips topped with gravy-thick Tennessee accents delivered by a couple of good-looking young men wearing goatees and cowboy boots.

At one point, Jarrod is trying to explain to the room the importance of having a good knife in an emergency, adding, to much laughter: "If the power goes out, I'm stabbing my way outta here, so look out! . . . clear a door path for me—because I'm GOAN!" Then he explains the presence of the stainless-steel coffeepot because "at the Bass Pro Shops, that's how we roll—if my house got blew up or run over by a torna-dah, I want me a cup-a-coffee!"

In other words, it was a lot more homey and less scary than what you'll hear in a typical hour of *The Glenn Beck Program*—nothing about the pending collapse of the worldwide monetary system or any talk of TEOTWAWKI , or "the end of the world as we know it." Then an elderly man at the far front corner of the room interrupts with a question.

"Have you addressed *The One Second After*?

"I'm sorry," replies Walter. "*The One Second After*?"

"The electromagnetic pulse."

"No."

"Well, I'd like to talk about that—but I'd like to talk about a Declaration of Emergency or official catastrophe . . ."

Walter makes a face. "You're going po-litical on us."

The man in the front row backpedals a bit. "I really don't mean that in a political sense, but it could happen for a whole series of nonpolitical reasons and we wouldn't know it and here we are unprepared for it."

He is referring to a book called *The One Second After,* by a North

Carolina professor and history writer named William R. Forstchen, about the fictional aftermath of an electromagnetic pulse explosion over the United States that renders virtually all modern technology unusable, not just computers and telephones but even cars built after the early 1980s, when they became increasingly computerized. Released in the early weeks of the Obama administration, as the world still reeled from the economic meltdown, *The One Second After* became a best seller—and while the book itself is not overtly political, it is a favorite among conservatives who became increasingly apocalyptic with the arrival of Obama. The book details an unraveling of American society as well as the food chain, devolving into civil wars fought by citizen militias—"the premise of which," according to *Booklist*, "Newt Gingrich's foreword says is completely possible."

There's nothing particularly wrong with either survivalist fact or survivalist fiction when viewed in isolation; an occasional apocalyptic sci-fi thriller can be a good stay-up-all-night read, and the emergency-preparedness tips offered by the blue-collar, quasi-comedians Walter and Jarrod on this day were good common sense for a natural disaster. But at the same time, this casual and all-too-frequent blurring of natural disasters, the Apocalypse, and the "po-litical"—end-of-the-world scenarios endorsed as "completely possible" by the GOP White House wannabe Gingrich—is also a toxic recipe for paranoia and fear. It is this background noise of terror that is used to sell irrational and counterproductive policies, and fear that is used to sell emergency products to consumers who in a rational world would have little need for them.

With little fanfare, the worldwide economic meltdown in 2008 that clinched the presidential election for Obama also triggered the biggest uptick in apocalyptic thinking—and shopping—since the so-called survivalist movement first entered the public consciousness in the 1980s and '90s. By April 2009, the *Kansas City Star* was chronicling how retailers were reporting shortages of items such as canning jars, water purification tablets, and of course ammunition amid worries over both the economy and natural disasters along the lines of

Hurricane Katrina, with its inept government response. Many believers in this new American Apocalypto were starting what some folks were calling "crisis gardens," which was a kind of "victory garden" in reverse. Indeed, a drive for food self-sufficiency was an important—if rarely discussed—element of new political movements like the Tea Party and the 9-12 Project, with even groups like the short-lived Sussex County Community Organized Regiment down in Delaware cultivating a vegetable garden when members weren't out protesting the new boardwalk in Rehoboth Beach.

The survivalist hoopla might have diminished over the course of 2009, a year in which the global economic markets and the U.S. dollar showed signs of stability and the Dow yo-yo'ed back over 10,000 (albeit with American unemployment remaining at ridiculously high levels). But then the right-wing media, led of course by Glenn Beck, came along to stoke the embers of paranoia. On February 20, 2009, the one-month anniversary of the Obama presidency, as Beck's popularity on the Fox News Channel was just taking off, viewers at 5 p.m. saw this announcement:

> Topics discussed on today's program may be disturbing to some viewers. The views expressed in this program are not predictions of what will happen, but what could happen. The panelists have been asked to think the unthinkable. Viewer discretion is advised.

It's doubtful that many viewers exercised their discretion and turned the program off after a warning like that—which sounded very much like the disclaimer on CBS Radio before it aired *The War of the Worlds* in 1938, the disclaimer that so many listeners missed or ignored. One of Beck's guests that night was a retired Army sergeant major named Tim Strong, who spoke about the "Bubba effect" of those who would know how to survive a possible apocalypse. Strong told Beck that "we'll go back to the segue of the survivalist attitude," that people could "lose that faith and confidence within the various politicians and the areas that surround them. They end up developing their own infrastructure, their own means to survive, to basically fend for themselves."

This kind of ominous foreshadowing is all too normalized in the current right-wing conspira-sphere—and not just through Glenn Beck. Commercials for "survivalist seeds" and related products don't underwrite only Beck; they host like the even more out-there Alex Jones and the politically incorrect Michael Savage. The proprietor of Survivalistseeds.com—a man named Big John Lipscomb, who claims to have lived in a straw house in Montana with no electricity or running water for the past eight years—told the *Kansas City Star* that he'd sold a couple of million dollars' worth of the seeds. And Big Daddy Lipscomb and Glenn Beck weren't the only ones cashing in on the latest wave of survivalism.

Consider James Wesley Rawles, the so-called survivalist guru who gained credence when some of his warnings of an economic meltdown came true in 2008. A former U.S. Army intelligence captain who claims he quit the military because Bill Clinton became commander-in-chief in 1993, Rawles touches all the right bases; he's a Christian fundamentalist and strict Constitutionalist who blogs from an undisclosed location (although it doesn't take Holmesian sleuthing to find his small town in northern Idaho), and in 2009 his book *Patriots: A Novel of Survival in the Coming Collapse* was a best seller that led to a new two-book deal. He advises people to buy farmland and then load up on tools, silver, and gold. "I encourage my readers to avoid trouble, most importantly via relocation to safe areas where trouble is unlikely to visit," Rawles writes. "But there may come an unavoidable day when you have to make a stand to defend your own family or your neighbors."

It was at the loudest peak of this steady background hum of the apocalypse that the Tea Party and all the related movements were born, which may explain why one hundred Tea Partiers in Nashville take an hour out from a busy weekend to ogle expensive gear from the Bass Pro Shops, even if it might be useful only in the next blizzard.

Useful or not, the man's question about *The One Second After* and the electromagnetic pulse touches off a rapid-fire flurry of questions and answers in the hotel meeting room.

"I want that gentleman in the front to know that you can harden things against a blast," a woman says from the back. "You can use an old microwave as a barrier cage against an electronic pulse . . ."

"But you have to get in there"—the microwave—"all the time," a man responds. Another woman nearby sounds equally perplexed.

"What are you talking about—an EMP attack?" she asks. "A terrorist will do something?" This anxious back-and-forth went on for a minute or so, until finally the discussion leader Walter Fitzgerald waded in to break it up.

"We're just trying to keep it basic with what would happen with Mother Nature—we're not trying to scare you with a terrorist attack," he says. "You can look up that stuff and I imagine there'll be more detail."

It is an instructive moment: with the anxious chatter in that room in Nashville about the electromagnetic pulse and the end of modern civilization and how to prepare for it, you feel as if you've just watched a history of the entire movement condensed into ninety seconds—a fearful proclamation about a man-made calamity uttered in a room full of intelligent but anxious people, amplifying fear as the conversation builds. After the panel ends, you wander over and talk to the man who asked the question about the EMP attack. He says his name is Jost Nickelsberg, and he used to be the mayor of Rensselaerville, a small town not far from Albany, New York, where he worked for a securities firm. Now he's living on his farm there with his fifteen cars, and he's wondering which ones might work in the event of an end-of-the-world-style attack. "I have grandkids now—but you can't sit in the sidelines," he says of his presence here at the Tea Party confab in Nashville. "There are some very unsettling things going on here. The leaders in Iran remind me of some of the worst people in our history."

Of course, other people here were saying the same kind of thing about Barack Obama. After all, you can't have The End of the World as We Know It without an Antichrist, and for some people the charismatic new president and his Nobel Peace Prize matches their interpretation of the great prophecies. Now that the Tea Party movement had arrived and was having its big media moment in Nashville, flocks of vultures were circling about—and if they weren't going after your wallet, they were going after your mortal soul. For all the talk that the Tea Party was a new kind of conservative movement—more libertarian, free from influence by the Christian right—it was clear in Nashville that the televangelist types saw in the Obama backlash an opportunity to be born yet again.

Indeed, two of the key figures at the Tea Party gathering were fiery leaders of the Christian right. Roy Moore, a former chief justice of the Alabama Supreme Court who'd been ousted for refusing to take down a monument to the Ten Commandments, told the convention that Obama "has ignored our history and our heritage, arrogantly declaring to the world that we are no longer a Christian nation." His rhetoric would have shocked people a year earlier but now sounded numbingly familiar; although Moore was supposed to be back in Alabama running for governor, he stuck around for the entire weekend, selling and signing copies of his book. Meanwhile, Texas pastor Rick Scarborough—who was ascending to the altar of the late Jerry Falwell as the nation's top practitioner of Judeo-Christian realpolitik—took to the floor of the Nashville confab for a prayer session laden with gay-bashing remarks; three attendees reportedly walked out—according to the *Washington Post*—but most applauded.

On the final morning of the convention, you learn that Scarborough and several ministers are having a strategy session far away from the main room, and so just after the appointed hour you find the small conference table where the Texas minister, a wide, balding ex–college football player, is holding court as a dozen or so followers munch on pastries. Their audacious goal is to get Scarborough's list of seven thousand "Patriot pastors" to somehow coordinate their efforts to stop what is seen as Obama's socialistic agenda. Another minster from here in Tennessee speaks:

"We've been told that unless you come across as kahnd"—kind—"you're not of God," he says. "I remind you that Elijah and John the Baptist didn't always come across as kahnd. Jesus—when he applied the whip to the money changers—didn't come across as kahnd. We should strive to be peaceful and strive to come across as kahnd but there is a time to stand up and say enough is enough!" A man across the table agrees, noting that some had asked Jesus if he were Elijah, but no one asked if he were Mother Teresa.

Eventually, Scarborough—hoarse from a cold, occasionally stopping to cough up some phlegm—holds court. "This is the same approach to Christianity as China, as Russia, as other lands of tyranny . . . In your sanctuaries, do whatever you want there—but don't let it come out here [into society outside the church] . . . It never stops with the last victory. They will then come into the churches as they did in Russia, and they will send you into court for indoctrinating children. That's what we're marching toward; that's not hearsay. I learned this in my own personal life, you know this in your own life—Satan never gives back ground that he's captured." You are still pondering just what exactly America's leading "Christocrat"—his own term—is getting at with all this, and who has said anything about coming into the churches, but now he's already moved on to that weekend's Super Bowl.

"How do you raise holy children today? During the Super Bowl you're going to see fifteen to twenty erectile dysfunction ads. How do you explain that to a ten-year-old child? The agenda is to sexualize these children because you have a bunch of fresh-faced hippies running this country who wanted free love everywhere—now they're riddled with disease and they want you to pay for it. This whole AIDS business is still primarily a homosexual-driven disease and for all these years and all the talk and all the billions, we're discovering that God will not be mocked."

For Scarborough and the others in the room it seemed as if the

Tea Party was just a new spin on an old culture war that started more than forty years ago, before the first hippie could wipe off the mud from Woodstock. Suddenly, one of the participants questions why the stranger over in the corner is scribbling so many notes, and you are asked to leave, but Scarborough agrees to talk with you later. He insists that the Tea Party is a spiritual movement, that the main thing driving it is "values based on the Ten Commandments." You ask Scarborough whether his fear of Obama's politics is motivated by a belief that the president is in fact the Antichrist.

"There are only two things that I've learned after all these years in the ministry, that there is a God and I'm not him," Scarborough tells you, but then he pauses to add: "If I were talking to another Christian in a private conversation, I might have an opinion on that . . . I do know this, that the reward for unrighteous living is unrighteous rulers, and I believe the rule of Barack Obama has been an unrighteous rule."

The next month, 24 percent of Republicans will say in a survey that Obama is the Antichrist. That headline obscures the deeper reality— which is that when it comes to politics, old-time religion was starting to fade. A *Newsweek* poll released around the time of the first Tea Parties in April 2009, for example, showed a drop in the number of citizens believing America is a Christian nation, and a steep drop since the Reagan era in Americans agreeing that a gay teacher should be fired—exactly the fire-and-brimstone stuff that was Scarborough's stock in trade. It's quite possible that more folks would have walked out on Scarborough's antihomosexual preaching had more than a couple of the convention-eers been under the age of fifty. But the economic apocalypse and the election of a newfangled, dark-skinned president who was so popular in secular places like Europe gave power to that new fundamentalist sales pitch that the Antichrist now walked among us.

Radical as this theory was, it was nothing new. In July 2009, WorldNetDaily—the same widely read Web outfit whose publisher, Joseph Farah, lectured the Tea Party convention on the subject of Obama's birth certificate—published an article entitled "Did Jesus actually reveal name of the 'antichrist'? Viral video makes Hebrew word connection to latest White House occupant." This weird article jumps through various hoops to find various quotes from the Bible about Satan and then Hebrew translations to end up with something that sounds like "Baraq Ubamah." The whacked-out WorldNetDaily article is now one of the 419,000 hits on Google for "Obama is the Antichrist." Obama's Antichrist-like-ness inspired various emails and the bizarre, unsupported accusation by obscure former *Saturday Night Live* cast member Victoria Jackson that the president "bears traits that resemble the Antichrist." Others even posted videos comparing Obama to the fictional Nicolae Carpathia in the 63-million-selling apocalyptic Left Behind novels of Tim LaHaye—Carpathia being a charismatic young politician who gains global power after one particularly good speech. LaHaye even had to publically deny to his huge fan base that Obama was the Antichrist, particularly after a strange 2008 campaign ad by John McCain that called his rival "The One" and seemed to be implying exactly what LaHaye denied.

IN THE WAKE of Obama's ascension—to the White House, that is—it seems as though the boundaries between these various movements of survivalism, religious fundamentalism, far-right politics, and outbreaks of raw hucksterism began to melt away. If there was a place where it all blurred together, it may have been in the entrepreneurial odyssey of one Brandon Vallorani. Vallorani is that uniquely American creation—a Christian entrepreneur. In the early half of the 2000s, Vallorani—father of six, active in his Grace Presbyterian Church in Georgia, with an MBA from the Benedictine Thomas More College—had one of the better gigs in that unusual career track, as chief operating officer of the outfit that was building an impressive Creation Museum in the Kentucky suburbs of Cincinnati.

But this heavenly job posting—Vallorani was reportedly on track to make well over $100,000 in 2004 after earning $90,344 in the first nine months of the year—didn't last forever. There was ugly infighting over both the science and the money, especially the money, and Vallorani was reportedly ousted from his job at the 70,000-square-foot Creation Museum, where adults pay $21.95 to see exhibits of humans walking the earth with dinosaurs, including a triceratops and a stegosaurus striding atop a scale model of Noah's Ark.

Like the ark, Vallorani made a safe landing, launching a business venture with a more political bent called Patriot Depot. Coincidentally or not, Patriot Depot and Barack Obama rose in tandem, starting in 2007. By the time that Obama became the Democratic nominee the following year, Vallorani's company had mastered the style of technology needed to bash the future president and lure customers to Patriot Depot at the same time.

That mid-tech tactic was email. Journalist Keith Thompson, writing for the Huffington Post, decided to trace the origin of the forwarded emails he kept getting with headings like "SEE OBAMA'S KENYAN BIRTH CERTIFICATE"; Thompson was amazed to learn how many traced back to Vallorani and his Patriot Depot. It turned out the company blasted out as many as 100,000 emails a day—funny-for-right-wingers stuff like "The Ten Commandments According to Obama." (Much of the material had a Christian bent.) Based on his interviews with company officials, Thompson estimated that the firm was making on the order of $3.5 million annually, including sales of roughly 100,000 anti-Obama bumper stickers that read, "Keep the 'change'!" In 2010, some of the items for sale at the Patriot Depot included bumper stickers hailing the acronym Obama as "One Big A [a picture of a Democratic donkey where two S's might go] Mistake, America" and a book *Born to Lie: From the Birth Certificate to Health Care*, conveniently next to a *Pictorial History of George Washington*. There is free shipping on orders over $100—more proof that not everyone was hurting in the Great Recession.

In fact, Patriot Depot was at the vanguard of a new industrial sector in America, the anti-Obama-bumper-sticker complex. This was driven home in early 2010 when a poll commissioned by the liberal Web site Daily Kos of more than two thousand self-identified Republicans showed that 39 percent of them favored the impeachment of President Obama, while another 29 percent were "not sure." The driving force—if it could be called that—for "the impeachment of Barack Hussein Obama" was a Web site operated by a longtime GOP muckcrawler named Floyd Brown, most famous as the small-time operative who did the famous 1988 racially tinged "Willie Horton" ad against Michael Dukakis. But the Obama impeachment drive posed one major obstacle even for a veteran like Brown: even the haters couldn't come up with a specific "high crime" or "misdemeanor"—the best that Brown could offer on his impeachment Web site was a quote from a radio host that Obama "seems to have, it seems to me, some malevolence toward this country." But a growing orbit of anti-Obama Web sites—which included ImpeachObamashirt.net and the Anti-Obama Super Store as well as ImpeachObamastuff.org, a subsidiary of Big Woody Productions—did share something, and that was "cool stuff," for a price, plus shipping and handling.

At the Tea Party Convention in Nashville, all of these old-school types—the DVD-and-jewelry hawkers, the televangelists, the political pros, and the newly arrived profiteers—mingled with the marks, the six hundred or so cash attendees, who swelled to over one thousand when Palin spoke on Saturday night. Many of the attendees were pretty much who they said they were—salt-of-the-earth folks, upper-middle-class (as virtually mandated by the admission price) retirees, small entrepreneurs, or homemakers, conservatively well-dressed but not stylish. They were almost all over fifty, almost all white, but their political views were not as monochromatic as some portrayed. A few minutes after the "emergency preparedness" session, you stay in the same room to hear Lori Christenson of Evergreen, Colorado, give a talk about how she'd founded a large Tea Party group there.

Christenson is fiftyish, with short wavy black hair in the style of TV's "Maude," and looked a little New Yorkish, with big brows and a bigger smile that she flashed with good humor and that she alternately turned on herself and like a laser beam against "Barry" from Hawaii, the same state where she grew up a few years earlier than Obama. She certainly had the power to smash stereotypes about the Tea Party, being a former corporate planner whose presentation on how she used Meetup.com and other social networking tools to turn out more than one hundred people for her meetings was slickly produced. A political neophyte, she said she and her CPA husband found themselves alarmed by the big-spending stimulus package proposed in the early weeks of the Obama administration and showed up for the April 15, 2009, Tea Party rally in Denver, attended, she says, by a crowd of seven thousand. "We felt empowered by all these people surrounding us who had similar values," she says. The Tea Party became her calling in life. Christenson and another leader of her Evergreen/Conifer Tea Party, Kathy Baker, had asked for and received donations from the rank and file to cover the high price of the Nashville junket.

But now that she was here, she felt a tad out of sorts among the old-line, Reagan-era-style conservatives who seemed to be leeching on the fresh blood of the Tea Partiers. Earlier that afternoon, while the Clinton-impeachment mavens Judicial Watch were thundering from the big stage, Christenson confided to a reporter from the *Washington Post* that she was uneasy with the right-wing social issues, that in libertarian Colorado her group refused to even discuss them. She told the reporter she was learning in Nashville "that we are very, very different in terms of our beliefs. So now what?" She now voices similar concerns to you, after her "Tea Party 101" presentation, and then, lowering her voice a few more decibels, she says something else a tad surprising: that she would actually like to see some kind of health-care reform, if not exactly the plan that Obama was pushing.

For Christenson, who revels in the details of how she recruits new members, slapping business cards on any car or SUV with a "McCain/Palin" bumper sticker, the movement itself is the message. She is typical of much of the big-ticket-buying public here. Over the course of two days, you spoke with or witnessed many who were like her—the retired doctor who was chartering boats off North Carolina in this stormy economy, the white-haired, lifelong local GOP activist from a rural Virginia mountainside who'd volunteered for Barry Goldwater in 1964, the couple that listened nonstop to local talk radio while they worked their farmland outside of Bakersfield. They had all spent in the low four digits to come here—perhaps to learn some grassroots organizing skills to bring back home but mainly just to be a part of this, something that seemed so much bigger than their atomized existence back home, away from this Nashville nucleus. There would be time for balancing the checkbook, both financially and psychically, at a later date—they believed that to have someone listen to them for a couple of days was priceless. They truly believed Christenson's credo that she voices at her seminar: "The celebrities are the nobodies in this movement."

Then, about twenty-four hours later, Sarah Palin waltzed into the Tea Party like she was walking onto a yacht, and blew that all up.

You see, it's pretty to think the Tea Party is all about Meetup.com and such, but "grassroots" don't sell $349 tickets for a fifty-minute speech. In Nashville, under the big brass chandelier, surrounded by the conventioneers now dolled up in their heartland-Saturday-night-out well-worn blue suits and leopard tops, the featured guest of the National Tea Party Convention had them at "Happy birthday, Ronald Reagan!" (his ninety-ninth, that day). The glamorous ex–half-term Alaska governor had been introduced by a leering Andrew Breitbart, who got a big laugh for saying he'd long "fantasized" about meeting the long-legged Wasillian in person. But to most of America, Palin, her biography, and her shtick needed no introduction.

Everything about Palin's persona—her you-betcha speaking style with random flights into eleventh-grade pep-rally snark, her know-nothing approach to the news media couched as heartland distrust of pointy-headed elites, her sexy moose-dressing right-wing brand of "feminism," and her Christian belief that her unparalleled rise to fame and now fortune was "God's will"—was anathema to more

THE NASHVILLE PREDATORS | 229

than two-thirds of Americans but pure catnip to the 26 percent on the far right. The fact that so much of her nationally televised Tea Party speech—blending the "culture war" that didn't interest some like Lori Christenson with a neoconservative focus on foreign affairs that was irrelevant to the antigovernment faction—was out of tune with the Nashville event mattered little when there was such a gut-level cultural connection. Palin made sure she threw in the one thing the Tea Parties wanted to hear: "This is about the people, and it's bigger than any one king or queen of a tea party." It was the brilliantly crafted opening line of her campaign to become exactly that, queen of a Tea Party, and before the closing music had already faded out she was long gone from her Opryland throne, chants still echoing of "run, Sarah, run."

Logistically, Palin—who survived the 2008 election debacle as America's Top Political Celebrity—couldn't really cash in on her new-found fame until she ditched the thing that was holding her back, her wonky responsibilities in her $125,000-a-year job as Alaska governor. She quit on July Fourth weekend of 2009, and in less than two months she'd signed on with a Washington speakers' bureau to arrange for speeches at $100,000 a pop—in other words, nearly as much money for less than one hour of talking as she earned in an entire year of govern-ing an American state. And then there was the inevitable book deal, which would eventually become the tome *Going Rogue*, for which she was paid an estimated five to seven million dollars.

The announcement that she'd also become a news analyst for the Fox News Channel—in a deal described by the *New York Times* as "lu-crative," including the construction of a television studio in her living room in Wasilla—was merely the whipped cream on the chocolate mousse. ABC News did the math and calculated that in the first ten months after quitting, Palin earned an astronomical $12 million. Just days after Palin resigned as governor, she and her husband, Todd, began construction on a large chateau-like house right next to her already good-sized lake house in Wasilla. "She has expanded her house and turned it into a compound," Rebecca Braun, the editor of the *Alaska*

Budget Report, told the *New York Times*. "She is basically invisible in Alaska but as big a celebrity as Princess Di everywhere else."

That was evident in Nashville from the moment Palin took her seat, as a flock of paying fans crowded up to a rope separating them from the VIP, focusing small digital cameras as if they were at the giant panda exhibit. The demurring queen had no interest in working a rope line either before the event of after, when she and her eight-year-old daughter, Piper, bolted out a side door to dash to Texas, the next stop in this only-in-America odyssey. "The governor is leaving the building," Phillips announced. If she didn't have the $100,000 check in her back pocket literally, she certainly did figuratively. Anthony Shreeve, a former ally who'd had a falling-out with Judson Phillips, told *New York Magazine* that Palin's contract also included $18,000 for a private jet for her and her entourage and even specified what type of airliner (according to later news accounts, a luxurious Hawker 800 or larger for travel to east of the Mississippi). "It was like when a rock star comes to town, the contract was that detailed," said Shreeve.

In that rock-star cameo, Palin revealed that on a certain level she was indeed using the backlash against Obama's presidency in the same way that so many of those in the audience had: as a vehicle for reinvention. But there was also something very different about it. Palin's born-again experience wasn't thrust upon her, but the result of cold—no Alaska pun intended—calculation. She hadn't lost her job, as so many people in the movement had—but rather she quit it when she saw a lucrative opportunity come along. Her radical views on some of the issues that were so important to the Tea Partiers—gun rights, for example—were no doubt genuine, but she also seemed to be both happier and wealthier espousing them in the consequence-free realm of paid speeches and Fox than acting upon them as an elected official. Of course, it was such intense anger over the American political condition that caused everyday people to pay $349 to hear a political speech in the first place.

The irony was that if Palin and some of the others who spoke here in Nashville or who came to the Music City hawking their wares instead spent their time working to solve the problems of citizens, that could be bad for business—now and down the road.

After the ex-governor has left the building, you wander over to the small Tea Party Emporium table, where there's a scrum that's now five or six deep, sturdily coiffed women fondling the tea-bag necklaces while a man in a suit and green tie is handing over his Visa card for the ritual of the swiping. Link is sitting at the table, beaming. You ask him how the weekend went, and there is no mention of Palin or upholding the Constitution or curbing the federal debt. "It's ecumenical," he says. For a split second you think that maybe he's talking about the conservative movement, but then you realize it's just another sales pitch, before this mad Tea Party convention vanishes down the rabbit hole. "It's good for a man or a woman."

Link doesn't want to stop the jewelry hawking, but one of the leopard-skin ladies interrupts with a question.

"Is there going to be a DVD for sale . . . of the speech?"

Link doesn't hesitate.

"I'm sure there will be a DVD—just check the Web site."

CHAPTER NINE

Hugewadsofmoney.com

Huge Wads Of Money From Websites That Work When The
Economy Doesn't! Basically The Worse Things Get . . . The
More Money You'll Make! . . . [I]t wasn't until the economic
crisis began in 2007 that I found a vein of pure gold. As the world
economy came to a screeching halt and the credit markets shut
down, I stumbled upon the most successful formula of my 30
plus [*sic*] in direct marketing, and this is your lucky day, because
I'm about to share with you exactly what that secret is.

From the website Hugewadsofmoney.com, run by the CEO of a
principal advertiser on the Web site GlennBeck.com.

Mary Sisack is not your stereotypical, angry, ripped-off consumer,
nor is she your stereotypical campus academic. An assistant professor
of chemistry at western Pennsylvania's Slippery Rock University, north
by northwest of Pittsburgh, Sisack is a fan of conservative talk radio
and conservative politics—joking there's actually an unlikely cluster of
like-minded thinkers in her small science corner of supposedly liberal
academia. The fifty-something Sisack, who lives in New Castle, Pennsylvania, also found in 2009 that she had come into about five thousand
dollars that she wanted to invest. Her thoughts turned to gold—not

surprising since one year into a global economic meltdown, there was a lot of chatter about a weak U.S. dollar, about further economic collapse, and how the tangible asset of gold could be the only truly safe haven for investors. And most of that chatter was coming from talk radio and cable TV news.

And so it was that Sisack turned on her radio one morning and heard Glenn Beck making a pitch for a seller of gold coins called Goldline International. She had heard some of her other favorite talk hosts—such as Mark Levin—also pitching for Goldline in recent days. "I wanted to buy some gold, and I heard that," Sisack recalled months later. But when she called Goldline—which is based in Santa Monica, California, and employs a large telephone sales staff—it wasn't quite the investment opportunity she expected. She later wrote about her experience on the consumer Web site Ripoff Report. "I can not believe how stupid I was," she wrote. "I thought 'how could I be mislead [*sic*] by Glenn Beck, Fred Thompson"—the ex–Tennessee senator turned radio host—"and Marvin [*sic*] Levin?'"

Here's how.

When Sisack called Goldline, the financial advisor encouraged her to buy Swiss francs, that they "had just become available and were such a good deal." Sisack later came to believe that she was steered toward the Swiss coins because the broker commissions were higher on them; she also noted that the advisor "strongly encouraged" her to buy between $20,000 and $40,000 worth of the coins, although she had told the salesman that she was limited to the $5,000 on hand. She noted in her online Ripoff Report, "I was warned about the gold confiscation (whatever that was)," and she also wrote that she was embarrassed that she'd revealed so much about her own personal finances to the advisor. "But again, how could Glenn Beck mislead me?" she wrote. "They must be reputable."

Indeed, the chemistry professor said she started doing her homework on Goldline only *after* she'd made her $5,000 investment. It was then that Sisack realized that she was paying on the order of a 30 percent commission to Goldline—which was typical for the company's customers, but that meant the commodity price of gold (which had already risen substantially since the start of the twenty-first century) would need to continue to climb sharply before investors like her realized a profit. What's more, Sisack said, her post-purchase Internet research showed she could have purchased the coins for considerably less elsewhere, that while she had paid $318 per Swiss franc, the same coins were available from other companies in the range of $208 to $218. That meant that—by her calculation—the gold coins that she'd just paid $5,000 for from Goldline could have been had for closer to $3,400. She headlined her December 2009 Internet posting "Naïve New Investor Down $1600."

Sisack was just one of millions who heard Glenn Beck touting Goldline International during the early months of the Obama presidency, as the fear of the rapid collapse on Wall Street at the end of 2008 rolled into more sweeping anxieties about government spending and the role of America—and its beleaguered dollar—in the future of the global economy. The increasing talk about gold was nothing new—throughout modern history, this hard-to-find-and-mine precious metal has been horded by investors as a safe harbor both in times of widespread economic or global unrest and as a hedge against runaway inflation of paper money; a prior peak price, for example, came in 1980 after the Soviets invaded Afghanistan and as the United States suffered a "stagflation" crisis. Of course, this also means that gold prices can collapse during stable times of economic growth, which is exactly what happened in the 1980s and much of the 1990s. The 2000s, with global terrorism and rising oil prices even before the crisis of 2008, was already a good time for gold investors—and especially for gold sellers—just as Glenn Beck was becoming a national figure.

And so even before the acceleration of Beck's rise to television fame that came with his move to Fox News in January of 2009, the conservative talk host had been doing regular promo spots for Goldline International on his popular, nationally syndicated radio show, and the Santa Monica–based firm was now a commercial sponsor of his TV gig as well. But there was something else. The weakening of the U.S. dollar and an even more apocalyptic meltdown of the American economy—a central part of the pitch by Goldline and other gold companies—had also become one of Beck's favorite conversation topics in the supposedly non-advertisement segments of his radio show, and an occasional subject of his nightly program on Fox News Channel as well.

One morning in early October 2009—around the time that Mary Sisack was beginning to think about her gold purchase—you are listening to the car radio as Beck is doing what frequently must be done to fill three hours of airtime before racing off to film his TV show, and that is riffing off the breaking news of the day. On this particular morning, there had been a noticeably large spike in gold prices, and Beck returned to his favorite theme, that here was another sign of the looming economic Armageddon. You scribble down a paraphrase of his words upon your return home, which are roughly: *Why is it not a big story when the price of gold shoots up $22 in one hour? You know, I was buying gold back when it was $300 and I believe it was $800 when I started telling you to buy it, and now it's at $1,040, and the way things are going I think this is just the beginning. . . .* Meanwhile, you see that Goldline International is running a banner ad across the top of GlennBeck.com touting its product as "trusted and used by Glenn Beck." And if you visit Goldline's Web site, there is a promotional video for Goldline that Beck himself filmed in his New York office.

It is a tangled web, indeed.

And in fact, the economic patter you heard in Beck's program that morning is just one tiny nugget in a veritable gold rush of such words over the course of 2009, the same year that Beck was elevated to *Time* magazine cover boy of American political punditry. "Tonight, are we facing the end of the almighty dollar? . . ." Beck started in his TV show on October 6, 2009. He went on in his opening monologue to talk about how gold would have been a safe haven against the investment losses that had battered and frightened his many viewers:

You don't have any gold, right? This is you. This is you. This is your savings. How much did you lose if you had any money in your 401(k)? Did you lose, let's say, I don't know, 40 percent of it? So, that's gone. Now, did you know that the dollar has lost nearly 29 percent of its value in the last seven years? Twenty-nine percent. OK, that's gone. Just gone.

Sound like a sales pitch? On this night, Beck invited on his favorite economist, Columbia University adjunct professor David Buckner, who amplified the host's message that runaway inflation was coming and that the little guy was going to get screwed once again.

"Any way to protect yourself?" Beck asked.

"Well, you invest in things that are friendly to inflation."

"Gold." It wasn't a question the way that Beck said it.

"Gold, real estate, and some realm of the world," replied Buckner. "It's kind of a twisted way of saying it."

Over the weeks that followed, Beck continued to double down on gold. On November 12, 2009, he even invited Goldline International CEO Mark Albarian onto his show as a guest, tempered only slightly by a disclaimer that Goldline is a sponsor of the program. Albarian used the platform of Beck's nationally broadcast show to tout gold as a scarce commodity and to say it was "reasonable" to think that gold could rise to $2,000 to $2,500 an ounce in an undefined "future," or in the range of double what it was then currently selling for. Beck used this as a jumping-off point for a monologue on one his favorite themes, which is the rise of Nazi Germany:

You know, I've said this for over, what, maybe two years. You have to think like a German Jew, 1934. Maybe 1931. You have to see that what we're doing here doesn't make any sense and it's been done before. So what do they do? People had food, diamonds, gold, artwork, anything of value that people would say, oh, you know what, things are going to change. So I'll be able to trade in gold or whatever.

On his November 23, 2009 show, Beck went back again to the theme of a looming economic meltdown and recommended to his listeners what could just as well be a mantra of the right-wing movement in this new decade: "the 3 G system" of "God, Gold, and Guns." Meanwhile, the lines between the Beck program and Goldline were so muddled and blurred that it was hard to know where one ended and one began. In that video that Beck had filmed for Goldline, he waxes nostalgically—just as he does on his TV and radio programs—about the Founding Fathers. "If you're like our Founding Fathers, Thomas Jefferson and John Adams, then you just know that what's on the horizon is temporary and this too shall pass," Beck says into the camera, now not the loud "Morning Zoo" jock but the earnest, soft-spoken, reassuring Beck. "Here's the deal: Call Goldline, study it out, pray on it." Goldline was even the chief sponsor of Beck's summer of 2009 "Common Sense Comedy Tour."

And there was something else that was a little blurry: Goldline referred to Beck as "a paid spokesman," a description that—given his frequent editorial comments about the economy and gold—set off ethical bells and whistles. By mid-December, Beck was instead a "radio sponsor," but the exact nature of the relationship between the TV star and the gold peddlers was buried as deep as a coin-laden Caribbean treasure chest.

Now, about Mary Sisack, the college professor from western Pennsylvania: she learned one more thing about her experience with Goldline International, which was that going to a consumer board like the Ripoff Report can bring results. She says she'd almost forgotten about her posting on the consumer site when an official from Goldline—not the original investment advisor—called her up and offered to buy the coins back. Others have told similar stories suggesting that Goldline is aggressive, often in a positive way, about responding to public complaints about the way the firm does business. That policy is reflected in a top rating from the Better Business Bureau, which focuses on dispute resolution. What's more, Goldline International engaged the founder of the Ripoff Report, Ed Magedson, to study its complaint resolutions, and Magedson gave a positive report, writing, "Rip-off Report feels Goldline has learned from all those who have complained . . . and they even seemed to be thankful for those who have brought problems to their attention."

But in May 2010, a liberal congressman from New York, Representative Anthony Weiner, announced that his office had conducted an investigation of Goldline International and that its initial findings were troubling. The Democrat told a news conference that his staff found evidence of both high-pressure tactics by Goldline and charging substantially more for gold coins than its competitors did. Specifically, he reported that the coins typically cost 90 percent more than the melt value—that is, the price of the gold by weight—and sometimes as much as 208 percent. Weiner sent letters to the Federal Trade Commission and the U.S. Securities and Exchange Commission requesting further action. And he singled out Beck and his aggressive sales pitches and monologues. "Commentators like Glenn Beck who are shilling for Goldline," the congressman said, "are either the worst financial advisors around or knowingly lying to their loyal viewers." However, Beck's enthusiastic shilling for Goldline does not mean he knows anything about the firm's alleged high-pressure tactics or overcharging; indeed, there's no evidence that he's aware of the firm's day-to-day business practices.

The problem that Weiner and financial experts have with Goldline and some of its competitors isn't the area of complaint resolution, but rather the core notion that Beck has pitched for so many months: that gold coins are a life-saving investment. There are two issues with this thinking. First, many experts seriously doubt that it is "reasonable"—in the words of the Goldline CEO—to expect that the price of gold is going to double in the coming years, even though that's the necessary level of appreciation for coin purchasers to see any kind of return on their investment once such high commissions are taken into account. In fact, just two short days before Beck's gold-hyping TV presentation about "the end of the almighty dollar," on October 4, 2009, the headline in the *Wall Street Journal* blared: "Gold is Still a Lousy Investment." Personal finance writer Dave Kansas noted that gold had already enjoyed a great run over five years; that with the economy so beaten down, inflation wasn't a problem in the short term; and that investors concerned about the end of "the almighty dollar" would be better served to put their money into overseas businesses.

More importantly, investment experts say there are simply better ways to buy gold than in the kinds of coins that Goldline offers—such as buying gold bullion through a firm or purchasing a gold fund that's traded on Wall Street. Either of these options does a better job of tracking gold prices without the commissions charged for gold coins. "If you want to buy gold because you're concerned about paper currency, which is very reasonable, I suggest you buy gold," the MSNBC financial pundit Dylan Ratigan said during an on-air diatribe. "Just don't do it with the extra subsidy that Goldline is delivering to Glenn Beck for his fearmongering, which is 90 percent more than you could buy the exact same gold if you just went to the financial markets. . . ." (The line about "gold confiscation" the salesman mentioned to Sisack is a reference to Franklin Roosevelt's 1933 drive to confiscate gold bullion as he propped up failing banks—a scenario that experts cannot foresee happening today but is typically part of the pitch by Goldline and its rivals.) A former Goldline sales agent named David Weishaar posted on the Ripoff Report that he left the company—along with several other brokers—in 2006 because "their prices were way too high for my clients to achieve a profit on their investments in a reasonable, timely way." (Weishaar, who now works for a rival company, declined to elaborate when reached by phone.)

Indeed, Mary Sisack was not the only unhappy customer in her dealings with Goldline after hearing an endorsement from Glenn Beck during those politically amped-up early months of the Obama era. In March of 2009, a customer who gave his name as "George from Santa Clarita," California, posted on the Ripoff Report that he watched Beck's video about Goldline and decided to simply request a brochure from the company. He was called by a Goldline rep two days later who "encouraged me to go ahead and make the purchase because the prices were going up rapidly and I would lose money if I waited for the brochure." The woman talked the Californian into buying $10,000 worth of English gold sovereigns, but there were credit-card issues that dragged out the order and gave George enough time to change his mind—as he calculated the markup for the coins was about 40 percent over the price of spot gold—and cancel.

Still, he wrote that he was shaken by the experience. "I am very disappointed in Glenn Beck for recommending Goldline," he wrote. "Why would I want to buy something for 40 percent more than it's worth and hope that it goes up 50 percent just so I can make $1,000 on a $10,000 purchase over maybe 3 years from now? I'm better off either with a CD or buying real estate."

This was the Glenn Beck behind the magazine cover stories, but the media glazed right over it. In the first phase of the Obama presidency, so much attention was lavished on the political motivations of the Russ Murphys or the Celia Hydes or the Lori Christensons of the new landscape, of what inspired their opposition to health-care reform or to immigration from Mexico, but only a few people were seeing what Beck and a few of his cronies were seeing across America: a surge in cash customers. The interplay between Beck's growing fan base—which seethed with anger over the economy and recoiled with fear at immigration and the changing face of America—and Beck's manipulation of those emotions for the sake of entertainment and commerce was dynamic and arguably explosive. The outrageous things that Beck said to keep his radio listeners and his TV viewers coming back—about the collapse of the dollar or President Obama's alleged contempt for white people or the need to stockpile food for a crisis—were often just outbursts of amusement, but they stayed with much of his audience, giving a shape and a direction to the backlash against Obama's presidency that at times was much more than Beck could control.

The nation had never seen anything like this—Beck was having an oversized influence on the national conversation, but his core motivations seemed not so much to better America's condition as to improve his own bottom line. Reflecting his rise as an entrepreneur, Beck even changed the name of his business venture at the dawn of the 2010s from Mercury Radio Arts to Glenn Beck, Inc.

The Goldline flap, which got some attention at the end of 2009, especially after Jon Stewart joked about it on *The Daily Show*, was just one noisy cog in an ever-growing messy web of often-overlapping business ventures—the obscure startup companies with their high-pressure pitches sponsoring the radio show and the TV program. That was the same show where Beck then relentlessly hyped his books, his movie-theater events, his "American Revival," and the comedy tours that were also backed by a TV sponsor. And then of course there was the 9-12 Project groups that staged political marches or rallies—events that then sometimes promoted books that were written—at least partially, perhaps—by Glenn Beck. With all these interconnected pieces, the world of politics—the thing that made Beck such a national icon during the town hall summer and into the Tea Party fall—could seem almost like an afterthought. Most importantly, Beck's apocalyptic worldview was the glue that bound the whole enterprise together, this brand-new hybrid that the media megastar should have more accurately called "the fusion of entertainment, enlightenment, and commerce." And there was a not-so-secret ingredient that made the entire recipe work:

Fear.

It was almost as if Beck was the bizarro-world version of Franklin Roosevelt, who in an earlier economic meltdown in 1933 had not only railed against "fear itself" but spoke of "nameless, unreasoning, unjustified terror which paralyzes needed efforts to convert retreat into advance." But in 2010, Glenn Beck Incorporated thrived on "nameless, unreasoning, unjustified terror," regardless of whether it helped to drive the body politic in the opposite direction of where FDR guided the "Greatest Generation." This was the thing that really placed Beck on a whole different level from even the Hitler-invoking Representative Paul Broun or the loose-talking Sarah Palin or the marketers and televangelists who worked the edges of the Tea Party convention—his willingness to touch the scariest parts of the American psyche, the deepest fears of citizens that often transcended mere politics. Beck was constantly straining to find the outer limits, exploring both the inner terrors of his audience and their hopes for restoration and a common purpose. And then he was brazen in taking hold of his public and using it to sell them things, with little care over the side effects.

The recession-simmered fear that Beck stirred up with his McCarthy-style allegations of Commies in the Obama White House was all boiling in the same giant pot with his relentless hyping of gold coins and with his taped promos for $249.99 "food-emergency kits" invoking 9/11 and his projections of a far greater American Apocalypto, and when you ladle some out, it all kind of tastes like the same rancid batch of scared-chicken stew. There's been far too much corruption in U.S. politics to get all misty-eyed about the notion of public service, but at least when the political agenda was set by elected officials there was some pretext of policy over profit; that has disappeared in a new era of entertainment-driven politics, of amusing ourselves to death exactly as the academic Neil Postman had predicted.

The perpetually self-educated Beck had stumbled—by decades of trial and error behind a microphone—onto the same thing that academics were working hard to confirm in the early twenty-first century, which is that fear is the greatest salesman, whether the product is freeze-dried food-emergency kits or a political ideology, or both. The newish field of neuromarketing looks closely at the basic level of brain stimulation from certain types of advertising; what top marketing expert Martin Lindstrom learned by studying the brain waves of more than two thousand people exposed to commercials was that fear moves product even better than sex, because of the way in which a well-instilled message of fear can stimulate the amygdala, the most primal area of the brain.

But experts also found that consumers can be motivated by something else, and that is religion, or the sense that in a world of great dangers they are part of a shared community of salvation. For four hours on most weekdays, Beck offers up a vision of an America created by divine right, under constant threat from The Other who would destroy it. There isn't a research laboratory in the world that could craft a better formula of fear and salvation for selling the Glenn Beck brand to America.

"There's a baseline level of fear in this country—and they're just plucking the strings," says David Altheide, a professor of social justice and inquiry at Arizona State University and the author of *Creating Fear: News and the Construction of a Crisis*, who sees Beck as a master manipulator of that emotion. He says the successful formula, straight from the American tradition of the tent revival, needs to offer both frightening consequences and a path to salvation, which could be a cause or might just be a consumer product. Beck's followers believe they have signed on for something larger than themselves. "They're doing something to save their country and doing something to engage their own identity," Altheide says of these followers. "That's powerful stuff."

Give Beck credit for one more thing: he is amazingly candid about his ultimate goals—it's just that his large community of fans is not paying close attention, or perhaps it doesn't care. "I'm a capitalist. I dig money," he told the *Wall Street Journal*'s James Taranto in early 2010. "But I'm not in it for the money."

Ironically, Beck's ceaseless gold-hyping in many ways mimics the lesser-known and more fringe-leaning radio host who has accused Beck of stealing his paranoid political style: Alex Jones. Indeed, the radio network—Genesis Communications—that broadcasts Jones and his 9/11 and "Camp FEMA" conspiracy theories from coast to coast is owned by a rival gold-coin merchant, Ted Anderson of Midas Resources, who frequently appears on Jones's radio show to talk about his products, and even, according to the *Texas Observer*, offers special deals for Jones listeners. Indeed, under the radar, Jones's small media empire is underwritten by the same bizarre assortment of survivalist-oriented products that also fuels the better-known Beck.

But Glenn Beck and Alex Jones are just the conduits for the gold rush and for other apocalyptic entrepreneurs making millions off of such panic. This is the bizarre story of Bill Heid of Thomson, Illinois, a man who has built a multimillion-dollar enterprise riding piggyback on Beck's popularity, with the same seamless appeal to fear.

NOT THAT LONG ago, Bill Heid made close to $5 million from selling a very different kind of fear—fear of getting fat. In the early 2000s, Heid ran a company called AVS Marketing. Operating from Main Street in the small town of Thomson—which is hard against the Mississippi River straight west from Chicago, the "Melon Capital of the World," population 559—Heid and his company placed ads in metro newspapers from coast to coast touting something called "The Himalayan Diet Breakthrough."

Readers flipping through the pages of the *Cleveland Plain Dealer* or the *San Francisco Chronicle* encountered an ad with a claim that was truly remarkable. These print advertisements showed grainy before-and-after pictures of women such as "Sara DuBerrier, Fashion Model" (who on Google has only one hit—which is the eventual federal complaint against the AVS ad). "New High Speed Diet Formula Used By Top Fashion Models Produces an Extremely Fast Weight Loss!" the ad announces in large type, including the aforementioned "Sara DuBerrier," who claims to have lost thirty-seven pounds in eight weeks without diet or exercising. How is this possible? AVS Marketing claimed its product was "a dietary supplement containing Nepalese Mineral Pitch, 'a paste-like material' that 'oozes out of the cliff face cracks in the summer season' in the Himalayas." The cheesy AVS Marketing newspaper ads were the kind of things that most readers see and ask: Who buys this stuff?

You'd be surprised. The Federal Trade Commission alleged that Heid and his AVS Marketing had sold some $4.9 million of the product by the time its agents started investigating "The Himalayan Diet Breakthrough" under its Operation Big Fat Lie, a crackdown on diet scams. But when the FTC finally reached a settlement with Heid's company some nine months after filing regulatory charges in October 2004, the agency agreed to a $400,000 payment because the remaining proceeds from "The Himalayan Diet Breakthrough" were nowhere to be found. Under the agreement that was signed by a federal judge on June 13, 2005, the feds claimed they would go after the rest of the $4.9 million— if the money could ever be located. Heid—who along with AVS Marketing did not acknowledge any wrongdoing—was also barred, according to the FTC regulators, "from making false or unsubstantiated claims about weight-loss products or other products in the future."

But five days before the judge signed the order against Heid and AVS Marketing, the Illinois man had already registered a brand-new company: Solutions from Science, Inc. (Heid did not return several phone calls seeking to learn more about the company.) The difference was that Heid's new venture wasn't seeking solutions to mundane problems like obesity, but rather to market products that would help customers cope with disasters, natural but also man-made, such as civil disorder or even a collapse of American society. And there was another important difference from Heid's past venture: with print newspapers experiencing accelerating losses in readership, when it came time to place advertising, Solutions from Science looked to the growing media of talk radio and the Internet—particularly sites with a gloomy political outlook.

Heid's new business took some time to incubate—there is a scant paper trail of what the company was up to in its first couple of years— but its profile was raised dramatically around the time of the worldwide economic crisis in the fall of 2008. By the following year, ads for Solutions from Science's first major product, the Survival Seed Bank, began popping up locally during *The Glenn Beck Program* on stations such as KTLK in Minnesota; on Web sites such as WorldNetDaily, the conservative online news source run by the well-known birther Joseph Farah; and most prominently with banner ads on GlennBeck.com, which Beck himself claims gets "millions" of monthly visitors (although the available stats, not always the most reliable, suggest a smaller but still substantial figure of 750,000). In 2010, *Forbes* magazine estimated that Beck makes some $4 million a year from his Web site—a sizable chunk of which comes from advertisers, and specifically from Bill Heid and Solutions from Science.

The online ad for the Survival Seed Bank—written in the same over-the-top fashion as the earlier promos for "The Himalayan Diet Breakthrough"—tells buyers that a $149.99 package of twenty-two varieties of not-genetically-modified heirloom seeds will grow an acre-sized garden that could produce thousands of pounds of food in the event of a catastrophe. The ad also notes that the seeds for products like "Giant Nobel Spinach" and "French Breakfast Radish" come in an "Indestructible" canister that "Can Be Buried to Avoid Confiscation." The ad copy includes some language that could have easily been borrowed from one of Beck's own monologues:

> You don't have to be an Old Testament prophet to see what's going on all around us. A belligerent lower class demanding handouts. A rapidly diminishing middle class crippled by police state bureaucracy. An aloof, ruling elite that has introduced us to an emerging totalitarianism which seeks control over every aspect of our lives.

Of course, some experts question whether the seeds that Heid and his Solutions from Science are peddling are really that special or worth $149.99. The same kinds of questions have been raised about the other major project that Solutions from Science promotes on GlennBeck.com, an "'Amazing' Solar Generator" that "Is Like Having A Secret Power

Plant Hidden In Your Home," an 1,800-watt solar generator that Solutions from Science sells for $1,597, plus a $95 shipping charge. Critics say the amount of power generated by this device could run a household appliance such as a freezer for a short period of time, but 1,800 watts is not nearly enough to power an entire house, as the ad implies. (The ad also shows a line of police in riot gear on a burning city street, noting that "Civil Unrest Might Even Cut Your Power.")

Other products that Solutions from Science has offered are darker than solar generators, pardon the pun. For a while, Solutions from Science was peddling for $49.95 (plus $9.95 for shipping) a book called *Understanding and Surviving Martial Law: How to Survive and Even Prosper During the Coming Police State*, said to have been written by "Sam Adams." The site for the book—which came with the controversial DVD called *Camp FEMA*, which promotes the underground rumors of already constructed concentration camps in America—was no longer up and running by the winter months of 2010. Here is part of Heid's over-the-top sales pitch: "Most Americans are 'sheeple' who truly display a herd mentality. Worst yet, most will do nothing and hope that evil will simply go away. (Most Jews in Germany did the same thing.)"

Some customers have not been satisfied with what they've received for their money from Solutions from Science. One who said he spent $29.95 plus $5 in shipping to purchase a book called *Survival Stockpiling* later complained to the Ripoff Report: "It is nothing more than a phamphlet [sic] that basicly [sic] tells you to buy lots of food, learn about firearms, grow a garden, learn how to can things. But rather than actually telling you how to do these things it says you can learn them from many online sources." Pete from St. Petersburg, Florida, reported similar problems when he paid $29.95 (plus $7.95 shipping and handling) for *The Debtors Secret Weapon*. "These folks are making credit remediation offers that are over the top of credibility," the customer wrote, adding that he was offered only a food survival kit on store credit to honor the money-back guarantee.

These disappointed customers might have been less likely to buy in the first place if they had seen another Web site operated by Heid—the one called Hugewadsofmoney.com. It is here that this major sponsor of GlennBeck.com—in searching for marketing affiliate partners—reveals his plans for making, well, huge wads of money off the economic crisis and customers' fears of a societal breakdown. If the inflammatory words are not enough—"Basically the Worse Things Get . . . The More Money You'll Make!"—there is the picture at the top of a suited man at a podium covered with a huge wad of money, naturally, fanning himself with $100 bills, in front of an array of headlines like "137,000 Jobs Vanish."

"It doesn't matter whether you share the same world view as these customers or not . . . but you'd be a fool to ignore the birth of a massive new industry right before our eyes!" writes Heid, who also mentions his partnership with the late direct-mail legend Gary Halbert, who served prison time in the early 1980s on a mail fraud conviction related to his marketing activities. "And the worse things get, the better you'll do, because many consumers are just now becoming aware of their dependence on a way of life which may be gone forever and which will require a dramatic process of education and preparation." By March 2010, Heid's enterprise was generating enough revenue to make a commercial for his Survivalist Seed Bank that aired on Beck's national TV show on FNC.

It's not clear whether Glenn Beck "share[s] the same world view" as these customers or not, at least personally, but professionally, the end-of-the-world-as-we-know-it ad copy of his Internet sponsor Bill Heid dovetails perfectly with Beck's frequent warnings of a U.S. society on the brink of collapse. In moving his act to the bigger platform of national television, Beck brought with him the radio practice of the "live read," the nearly seamless segue from editorial content to a paid commercial spot, refined to an art. It's one thing when a guy on a local sports station makes a smooth transition from why the Eagles needed to trade Donovan McNabb to why you should visit your local Toyota dealer. But Beck was essentially doing a "live read" on the national political debate. Was his February 2009 TV show in which he asked experts to "think the unthinkable" driven by a political commentator's sincere belief that America faced looming food and electricity shortages? Or was Beck motivated by his sponsors like Goldline International, Solutions from Science, and Food Insurance, the freeze-dried food peddler for whom Beck taped a promotional video that alludes to the 9/11 attacks?

Interestingly, as Beck's national political clout grew, his advertising base—even on the profitable confines of the Fox News Channel—began to shrink, with well-established and reputable national brands like Wal-Mart and Bank of America removing their commercials from his TV show. A good deal of this was the result of a highly focused liberal pressure campaign—launched after Beck's most controversial statement on Obama's supposed hatred of white people—under the auspices of Color of Change, a group that was tied to Obama's special advisor on green jobs, aide Van Jones. It was that tie, progressives alleged, that was the real reason Beck focused a series of McCarthy-style broadcasts on past statements by Jones. Beck scored a major public relations triumph when he struck pay dirt with the discovery that Jones had once signed a petition alleging the U.S. government had advance knowledge of the 9/11 attacks. Jones's September 2009 resignation was proof to the mainstream media of Beck's growing clout.

Despite the Van Jones victory, the damage had been done with the loss of Beck's bigger advertisers after his "hatred of white people" remark. What remained when these name brands parted with Beck was an odd assortment of smaller companies that all seemed to be selling a certain kind of fear, even if it was not always apocalyptic. It was a scary world out there—in addition to the possible collapse of the United States, there were identity thieves and other technological risks, such as losing all your computer files. The other common bond was Beck's silky transition from political anger to his calm reassurance that these products will keep you safe—even though most of Beck's remaining sponsors are companies that spend millions on radio and TV promotion but have delivered mixed results with their actual products.

If you listen to Beck's radio show for even a short period of time, you will probably hear him lavishing praise on his sponsor Lifelock, an identity-theft protection service. Not surprisingly, Beck doesn't inform his listeners that Lifelock has been panned by some reviewers who say what the company really offers—paying home workers to place "fraud alerts" in customers' names with credit agencies that would make it harder, in some situations, for an identity thief to obtain credit—isn't worth the $10-a-month fee. He also doesn't tell people that the firm has been sued both by unhappy customers and by the credit agency Experian, which won a major ruling in 2009 suggesting that Lifelock's core business practice was a violation of public policy. And there is no mention that a co-founder of Lifelock resigned in 2007 when a newspaper revealed his history of bankruptcies as well as a Federal Trade Commission investigation into his previous company.

In other commercials for Lifelock, the firm's current CEO, Todd Davis, gives out his real Social Security number as supposed proof that his service can stop anyone from using it, but doesn't reveal that a Texas man once successfully used that broadcast information to fraudulently obtain a $500 loan, one of thirteen such cases discovered by the *Phoenix New Times*. Davis also acknowledged in 2008 that 105 Lifelock customers had been victims of identity theft; although the company also touts a $1 million guarantee, it's not spelled out in the commercials that the money applies only to the costs associated with restoring credit and does not cover any actual theft losses. In March 2010, Lifelock finally agreed to pay $12 million to settle claims by both the FTC and some thirty-five states that it had overstated the value of its service. FTC chairman Jon Leibowitz said "the protection it [Lifelock] actually provided left enough holes that you could drive a truck through."

Another company that Beck frequently flogs on his radio show—and which advertises on his Web site—is Carbonite, the online file-backup service for home or office PCs. "I own a small business and we protect our files with Carbonite," notes Beck in an online ad. "You can't beat the value or peace of mind." But here, as with Lifelock, the company has garnered mixed product reviews for what the heavily advertised service actually does. The Boston-area company even filed a lawsuit against one of its vendors because of some customer files that were lost in 2007. Businessman Joe Hegreness of Scottsdale, Arizona, told the Ripoff Report that over a nearly six-month period "my computer has failed to make its initial backup. I have been told numerous times by the company that the internet connection is the problem, my files are the problem etc.," he wrote, calling it "a total ripoff." There was also a scandal involving Carbonite's eagerness to promote its product; when it appeared on Amazon.com in 2006 it received a string of glowing five-star reviews from the Boston area. When a disgruntled customer who was unable to retrieve his files investigated, he discovered all were written by top officials of Carbonite. In the reality-based world, in early 2010, some forty-eight out of eighty-one Amazon reviews (or 59 percent) of Carbonite were in the most negative one- or two-star range. The editors of *PC Magazine* did give the product a "good" rating, although its readers rated Carbonite only "fair."

A company called Food Insurance, which also sponsors Beck's radio program, sells freeze-dried food and related products in a shiny red canvas backpack. Beck even taped a several-minute video testimonial for Food Insurance, in which he talks about watching the planes from his office window in Manhattan, and how he once used to be able to see the World Trade Center from there. He says, "We live in a crazy world. I live in a nuts town where anything can happen, not just a natural disaster but a hurricane or a man-made disaster—you just want to be able to have some peace of mind." He said the Food Insurance backpack—kits for sale on its Web site start at $199.99—has everything you need "in case the world goes to heck in a hand basket."

Carbonite and Food Insurance are like many of the companies that sponsor Beck's show or Web site—fairly recent startups peddling a product that is newfangled or gimmicky or both. In early 2010, Beck began aggressively touting a startup rival to Craigslist.org called Upillar.com founded by a twenty-seven-year-old Utah entrepreneur named

Trevor Milton that bills itself as a less-raunchy alternative (Milton, like Beck, is a Mormon). Utah, in fact, is a nexus of Beck-promoted start-ups, including Upillar and Food Insurance. In June 2008, Beck gave the keynote speech there for five thousand salesmen for the controversial mortgage-software company United First Financial, or UFirst. The company, which recruits its salespeople with Amway-like fervor, peddles its plan to help homebuyers pay off their mortgages more quickly—but with the help of software that costs $3,500 upfront. Skeptics including the popular-with-conservatives financial guru Dave Ramsey have questioned the need for the UFirst project, writing that "there is no magic software"—but Beck told the salespeople they were doing God's work, saying, "you may well be the calling, doing the Lord's work to save our country . . . you're going to save families. You are going to save people's houses . . . You have the answer."

But truth be told, there is no product that Beck promotes with greater zeal and religiosity than Glenn Beck himself. The same *Forbes* article that estimated the entertainer makes $4 million from his Web site said that figure is dwarfed by the amount he makes from speeches—such as the one that he delivered to UFirst—live appearances, and books, which alone bring in some $13 million a year. From the moment that Beck went national on the radio in the early 2000s, he has looked for every profit angle to exploit—offering listeners special "insider" packages that even come with a magazine produced by Beck's staff, called *Fusion* (in early 2010, it was $34.95 a year for ten 16-page issues). All of Beck's extracurricular activities are relentlessly flogged on his radio show and occasionally on his Fox News program—none more than his avalanche of best-selling books.

Since 2003, when he did the obligatory-for-national-radio-hosts, what-I-believe-with-a-smidgeon-of-autobiography book called *The Real America: Messages from the Heart and from the Heartland*, Beck has published or has committed to producing a total of eight books, with the pace increasing to the rate of two every year—even as he continued to go on the radio for three hours in the mornings and do his nightly one-hour show on TV, as well as live appearances on many weekends. You may ask yourself: How does he do this? Typically, Beck's books are shorter than the average tome, with lots of white space (or in the case of 2009's *Arguing with Idiots*, with large graphics and the like to illustrate his points). It would also be an understatement to say there is a stream-of-consciousness feel to Beck's work, perhaps reflecting the author's admitted struggles with attention-deficit disorder but also the what-did-you-expect outgrowth of churning out all these books at the same time as so many other paid gigs. (Although Beck signed a lucrative multi-book deal with Simon & Schuster in 2009, he increasingly works with others including Kevin Balfe, senior vice president for publishing for Glenn Beck, Inc.)

Beck's 2009 best seller *Common Sense* is the archetype of his book empire—especially in its lack of depth, not to mention its lack of focus. Nearly half the volume is a reprint of the original *Common Sense* by Thomas Paine, which of course has long been in the public domain; the "meat" of the tome—aided by Beck staffer Joe Kerry—clocks in at just 107 pages, much of it boilerplate diatribe against out-of-control government spending. Thomas Paine rarely gets a mention, although at one point Beck (or maybe Joe Kerry) writes, "Thomas Paine wrote, 'The cause of America is in great measure the cause of all mankind.' These words are as true today as they were then."

Really? Beck—and probably many of his listeners—would be turned off by many of the views of the real Thomas Paine. For one thing, while Beck has tried to argue that America's true roots lie in Christianity, the real Thomas Paine was a Deist who loathed organized religion, writing in *The Age of Reason* that all churches "appear to me no other than human inventions, set up to terrify and enslave mankind, and monopolize power and profit." Increasingly as the 2010 elections approached, Beck inveighed against the modern progressive movement that gave America a progressive income tax; yet in *The Rights of Man* Paine argued aggressively—even with elaborate charts—in favor of redistribution of wealth, with the goal of "[r]estoring justice among families by a distribution of property." And there's more: Paine authored a pamphlet called "Agrarian Justice" that even advocated for a guaranteed minimum income, the kind of idea that would not go over well with the legion of Beck followers who rail against "the handout state." If Paine could be brought back to life, one could easily see him reenacting the legendary Marshall McLuhan scene in Woody Allen's *Annie Hall*, informing Beck that "you know nothing of my work." It certainly wouldn't matter. More than two million copies of *Glenn Beck's Common Sense* have been sold.

On December 3, 2009, Beck took over hundreds of theaters from coast to coast for an intensely promoted event, a simulcast of a live show based on his nonpolitical fictionalized account of his childhood, *The Christmas Sweater*. The event was revealing of Beck's demographics: there were decent crowds and even some sellouts in small towns and in the Deep South, but theaters in large cities like New York and Boston and even in Seattle, where Beck had started out in radio, were virtually empty. One account said that only seventeen tickets were sold in Manhattan. In addition to the regionalism of Beck's appeal, the crowds may have been a testament to the low-end production values, as much of the show consisted of Beck sitting there and recreating the characters in his "Clydie Clyde," "Morning Zoo" kind of voices, but the biggest problem was arguably the price. Tickets to the theatrical event were $20—more than what theatergoers paid to see the big-budget special effects of *Avatar*. Yet Beck continued to raise the stakes on ticket prices as his popularity soared. For his seven-hour political talk-fest called *The American Revival Tour* in the spring of 2010, Beck asked a top ticket price that came with service charges to $134.

High ticket prices may explain why Beck's income had soared to at least $32 million by 2009, according to the estimates compiled by the *Business Insider* and *Forbes*. When Beck moved up to television and his stint on CNN Headline News in 2006, he and his family moved into a spectacular, newly constructed sixteen-room, 8,750-square-foot four-story house on a sweeping hillside overlooking the Laurel Reservoir in the upscale enclave of New Canaan, Connecticut. There's a sturdy American flag in the front near the four-car garage, a built-in pool and a spa amid the lush lawn out back, and a spectacular brass-chandelier foyer, leading to rooms with arched doorways and crown molding surrounding impressionistic objets d'art.

Beck once wanted to add something else: a six-foot-high fence surrounding the property on all sides. In June of 2008, accompanied by his wife Tania and a security guard as well as his attorney, Beck arrived at a zoning board hearing in New Canaan to successfully lobby for the fence, which his lawyer said had been recommended by "their security people." The man making millions for his ability to talk let his attorney, James D'Alton Murphy, do all the speaking this time. Murphy said that Beck needed to erect this kind of Berlin Wall around the perimeter of his property because he was under siege from friend and foe alike. "[The fence] won't stop them, but it will slow them down," the lawyer said, adding a Beckian, apocalyptic flourish: "It will stop anything people send into the property, whether photographs or bullets."

(Beck's next-door neighbor in New Canaan, Ilona Sheehan, said Beck ultimately put up a lower fence but still remained obsessed with security, erecting an ugly chain-link fence between their properties and flooding the house with bright floodlights. She also said by telephone that she's never seen any fans, detractors, or other strangers coming unannounced to the house, as Beck's attorney claimed.)

One thing that Beck's fence might have prevented was rank-and-file citizens from seeing how his public character differs from his private life, where he is, among other things, an apparent believer in the manmade global warming he has ridiculed on his show. In February 2010, Beck told an interviewer from USA Weekend that he was using energy-saving products around the home in part because of his belief that humans were partly responsible for climate change, that "[y]ou'd be an idiot not to notice the temperature change." That only added to the sense that just like the conservative pundit "Stephen Colbert" of TV's

The Colbert Report, "Glenn Beck" the reinvented entertainer, pitch-man, and political avatar was merely another character, just a much more effective one than "Clydie Clyde." Nevertheless, Beck apparently decided in late 2009 that it was time to move on. He placed the New Canaan house on the market for $3.99 million, or a quarter-mil less than what he'd paid for it four years earlier.

The investment loss was immaterial—Beck's income was still rising astronomically, and presumably his next mansion would be even more spectacular. It was as if Beck had truly taken to heart the words of his sponsor Bill Heid, that "Basically The Worse Things Get . . . The More Money You'll Make!"

But like any consumer brand, Glenn Beck Incorporated found that to keep the customer engaged he had to constantly increase the noise level. With his arrival at Fox News in early 2009, Beck unveiled the now-famous chalkboard that he used to sketch out an ever-elaborate series of conspiracies involving the Obama administration and some of the president's mid-level officials that Beck bludgeoned for past statements—some of them accurate and some of them taken out of context. In Beck's new world, Obama's commonsense proposals to create "green jobs" in alternative energy, for example, were seen as part of a Marxist-inspired plot to "transform" America and undermine the Constitution. A classic example of Beck's muddled yet influential message came on his broadcast of September 18, 2009—six days after the successful Beck-inspired rally in Washington, D.C.—when he drew an elaborate "Tree of Revolution" that somehow linked Barack Obama and the liberal community-action group ACORN with the 1960s campus-protest group the Students for a Democratic Society and a long-dead ex-president, the early-twentieth-century progressive Woodrow Wilson. Increasingly, Beck casually mixed comments that the United States was marching toward either socialism or Marxism or Maoism or a Hitlerian kind of authoritarianism or fascism—despite the fact that those ideologies are not only contradictory but often warred with each other throughout the twentieth century.

As time went on, his regular broadcasts grew more and more fre-netic. In January 2010, Beck's program on Fox News switched gears and broadcast a documentary that the host called "Revolutionary Ho-locaust," a shock-and-awe bombardment that was stunning even in the context of his long-running crusade against a century of progressivism in America. It leaned heavily on the much-criticized writings of conser-vative polemicist Jonah Goldberg, author of the book *Liberal Fascism* and—against a backdrop of Hitler salutes and massive Nuremberg Nazi rallies—used a series of obscure and sometimes out-of-context quotes to blend the rival philosophies of Nazism and communism and, more importantly, imply this all had something to do with the complex American political condition in the second decade of the twenty-first century.

The following month, Beck capped his year-long hijacking of the national conversation with an attention-grabbing speech to the annual conservative talk-fest known as CPAC. A lot of people were surprised by the rambling lack of focus or the occasional shock-jock references to "vomit," which just means that they hadn't been paying close attention before. There was something else that Beck had said before that was nonetheless shocking in this context, that "progressivism is the cancer in America" and that "[y]ou must eradicate it. It cannot co-exist." In other words, those who disagreed with Beck were not to be bested in debate or at the ballot box; they were to be wiped off the earth.

By early 2010, after a year of this kind of pounding had elevated the fear alert level to red, Beck seemed poised at the next step, which was somehow converting this angry stir-fry into a more focused move-ment. If Beck was really trying to emulate that fictional mad-as-hell-and-I'm-not-going-to-take-it-anymore TV anchorman Howard Beale of *Network*, this next part had no script to follow. As the midterm elections moved toward the front burner, Beck gave a talk to "his base" at the retirement-heavy The Villages, Florida, near Orlando and an-nounced he was working on something that might have struck a few of the senior citizens wistfully, that he was working on a hundred-year plan for America. "It will require unconventional thinking and a radical plan to restore our nation to the maximum freedoms we were supposed to have been protecting, using only the battlefield of ideas," he said. The culmination would be a book called simply *The Plan*, and he announced that he would unveil it at a mass rally at the Lincoln Memorial on August 28, 2010, the forty-seventh anniversary of the day that Dr. Martin Luther King gave his "I Have a Dream Speech," at roughly the same spot. Like everything else that Beck did, his political ambitions thinly disguised his desire to move a couple million more books.

But over the coming weeks, the plan for *The Plan* changed, partly because of the estimated $2 million cost of the Washington event. By early 2010, the event was rebranded as "Restoring Honor," now described not as the unveiling of a political plan or related to a Beck-authored book, but as a "non-political, non-partisan rally that will recognize our First Amendment rights and honor the service members who fight to protect those freedoms." To pay for this, Beck said he would donate $1 million—either a magnanimous gesture or a down payment on book promotion, depending on your level of cynicism—but that the other $1 million would be funneled through Glenn Beck radio listener donations to the Special Operations Warrior Fund, a highly rated charity that offers aid to the families of service members who are wounded or killed in combat. In other words, this second $1 million being donated to the Special Operations Warrior Fund specifically for Beck's rally would not be helping send the kids of slain soldiers to attend college, but it would be diverted toward a rally that—whatever other purposes it served—would raise the national profile of Glenn Beck into a higher orbit.

The announcement of *The Plan* and the grandiose scheme for a massive rally in Washington in the metaphorical shadow of Martin Luther King dramatized both the risks for Beck and for a nation struggling to come to terms with the increasing fervor of his followers. In the pressure cooker of political entertainment, the ability of Beck not only to move people but also move product depended on an ever-ready ability to shock people and say surprising things, and it was getting harder to top some of the outrageous things he had said in those early days of the Obama administration. His ambitions for his entertainment empire—Glenn Beck Incorporated—had grown to outsized proportions, which put pressure on Beck to say more outrageous things to keep new customers flowing in.

In the spring of 2010, perhaps fueled by the difficulty of the challenge he had created for himself, Beck told his audience with surprising candor of how far he had taken things when he was first trying to build an audience on Fox News: "When we were, and I've never told this story before, when we were starting the TV show, there were things that I did that I wouldn't do now because I had to be more of an entertainer to get people to go, what is this show at five o'clock? I never said anything I didn't believe, but I may have said things in an entertaining fashion."

The worry for America was that some of those viewers wouldn't be able to discern where the entertainment ended and where reality started. Indeed, those lines have been blurred before—with lethal consequences.

CHAPTER TEN

"Pop"

The face of evil is riddled with zits. That's the first thing you can't help but notice about Richard Poplawski when you finally see him in person for the first time—acne pockmarks all over ghostly pale skin that has seen little natural light since the events that occurred on April 4, 2009, some eight-and-a-half months earlier.

Indeed, Poplawski looks nothing like the pictures that have been plastered all over the Internet since that fateful day—the ones showing a young scowl under a sharp buzz cut, glaring into the camera, his tattoo, the one he once described as "a slightly Americanized version" of the Nazis' Iron Eagle, poking out ominously from underneath his neckline. Now, inside Room 324 of this vaguely castle-like, Renaissance-style Allegheny County Courthouse, he's just a scared kid, a kid who has recently gunned down three grown men. In fact, in his faded white T-shirt and crimson sweatpants, and with all the acne scars, Poplawski at 10 o'clock on this dead-of-winter morning looks like nothing more than a jobless slacker who just stumbled down the stairs, about to pour himself a big bowl of Cap'n Crunch while he plays another game of Halo 3.

Poplawski keeps his narrow eyes forward the whole time, always focused on the judge, Jeffrey Manning, his expression completely drained of affect—even when his own court-appointed attorney reveals that an online petition calling for Poplawski to die by lethal injection has exactly 36,916 signatures, or when a quote is read back from a neighbor calling him "the monster of Stanton Heights," the sturdy redbrick, middle-class Pittsburgh neighborhood where he once lived. Poplawski's intense focus on the orderly and often tedious legal proceedings directly in front of him serves another purpose; it keeps him from seeing the mess that he has left behind him, quite literally. About twenty feet to the rear of the defense table, right there in the front row of the spectator area, sits the thin, dressed-in-black line of survivors, relatives of police officers Eric Kelly, Stephen Mayhle, and Paul Sciullo II. They are the living monuments to the paranoid torrent of hate that young Poplawski unleashed from a weapons cache that included a Romanian-built assault rife on the forty-first anniversary of the assassination of Martin Luther King.

Later on, former president Bill Clinton will give a speech to mark the fifteenth anniversary of the Oklahoma City bombing but also to bemoan a resurgence of the same type of hatred that led to the insane antigovernment actions of the murderer, Timothy McVeigh. "But what we learned from Oklahoma City is not that we should gag each other or that we should reduce our passion for the positions we hold, but that the words we use really do matter because there are—there's this vast echo chamber," the forty-second president said. "And they go across space and they fall on the serious and the delirious, alike; they fall on the connected and the unhinged, alike."

Bill Clinton didn't mention Richard Poplawski by name, nor did he single out Glenn Beck.

He didn't have to.

ON MARCH 3, 2009, *Fox and Friends*, the unintentionally goofy morning program on the Fox News Channel, invited on a special friend—Glenn Beck, whose 5 p.m. show had been on the network for roughly six weeks and was already picking up steam, but still building an audience and looking for attention in what Beck would later call that "entertaining fashion." The topic of the conversation started out with revelations of a (briefly) secret letter that the also then new president, Barack Obama, had sent to his Russian counterpart. Then, with no warning, the discussion swerved to the far, far right.

Beck told his Fox colleagues that American allies in the Czech Republic "understand freedom. We don't even understand freedom anymore. We are a country that is headed towards socialism, totalitarianism, beyond your wildest imagination. I have to tell you, I'm doing a story tonight that I wanted to debunk these FEMA camps. I'm tired of hearing—you know about them?"

"Sure," responded the ever-chipper co-host of *Fox and Friends*, Steve Doocy.

"I'm tired of hearing—I wanted to debunk them," Beck went on. "Well, we've now for several days done research on them. I can't debunk them. And we're going to carry the story tonight."

The other co-host, Brian Kilmeade, wasn't sure what to say in response. "I don't know anything about them, so . . ."

Beck: "It is—it is our government. If you trust our government, it's fine. If you have any kind of fear that we might be headed towards a totalitarian state, look out, buckle up. There is something going on in our country that is—ain't good."

For years, there have been rumors and conspiracy theories bubbling under the American surface that the Federal Emergency Management Agency, or FEMA, was building or had already built as many as eight hundred prison camps, or concentration camps. Frankly, who was spreading the rumors depended heavily on which party was in power. They started to gain steam on the extreme right in the Bill Clinton years, concurrent with the rise of the militia movement, especially across the American West. As noted by the writer Dave Neiwert, who has been investigating the far-right radical fringe since that era, the supposed list of the eight hundred camps includes locations like Minidoka, an Idaho site that really once had been an internment camp for Japanese-Americans during World War II and was being renovated not as a holding pen for American "patriots" but as a historical site. Other alleged camp locations, such as Montana's Malmstrom Air Force Base—also the alleged location of "UN aircraft groups"—were just made up from thin air. Still, some on the far left—during the nadir of the second George W. Bush administration, and inspired by a real-life contract from the Homeland Security Department to a unit of then vice president Dick Cheney's former firm of Halliburton to open emergency centers in the event of a crisis such as an influx of Haitian boat people—revived the rumors in the 2000s. Those facilities were not constructed, but reports of the supposed "FEMA camps" began bounding around the Internet all over again with the election of Barack Obama; indeed, the establishment of such camps was one of the ten orders that the fast-growing Oath Keepers said they wouldn't obey.

Legislation proposed in Congress dealing with the potential for a national emergency—again, along the lines of a Haitian or Cuban refugee crisis—gave new life to the movement. As noted in an article posted on the PrisonPlanet Web site—the Web home of Alex Jones—on February 21, 2009, or roughly ten days before Beck's appearance on *Fox and Friends*: "Ominously, the bill also states that the camps can be used to 'meet other appropriate needs, as determined by the Secretary of Homeland Security,' an open ended mandate which many fear could mean the forced detention of American citizens in the event of widespread rioting after a national emergency or total economic collapse. Many credible forecasters have predicted riots and rebellions in America that will dwarf those already witnessed in countries like Iceland and Greece."

By now, the alleged FEMA camps were once again all the new paranoid style, especially on extremist Web sites such as Stormfront, an address frequently given over to white supremacist ranting. Ironically, when Beck took to the airwaves on the afternoon of March 3, he did not deliver the supposed goods that he'd promised that morning. He told viewers, some of whom were surely disappointed: "This is something that I snapped on the air, because somebody called me up and said, 'Why don't you talk about the FEMA prisons.' And I said, 'Can we just settle the FEMA prison thing?' I don't believe in the FEMA prison. If you don't know, I'll tell you about it in a couple of days. I was going to talk about it today, but as I came in—I came in and did the show this morning, and then I went in to my office, and I was looking at all the research that are [*sic*] being compiled, and it wasn't complete. And I am not willing to bring something to you that is half-baked."

Well, thank God for that . . . but the reality is that the damage had already been done. For many people on the paranoid fringe, the only takeaway was that an increasingly popular new host on the most-watched cable news channel, with as many as three million viewers on a given night and millions of TV viewers and radio listeners over the course of a month, had told the world that he "can't debunk" the notion that concentration-style camps were under construction in the United States, and that if you thought a totalitarian state is coming in America you should not go straight to a psychiatrist but rather you should "buckle up." Such rumor-mongering from under-the-radar new media on the Web or on Internet radio was already a problem, but a more manageable one than when a well-known Fox News host had waved a giant red permission slip in front of his audience, saying in effect, in the words made famous by sportscaster Jack Buck, "Go crazy, folks! Go crazy!"

Here amid a Pittsburgh neighborhood of sturdy ranch houses was the grave threat that came with "amusing ourselves to death," while slick talking heads on seemingly respectable TV networks and their well-dressed compatriots in the corridors of Congress kept shifting the "Overton window"—in Beck's beloved political theory—to a place of whacked-out conspiracy and an extreme-right philosophy. Those who dismissed Beck's melodramatic televised antics as "the tears of a clown," or laughed at the black-helicopter theories or anti-Census rants of politicians like Michele Bachmann or Paul Broun or the over-the-top sales pitches for survivalist seeds and freeze-dried foods, were forgetting about "the unhinged"—in the words of ex-president Clinton—that these words were assaulting on a daily basis. The hucksters like Bill Heid pitching the apocalyptic necessity of solar generators and heirloom seeds tried to convince themselves that, in Heid's own words, "[i]t doesn't matter whether you share the same world view as these customers or not," but so-called customers like the overstressed and delusional young Rich Poplawski put an end to all of that.

Poplawski was a rootless misfit who was smart enough to sop up all the poisonous information that was floating in the media ether—starting as a teenager with radio's "shock jocks" before graduating to the theories of economic collapse and food preparedness that he heard from Glenn Beck and Alex Jones—and yet delirious enough to channel them into violent fantasies that became a horrifying reality when he finally lost his ability to distinguish between the two. Selling the ideas that America in the Age of Obama was devolving into a replay of Nazi Germany or that paper money was going to be worthless moved a lot of product, sent ratings skyward, and swayed voters on the far right. You have seen first-hand how these messages motivated people like Russ Murphy into political activism—and how they could move a television viewer like Larraine Whayland to tears. But these warped messages also pushed a small fraction of those people toward unspeakable acts—in ways that are so unpredictable that the potential for random outbreaks of violence threatens us all. Rich Poplawski is a young man who in just a few short years amused himself into a murderous rage.

Other Americans were swayed in the same directions. Into this paranoid web also wandered a fifty-three-year-old Glenn Beck fanatic and mother of three from the East End of Long Island named Nancy Genovese. In the summer of 2009, some writers and liberal bloggers described Genovese as, in effect, the Real Paranoid Housewife of Long Island for her seemingly unusual picture-taking outside a nearby military base; Genovese claims—in a lawsuit—that she was wrongly arrested and wrongly harassed by the authorities who called her a domestic terrorist. The truth is out there.

At least this much is not in dispute: Genovese was indeed

apprehended by the local authorities for taking photographs over the fence of an Air National Guard base in Westhampton, New York, not far from the tony beachside resorts for rich Manhattanites. It happened on July 30, 2009, when Genovese, who told reporters that she is retired from her career as a building-supply sales rep, was on her way home from the shooting range in her Saturn Sky convertible. She said that when she saw the HH–3E "Jolly Green Giant" helicopter that sits near the base entrance, she pulled over to snap a picture because she wanted to post it online to show support for the U.S. troops overseas.

Base officials and the cops didn't see it that way. A major from the Air National Guard claimed that Genovese had already been warned to stay away from the base after attempting to take pictures there a couple of weeks earlier, and that her information had been recorded in case she returned. When an off-duty officer spotted her there a second time, that triggered a chain of events that not only led to Genovese's arrest on misdemeanor trespassing charges but a search of her trunk that revealed an XM–15 assault rifle and a shotgun—both legally registered and unloaded—and five hundred rounds of ammo. A judge set a high bail—$50,000—and Genovese spent four days in jail; however, the trespassing charge was later dropped and that led to a lawsuit by Genovese, who claimed she was merely a patriotic America wrongly arrested by overzealous authorities.

In the days following her midsummer arrest, several liberal bloggers and journalists reported on Genovese's enthusiasm for Glenn Beck and Alex Jones. Indeed, a quick peek at her MySpace page—which is now set to "private" but which was archived by bloggers last August—included the posting of a Beck video; below it she wrote: "I just saw Glenn Beck tell it like it is! Yes, he was firm and he is talking to congress, for all of us. . . . we the people." But scrolling down to the time frame shortly before her arrest, Genovese also makes it very clear that she was indeed conducting her own investigation of the possibility of the "FEMA camps." In fact, she writes specifically of her obsession with a crisis/terrorism response drill that was called the National Level

Exercise '09 and was slated for July 27 through July 31—the exact time frame that included her arrest at the base.

Genovese wrote on MySpace of several calls and phone conversations she had with officials, including one from the Department of Homeland Security, in which she pressed her belief that foreign troops would be conducting drills on American soil as part of the exercise. She wrote of her conversation with the DHS man:

> He says there is no way right now, marshal [*sic*] law will be imposed in the USA. He told me it would have to be dyer [*sic*] situation for the President to make such a declaration. I presented a scenario of dyer straits to him, like, the dollar goes down to the predicted 15.7 cent in value, swine flu is killing people and they have a few million dead bodies to deal with, people have no homes, no food, looting is going on. Um, yes, martial law would be something the country would need. He did insist Americans would never put up with being put in any camp and stopped me when I even mentioned the word camp. He told me FEMA owns NO camps. None.

In pressing the unnamed Homeland Security worker, Genovese said she asked him about an Alex Jones "exclusive" on the alleged purchase of 500,000 specially designed coffins. She even uploaded a Jones video to her MySpace page, adding: "They are counting on us not finding out, and they are counting on us that do find out to do nothing. Well I am not just going to sit on my hands any more, something needs to be done before me and everyone I know ends up in one of these coffins."

"They were telling me I was a terrorist," Genovese told a local newspaper, the *Southampton Press*, on the day that she was released from jail. "I said, 'This can't be happening in America.'" She had invited the reporter into her home, and she told her, "This can happen to anybody."

In the background, the reporter later wrote, *The Glenn Beck Program* was blaring from a television.

. . . .

"RICH, LIKE MYSELF, loved Glenn Beck."

"Myself" is Eddie Perkovic—and "Rich" is Perkovic's lifelong best friend, Rich Poplawski, the accused murderer of three Pittsburgh police officers, a national event that still has this iconic Rust Belt shot-and-a-beer city reeling months later. It was not hard to track down the twenty-three-year-old Perkovic, who was wearing pajama bottoms and an ankle bracelet—under house arrest after an incident that involved drunk driving . . . among other things. He lets you into the cluttered front room of a narrow row house sharply angled into one of the steep hills hurtling down toward the Allegheny River, ten minutes east of downtown, and he turns down the volume on the afternoon *Law and Order* reruns and launches what starts out as a lengthy political and personal monologue, until Perkovic's mother, Pamela, wanders in, perking up at the discussion of the "FEMA camps."

Pamela Perkovic, who has black curly hair and is wearing a baggy sweatshirt, occasionally chides her son's more way-out statements but is nonetheless a big believer in the "FEMA camps," which she's read about on the Internet and heard about on the radio, and she also remembers hearing Glenn Beck confirm their existence. "Oh yeah, we did see the little thing —but I wasn't paying that much attention at the time—but, yes, there was a thing on *Glenn Beck* about the camps— and they're there and we know they're there."

"Rich was . . . you know, he really felt strongly about these camps— that people better watch out," Eddie added. "He saw it on *Glenn Beck*, too." Actually, it had already been reported in the media that Poplawski, exactly one month before the killings, was clearly familiar with Glenn Beck's back-and-forth on the "FEMA camps"; he'd even posted online a YouTube clip of Beck interviewing Representative Ron Paul that night of March 3, the same day as his *Fox and Friends* appearance. The interview is a classic example of how both Beck and presidential wannabe Paul are masters of the new paranoid style. Both men sort of denied the camps but sort of didn't; Paul, the national political figure, told Beck, "So in some ways, they [FEMA] can accomplish what you might be thinking about, about setting up camps, and they don't necessarily have to have legislation, you know, to do the things that we dread. But it is something that deserves a lot of attention."

Perkovic's mom adds that Poplawski "also had a stockpile of food—sugar, water, rice."

"Yeah, he brought it to my apartment, because I guess he also thought the economy might collapse really soon—and then said, 'Maybe I made a mistake,'" Eddie chips in. "But he brought me, like, a box with inside like a bag with a gallon of water. He brought me two gallons of rice and he would always say, stock up on canned goods, if anything happens like where America does collapse, you want to stock up on food, water."

"He had toilet paper," Mom adds after a pause.

"Oh yeah . . . toilet paper."

Eddie Perkovic—like his friend, the accused cop-killer—is a hard one to pin down. He is not someone that you'd cast in a movie as "the murderer's best friend"; not only is Perkovic blond and boyishly clean-shaven, with no apparent tattoos and a big-toothed smile, but he is also unfailingly polite and well-spoken, a kind of a low-brow conspiratorial Eddie Haskell, even as he is presenting wacky ideas that are completely or nearly completely bouncing off the confining walls of his house-arrest haven.

Perkovic insists to you that he turned down a job offer in New York with XM Radio (which is actually headquartered in Washington); of his recent arrest he says, "I didn't know you weren't allowed to sit in your car in your driveway, drunk," failing to mention what was reported in the local news: that the police were in that driveway because the mother of Perkovic's baby said he'd threatened her with a loaded rifle. Perkovic is chain-smoking during this manic monologue, although at one point you look down at your notebook and when you look back up the cigarette is gone and instead he is now waving around a half-eaten Hot Pocket in his right hand as he continues his rapid-fire riffing.

"A couple of things that I had mentioned to him [Poplawski]—not that he had mentioned to me—were the fact that there is more than one Guantánamo camp and that things like that don't really belong—and it's not that they don't belong . . . it's just that they're not talked about because they're kind of kept hush-hush because they don't want the American people to know about that sort of thing."

So where are these camps, you ask.

"Oh, they're spread across the United States." Perkovic's tone is firm, unwavering. "There are Guantánamo camps—it's been documented, it's truth . . . it's not like, it's not a conspiracy you believe it or you don't—it's been documented. President Obama started to uncover a couple of them—more than one I know . . . It's scary."

Rich "Pop" Poplawski has been behind bars for months now, but the contours of his paranoid world on the outside remain in place—this American Apocalypto that is underemployed and overstimulated by a bombast of half-baked electrons, boiling over in moments of occasional rage. Not everyone inside this growing end-times bubble is armed to the teeth, thank God, but Rich Poplawski was. He owned a powerful AK–47-style assault rifle, a .22-caliber shotgun, and at least a couple of handguns, including a .357 Magnum, all of them purchased legally.

THE MARTIN LUTHER King holiday is a pretty peculiar day to spend inside a gun store, especially to talk about a cop killing that happened on the anniversary of the King assassination in Memphis. But here you are, standing at the counter of the Braverman Arms in the adjacent-to-Pittsburgh borough of Wilkinsburg—the best-known gun shop in the urban center of the western Pennsylvania hill country that gave us *The Deer Hunter.* You walk in past the posters for "Firearms Owners Against Crime" and a couple of large trash cans piled high with holsters and then through a narrow selling floor, the walls lined with antique rifles and even a couple of long swords, no doubt relics from Pittsburgh's peak of industrial revolution prosperity. Right behind the cash register, you note the official White House picture of President Obama—all glossied up and distributed by the National Rifle Association. The headline reads, "Firearm Salesman of the Year."

Buddy Savage, the owner of Braverman Arms, is waiting in the dank back room lined with ammo cases. Savage is seventy years old now and he's been at the gun shop ever since it opened in the late 1950s, when Wilkinsburg was a thriving borough of about 37,000 and Main Street was lined with shoppers, flush with postwar paychecks from the steel mills pumping black smoke into the Mon Valley down the road. Savage is a thin man with a surprisingly preppy look—fashionable sweater, square-rimmed glasses—and a weariness about explaining to reporters and the like that everything they think they know about guns is wrong, that for example, the rapid-fire AK–47 started out with the imprimatur of "the Geneva Convention" (he was apparently referring to the Hague Convention of 1899) because it fires less lethal nonexpanding bullets. You change the subject and ask him about Obama and the gun control issue.

"I think down the road, eventually . . . I think when he gets control, I can easily envision confiscation."

Really?

"I think it's reasonable down the road. I think it's unreasonable now. There's too many people that are armed and he [Obama] doesn't have that type of control yet. He's working at it. It depends on how successful he gets. If I were him . . . he's doing it in the right order. He's staying away from the crust of it right now—I would say there'd be a backlash. If he were to get enough power and appoint people to where guns are the issue, it doesn't make any difference—I've already lost my rights, you know what I mean?"

Not really. You were in fact talking to Savage on the very week that it looked as though the Obama administration and his Democratic allies had once again flubbed their chance to extend health care to most Americans, with their short-lived high-water mark of sixty Senate votes about to disappear the very next night in a special election in

Massachusetts. At this moment, the idea that Obama is "gaining control" over anything seemed absurd. The best-known firearms merchant
in a major American city ranting about the coming "Obama gun confiscation" would have sounded startling a few months back, but by the
dawn of 2010 you've heard it all before.

If you're under the impression by now that Pittsburgh is a hidden
hotbed of paranoia, that may be a surprisingly rational conclusion.
It's hard to imagine an American place with more of a land-that-time-
forgot feel than this rust-worn Steel City, with so many faded bridges
across giant chasms, hints of redbrick, middle-class stability on one
hilltop and graffiti-scrawled squalor on the next one over—a visually
arresting nineteenth-century polyglot of faded Romanesque and Itali-
anate homes, some that appear to be clinging for their life on the impos-
sibly steep slopes. When the steel industry began to go south—literally,
at first, but later on a slow boat to the Far East and elsewhere—in the
1950s and '60s, more than half of Pittsburgh's population disappeared
along with it, either to Florida or to a more permanent retirement community. In the early 1980s, most of the mills were already in an early
state of imperial decay, a few still illuminating the cascading hillsides
with magical nighttime torchlights of fire. All are extinguished now.

Many of the mill sites have been reinvented atop the once-toxic fields
of muck as gleaming glass campuses—or at least a new Wal-Mart in
some spots—and some of the best-trained grads of colleges like Pitt or
Carnegie-Mellon do now have a smattering of high-tech jobs in things
like robotics to stick around for. But the broader middle-class economy
of Pittsburgh is a remarkably nonprofit affair—with the bulk of these
barely livable, nothing-like-the-steel-heyday salaries found in a massive
hospital sector that takes care of the aging population, and much of the
rest in necessary civic functions like the firefighters trying to save the
aging housing stock and the cops dealing with a violent crime rate that
is double the national average.

And to explain what the hell just happened, the blue-collar politics here went through more ups and downs than the Mt. Washington

tramway, from rock-solid, trade-union, economic liberalism straight through to the 1970s, reversing fields as the majority became socially conservative "Reagan Democrats" in the 1980s; when the so-called Reagan Revolution never showed a payoff in the Rust Belt, what largely remained wasn't really politics anymore so much as rage, tempered by the opiate of the Steelers and the Penguins, both 2009 world champs. Talk radio flourishes here—it used to be mostly local, KDKA railing against midnight pay raises for Pennsylvania state lawmakers, until the 50,000-watt national sound waves and satellite transmissions of Fox-fired discontentment began to echo off these once-hallowed hills.

Savage's Braverman Arms is a strange kind of oasis—at least in terms of commercial activity—in Wilkinsburg, a particularly distressed section of the Pittsburgh area, in a valley surrounded by dilapidated homes, some of them even boarded up. Likewise, the businesses next door to the gun shop appear to be long shuttered and dark—the butcher shop with 1950s Deco signage that became a 1990s video-rental store is now just a shell, as is the dark and apparently short-lived "Negril Caribbean" storefront next to that. In fact, metered parking places are completely empty for a block or two on either side of Braverman Arms, a beehive of activity, where a steady stream of minivans and pickup trucks pull up—mostly driven by middle-aged white men, scurrying out with boxes of ammunition and driving home through a mostly African-American shopping strip where a man in Uncle Sam suit and pants advertises a local tax service—"Get Paid $50!"

One night in 2000, a black man named Ronald Taylor wrote a long, rambling note that praised Adolf Hitler and the Oklahoma City bomber McVeigh and said "the United Snakes of America will burn in hell," and then he went out and started gunning down all the white people he could find in Wilkinsburg. He killed the maintenance man in his apartment building, then a seventy-one-year-old retired Catholic priest who was eating at the Burger King, and then finally the twenty-year-old kid working the drive-through window at McDonald's. It turned out that the .22-caliber handgun he used was bought by his grandfather some eighteen years earlier right here at Braverman Arms, and then passed down, as if a family heirloom. Buddy Savage says he's heartsick that he sold that gun to Taylor's family, heartsick that he sold at least one of the weapons that Richard Poplawski used nine years later, even though the alleged cop-killer's AK–47 was reportedly obtained over the Internet.

Savage says he tries.

"Truthfully, we're tough," he says, suggesting that with fifty years of experience he sometimes knows when to halt a sale. "If you're black or white . . . if it's an asshole, it's an asshole. We refuse a lot of sales, but we know that when they walk out the door, they've educated them-selves"—on how to legally buy a gun somewhere else. When the police came to him after the April 2009 cop killing, Savage had to pore through store records, since he had no recollection that he'd indeed once sold a gun to a just-turning-twenty-year-old kid who'd already been booted from Marine boot camp, with an expired protection-from-abuse order and with few job prospects.

Richard Poplawski just didn't seem that unusual around here.

It is not long after the visit to the gun shop that Pamela Perkovic is handing you a framed photo from her living room of Braverman Arms' most notorious customer, Richard Poplawski. Inside the picture frame, he is an All-American Everyteen, wearing a polo shirt and a baseball cap, clean-cut and leaning forward on a sofa with a video-game con-troller in his hands.

"Let me say one thing—people show a picture of Rich as being a skinhead and blah blah blah," says Perkovic's mom, who is still not ashamed to portray herself as a kind of surrogate mother of the jailed death-penalty candidate. "Well, this is Rich Poplawski right here. This is the real Rich Poplawski. But nobody wants to see that picture."

But no single snapshot can explain exactly how this happened—not the Perkovics' photo of Poplawski as a prepped-out couch potato, and not the one that you see in the newspaper all the time, the skinhead wannabe with the vacant look and that menacing tattoo across a bare chest. No individual photograph could capture the essence of a guy who'd take young nieces to the playground or help Mrs. Perkovic with her groceries and stay to watch the Penguins when she was all alone, and then go home and post hate-filled drivel on a racist Web site; a guy who'd failed at everything important he'd tried, often with a history of violent actions. It is an enigma that a team of court-appointed psychiatrists is spending thousands of dollars to solve, and even then there will not be an answer that satisfies.

A cynic could certainly find irony in the birth date of the future Glenn Beck fan—9/12, or September 12, 1986, to be exact. But this "September 12 person" seemed programmed for failure from day one. His father—some fifteen years older than Poplawski's mother, Margaret, who was just seventeen when their only child was born—pretty much vanished when his son Rich was only two, after allegations, made in court filings, that he'd thrown Margaret Poplawski into a wall and kicked her in the ribs. "Dad" resurfaced at length only to talk to the newspapers after the events of April 4, 2009. Rich Poplawski's mother—who had convictions for drunk driving, just like Poplawski's father—found work in the belly of the Pittsburgh hospital behemoth as a registered nurse, but she has been described by those who know her as not much of a caregiver. "His mother was the whole problem," said best friend Eddie Perkovic, citing a string of alleged screaming matches and drunken incidents, including one just a week before the 2009 shootings in which she humiliated her son at a pizza shop and wouldn't take his phone calls.

As the only child, Rich Poplawski seemed as unsteady as the foundation his parents provided—conscientious enough to watch over younger kids in the park, with signs of an intellect, yet ultimately always sabotaging himself along the way, usually with a final flourish of violence. Poplawski was asked to leave Pittsburgh's North Catholic High during his junior year there. He earned a GED and joined the Marine Corps in 2004—the same year that he registered to vote as a Republican—but was asked to leave boot camp after just a few weeks, reportedly because of an incident in which he tossed a tray at a drill instructor. His only steady girlfriend ended up seeking a "protection from abuse" order, or PFA, against Poplawski just six weeks after that, claiming in legal papers that he'd pulled her hair in a fight and spoke of a buried gun.

Over the next four years, Poplawski sought to drop some kind of anchor—he tried living in Florida for a time and spoke of dental school and computers and learned glass-making, but there just wasn't a lot of work, especially for someone with his increasingly checkered résumé. "He liked to watch the Pirates and the Penguins, but he also was always looking for a job," his friend Aaron Vire told the *Pittsburgh Review-Tribune*. "He talked to me like a man who was like, 'Dad, I'm going to make some money, I'm going to make a lot of money, I'm going to find a way to succeed,'" his father later said.

That never happened. In the old Pittsburgh, there might have been plenty of decent-paying jobs for someone with Poplawski's background in the fire-belching mills, but there was nothing for him or his kind in the handful of shiny glass offices that replaced them. On the surface, there are certainly parallels between Poplawski's grim American odyssey and the people you met elsewhere. His dim prospect of getting a steady, well-paying blue-collar job were no better or worse, really, than that of let-go-in-his-late-forties Joe Gayhan or of the laid-off mortgage specialist Al Whayland, and his fetish for heavy firepower would have made him just another face in the crowd milling about the vast pole tent at Knob Creek. But not all customers are created equal; many of those others still had the rudiments of a support network in their family or their home or their church, as well as the restraint of their advancing years. Poplawski had none of these safety cushions.

Unemployed much of the time after he moved back to the city in late 2007, he was spending more and more of his free time on the Internet, especially on the Web site called Stormfront, which was created in 1995 by a former Ku Klux Klan leader and which established itself, in those early days of the Internet, as kind of the Yahoo!-like content king of white supremacy. According to the Anti-Defamation League, which later conducted an in-depth investigation of Poplawski's online postings, he visited there briefly in 2006 or 2007 to show off his Iron Eagle tattoo, then returned in late 2007 for a series of racist rants. Poplawski wrote that "Negroes especially have disgusting facial features. The fat nosed flaring nostril look is putrid. Nappy hair makes me want to gag"—views on race that he attributed to a "solid upbringing" by his mother.

November 2008 was the month that Barack Obama was elected president, that the economy still reeled from a worldwide meltdown, and that Poplawski, in the midst of a last long stretch of joblessness, began spending a great deal of time again on Stormfront. This time, however, his chatter was less old-time ugly race hate and more a reverberation of the end-of-the-world, fiscal-collapse talk he was hearing on the radio and all around him, from the Internet conspiracy-monger Alex Jones and soon to be echoed by Glenn Beck. More to the point, Poplawski's online rantings and his conversations with friends sounded like Beck's advertisers at that time—selling the idea of a pending collapse of the U.S. dollar and the need to stock up on food. In the days right after Obama's election he wrote about seeking "ultimate victory for our people" by "taking back our nation." By March of 2009, he posted there would be a "slow, drawn out national demise" that would "allow the masses to remain asleep while the power at the top is consolidated."

Sometime in March 2009, Poplawski adopted a new screen name on Stormfront, "BracedForFate."

Increasingly, Poplawski was becoming so paranoid about the rumors of the FEMA camps that he wasn't even able to fully enjoy the civic eruption when the Steelers won the Super Bowl that February. He later reported online that when he took to the city's clogged streets, he yelled to the officers straining to keep the peace, "Hey! When the shit really hits the fan, I hope you guys are on our side. . . . !! I can only hope that at least some [of] our men and women in uniform have their heart in the right place." He also wrote: "It was just creepy seeing busses [*sic*] put into action by authorities, as if they were ready to transport busloads of Steeler fans to 645 FEMA drive [*sic*] if necessary."

Two months later, when it really did hit the fan, his mother told police in a sworn statement that her son had been "stockpiling guns and ammunition, buying and selling the weapons online, because he believed that as a result of the economic collapse, the police were no longer able to protect society. He only liked police when they were not curtailing his constitutional rights, which he was determined to protect."

For months, Richard Poplawski had been a damaged sponge absorbing practically every one of the toxic clouds you'd see drifting across America at the end of the 2000s—all that talk of the "Obama gun confiscation" so rampant at Knob Creek; the rumors about "FEMA camps" and the mythical crackdown on constitutional rights that animated the Oath Keepers; the runaway fear of The Other, which may have been Latinos down in Arizona but for Poplawski was mainly blacks. It was the winter when politicians like Paul Broun first spoke of Obama as a potential Hitler in a naked appeal for attention and for votes, but those like Poplawski weren't interested in the soapbox or the ballot box, only the cartridge box. This was all saturated in the poisoned additive of talk radio, where people like Beck and Jones were selling gold and survival seeds and themselves to a faceless universe of customers.

Rich Poplawski loved the shock jocks so much that he desperately wanted to be one—not even so much like Glenn Beck but like his favorite nonpolitical radio personalities, the foul-mouthed pranksters Opie and Anthony, the New York–based disc jockeys continually in hot water for pranks like encouraging a couple to have sex in the pews of St. Patrick's Cathedral. Perkovic and mom still swoon over a time they traveled to the Big Apple to see Opie and Anthony in person. A couple of years ago, Poplawski and Perkovic recorded their own radio shows for a site called Pirateradio.com—"The Eddie and P.O. Show."

Perkovic asks if you want to hear one of the episodes, from May

2007. It was based on an incident when Pamela Perkovic saw someone that she believed to be a Muslim putting up posters in their Lawrenceville neighborhood that read, "Eternal Happiness Flying Through the Sky." Convinced that it was a celebration of the 9/11 attacks (although a twenty-second check of Google revealed the whole thing to be a very non-Muslim public art project), it was the basis for a ten-minute radio show that is completely unlistenable, much of it a string of f-bombs and other expletives linked together in most unfunny ways. Only later do you read that the Pittsburgh police had undertaken an extensive effort to get this episode of "The Eddie and P.O. Show" because of its opening, which they described as "a hit list."

The program begins with riffing heavy metal and with Poplawski and Perkovic trading their crude banter, much of it centered on the mass murder of thirty-three people on the Virginia Tech campus just days earlier. The metallic music is punctuated every so often by the sound of gunfire.

> Pull the trigger. . . . Pull the trigger. . . . All I have to do is reach for the trigger and, Pow! . . . I plead not guilty . . . I plead not guilty . . . I plead not guilty . . . thirty-three people dead, I'm fairly impressed by that . . . thirty-three people dead. I'm fairly impressed by that. . . . That is fucking doomsday status.

The final voice is unmistakably that of Richard Poplawski:

> I want to kill my ex-girlfriend, her mother, her pets, my father, people I don't like—and in a random measure a couple of members of the Pittsburgh police.

Followed by the loud blast of a shotgun.

Most incongruously, the show then segues into the opening bars of the theme song from *Friends*—"I'll Be There for You."

. . . .

Early morning, April 4.

It is 7:03 a.m., to be exact, and Margaret Poplawski is on the phone to 9–1–1. The Poplawskis, mother and son, had gone out to an animal rescue shelter a while back and picked up a couple of pit bulls. It seemed like a good idea at the time, but now one of the dogs has peed on the rug, and Margaret Poplawski is yelling at her son, who was out until all hours of the night at a party, to clean up. But the argument has spiraled out of control, and Rich Poplawski's mother is talking to the dispatcher. "Look, I'm just waking up from a sleep," she says. "I want him gone."

Until this moment, nothing had seemed out of the ordinary—ordinary for the conspiracy-minded Poplawski, anyway. The day before, Rich Poplawski had strolled through the middle-class neighborhood with the two dogs and a .380-caliber pistol strapped to his waist, where he stopped to shoot the breeze with about ten teens hanging out in a kid's garage on a Friday night. The *Pittsburgh Tribune-Review* said he talked to the teens "about the Penguins' playoff chances and his conspiracy theories of how the government was going to collapse."

Poplawski was clearly obsessed with politics in those final days before the incident. Poplawski's grandmother Catherine Scott said in a television interview that her grandson was depressed over his lack of prospects in Pittsburgh, that "[t]here is no life for these young kids coming up." She and others said Poplawski—convinced that money would soon become worthless—racked up $13,000 on a credit card buying guns and other items, and then became furious at the banks and their government bailout when his interest rate got jacked up from 9 to 30 percent. Scott also told the interviewer:

He says these people losing their jobs will probably be on unemployment around the fall of the year and there will probably be civil unrest and you should have extra food, you should have extra water, because water's essential. . . . If people are going to bombard your house, how else are you going to protect yourself? The reason he went out and bought that AK–47 is because he knew Obama was going to ban those.

That was all on Friday night, but now it is Saturday morning and Poplawski has been drinking and the dogs are barking and the police are coming to the house on Fairfield Street, as they have reportedly done a number of times before. Except this time, Poplawski is in the basement putting on his bulletproof vest and collecting his arsenal that he's assembled from Braverman Arms and the Internet and God knows where else.

It is 7:11 a.m. when the two on-duty officers, Paul Sciullo and Stephen Mayhle, arrive at the house. According to Margaret Poplawski's affidavit, she answered the door and let the two officers inside.

"Come and take his ass," she reported saying.

But Sciullo and Mayhle made it only about ten feet inside the house before they were gunned down in a hail of bullets from Poplawski, who was standing six feet away. It is believed that Mayhle survived long enough to return fire and hit the gunman in the leg. Margaret Poplawski said she turned to her son and said, "What the hell have you done."

But Richard Poplawski was not finished. There are a number of Pittsburgh cops who lived in Stanton Heights, and one of them—Eric Guy Kelly—was just getting home from the overnight shift when he heard the shots. He raced over—but Poplawski came out onto the porch and shot Kelly before he could make it to the front door. By now, other officers were responding—one of them, Timothy McManaway, was shot in the hand before he could drag the dying Kelly's body behind an SUV and out of the line of fire.

The modest cul-de-sac looking down toward the Allegheny River was a war zone now, surrounded by SWAT teams, and the standoff lasted nearly three hours before the wounded Poplawski gave himself up. "I'm standing down, come in and help me," he cried, and he was taken out on a gurney. Later that day, Poplawski told the cops he had pondered "going out in a blaze of glory," but decided against it—because he now wanted to write a book about what happened.

Since then, the case has stayed in the news, as the wheels of justice turn ever so slowly over Poplawski, and as Pittsburgh struggles to honor the three fallen cops and provide ongoing comfort to their families. But both Eddie Perkovic and his mother, who say they have received frequent phone calls from Poplawski in jail, said he has insisted there is something else that has not been reported about that morning.

They said Richard Poplawski has told both of them that right before the police showed up, his mother also said this to him:

"You're not going to shoot anybody, you fucking pussy."

In 2007, the Roman Catholic Church threw a batch of cold holy water on the notion of a "Limbo" after death, but then Pope Benedict XVI and his theologians never spent the better part of a day inside the edge of Hell known as Room 324 of the Allegheny County Courthouse. The courtroom is a nineteenth-century palace of monochrome, lit by sickly fluorescent bulbs with a droning HVAC soundtrack, half-open window shades revealing only the bleak gray of mid-January, not even a hint of spring.

Poplawski's public defender—a blond, simmering volcano named Lisa Middleman, equipped with a briefcase with so many motions she's already nearly run out of letters in the alphabet—has called to the stand a private investigator named Jessica Milko, who'd been tasked with pouring over literally hundreds of local newspaper articles and TV stories about Middleman's star client, aiming to show there was no way that Poplawski could ever receive a fair trial in this Pittsburgh-centered county.

Towards the end of the long hearing, the seen-it-all-before Judge Manning is droning over the sound of the heaters as he patiently explains why one intemperate remark by Pennsylvania's perpetually foot-in-mouth governor Ed Rendell was hardly grounds for granting Middleman's over-the-top motion to dismiss all charges against an accused triple-cop killer. But even in his own private Limbo, the onetime shock-jock wannabe can remain silent for only so long. Suddenly, there is a commotion in the courtroom. Poplawski has leapt to his feet, tossing his handcuffed arms skyward.

"Can I speak?!" he yells. Two courtroom officers respond to his request by jumping up from right behind him and forcing Poplawski back into his chair.

"Is it his neck?" The second voice is that of Margaret Poplawski—suddenly maternal, too little and too late. And now the deputies are leading her out of the courtroom, as the judge declares a short recess.

In the front row, Frances Kelly watches the entire spectacle—eyes arched upward in an expression of resigned frustration. Without uttering a word, Kelly—sixty-one, a longtime teacher's aide, deeply religious, still dressed for mourning, in black pants and blouse—is the moral center of the proceedings, caressing the shoulder of her granddaughter as the hearing drags on and patiently acknowledging the deputies as they come forward and say things about the late Eric Guy Kelly like, "I heard he was a great man." There is little doubt that she would like to tell the world about the son she lost that morning, but she cannot. She is included in the judge's sweeping gag order—because some day prosecutors hope to call her to the witness stand, to convince a jury that Richard Poplawski must die for his crime.

"I can't say a word about anything," she tells you in the corridor, politely but firmly. "Anything I say, she's going to throw up against the case," referring to Poplawski's attorney Middleman. Indeed, Kelly had just been singled out inside the courtroom for potentially violating the gag order, all because she had simply told a Pittsburgh TV news crew in the days after her son's murder, "It hurts so bad. I still think of it like he's living. I can't accept that he's passed."

Pittsburgh police officer Eric Guy Kelly had just worked the overnight shift, 11 p.m. to 7 a.m., and he was due at a private security job at 10 a.m., after just a three-hour break. When you're supporting a wife and three kids on the hillsides of Pittsburgh, that's just what you do. He lived right there in Stanton Heights, just a couple of blocks away—in fact he was in his driveway when he heard the gunshots. He'd just driven home his daughter—who at twenty-two was the exact same age as Poplawski and had also worked an overnight shift, as a nursing assistant at one of the hospitals. Upon hearing the gunshots, he dropped her off and decided to head over to the house where they seemed to be coming from. That was just like Kelly—ex-Marine, football player at the University of Tennessee, now a cop always doing things he didn't have to.

On the job for fourteen years, he was the kind of officer who always went to the scene. "He lived in Garfield for awhile when we were working night turn, and if a call came in for his neighborhood, he was the first one to step out of his house and offer help," a former partner, Detective Dan Sullivan, told a local paper. So going to Poplawski's residence that morning was routine—but he also knew the risks. In fact, he always told his wife, Marena, that if there was a knock on the door and a white car parked outside, it would be bad news.

And then, late that April 4 morning, a knock came and the white car was outside, exactly the way Eric had told his wife it would go down. A few days later, Officer Timothy McManaway—the one shot in the hand trying to rescue Kelly—dropped by to pay his respects. Said Marena Kelly: "He told me that Eric's last words were that he loved me and the kids."

Eric Guy Kelly didn't know anything about the "FEMA camps" that didn't even exist, he wasn't in on any scheme to knock on the doors of Stanton Heights and confiscate his neighbors' firearms, nor was he thinking at all—in the words of the statement that Margaret Poplawski later gave—about curtailing anybody's constitutional rights. Whatever Kelly's own political views might have been, it wasn't something that he wore on his sleeve—how could he have time for that stuff, working two jobs and picking the kids up at school and running across town to his mom's to fix her leaky toilet? He'd learned in the Marines—the same Marines that Rich Poplawski had flunked out of—to leave no one behind, certainly not his fallen colleagues Stephen Mayhle and Paul Sciullo II. But he didn't know what he was walking into that morning. He was a casualty in a war—a bogus war that mostly existed in angry electrons and loose radio waves and the discombobulated brains of some of the people receiving them. Kelly was a guy who was murdered for wearing a uniform, when in reality he was just another American from a different side of the same hill.

And Kelly, Mayhle, and Sciullo weren't the only casualties in this insane war. There were Greg McKendry and Linda Krieger, two sixty-somethings sitting in the pews at the Tennessee Valley Unitarian Universalist Church in Knoxville on July 27, 2008, when an unemployed man named Jim David Adkisson took a 12-gauge shotgun out of a guitar case and began firing; police found books by Michael Savage, Bill O'Reilly, and Sean Hannity in his apartment near the killer's own antiliberal "manifesto" that targeted—among other things—Bernard Goldberg's *100 People That Are Screwing Up America*. The police reported he chose the Unitarian Church because if "he could not get to the leaders of the liberal movement that he would then target those that had voted them into office."

The war's casualty list also included Stephen Tyrone Johns, the security guard at the U.S. Holocaust Memorial Museum in Washington, gunned down on June 10, 2009, with a .22-caliber rifle by James Wenneker von Brunn, an eighty-eight-year-old lifelong white supremacist who went to the museum carrying not only a gun but a notebook that read in part, "The Holocaust is a lie. Obama is created by the Jews." An Adolf Hitler enthusiast, von Brunn had sent out a mass email suggesting that, among other things, Obama was a citizen of Kenya, the same birther theory that would be cheered on in Delaware a few weeks later.

And then there was victim George Tiller, the Wichita, Kansas, abortion doctor who was shot and killed, also in a church, by Scott Roeder, who confessed that he committed the murder because "preborn children's lives were in imminent danger." For years, Tiller had been called "Tiller the Baby Killer" by the likes of the Fox News Channel's Bill O'Reilly and others in the conservative media.

In May 2010, two more cops were killed by right-wing fanatics. Brandon Paudert and Bill Evans, police officers from the Arkansas city of West Memphis, were gunned down at a traffic stop by forty-five-year-old Jerry Kane and his sixteen-year-old son. Kane had, just before the incident, uploaded a video to YouTube.com that said "you have to kill them all," and he espoused extreme right-wing, antigovernment views on a Web site for his unorthodox foreclosure-advice business, including his idea that paper money is worthless.

Meanwhile, also on the Fox News Channel, Glenn Beck finally did get around to debunking that "FEMA camp" theory that he had claimed famously he couldn't debunk. He invited on his program the editor of *Popular Mechanics*, who showed a video that was circulating on the Web that purported to show the American Auschwitz when in fact it was an Amtrak rail repair facility in Indiana. Beck told his audience, "And quite honestly, I don't believe that there are FEMA concentration camps. I think that sounds kind of nuts." Unfortunately, Richard Poplawski wasn't able to watch the program that afternoon. It aired on April 6, 2009—two days after Poplawski's paranoid cop-killing spree.

On the same day, Beck was also outraged that some bloggers were so quick to connect him and Poplawski. "Blaming anyone except the nut job for what happened in Pittsburgh is crazy," Beck said. "Police officers over the weekend were killed by a crazy with a gun and blaming anybody else besides him is like blaming the flight attendant after a terrorist takes down a plane." His point is partially valid. Knowing the toxic cloud in the mind of Richard Poplawski, the absent father and the difficult-mother issues that were taunted to the surface that day, his inability to find a steady job or a steady girl, the racial hate, it would be foolhardy to lay a simple, direct cause-and-effect rap on Beck, Alex Jones, or the other far-right media. After all, most people who respond to Beck's message—like Russ Murphy down in Delaware and all the other "September 12 Americans"—do so in ways that are legal and legitimate, usually exerting their free-speech rights on signs and at rallies.

But for all the thousands of law-abiding Russ Murphys, there are X number of Richard Poplawskis scattered across America, and we shouldn't have to do the math to learn the real value of X because simply put, one is too many. He is the living embodiment of an American Nightmare, an individualized worst-case scenario of all that you had seen from the drill fields of revolutionary Massachusetts to the sun-baked powder keg of Arizona. He was channeling the Internet not as a conduit for civic involvement but as a tool for buying the latest exotic assault rifle and then finding a reassuring online community of "like-minded" racists, smart enough to find all the trendy sources of foul-mouthed misinformation but not educated enough or focused enough to find a steady job or a stable life that would free him from a World Wide Web broadcasting cynical political messages that didn't offer engagement or hope but only paranoia. It was only the last match that was tossed by a multimillionaire who comes into the nation's living rooms just before supper time and regularly yells "Fire!" into all the crowded minds, terrifying the people who were already standing mentally near the exit signs.

The morning after seeing Richard Poplawski in the pockmarked flesh, you are hurtling up and down the steep inclines of the Pennsylvania Turnpike, the first great American superhighway, and the waves of AM radio are straining to clear the Allegheny ridges, sneaking through narrow tunnels and struggling to carry Glenn Beck to the good people down in the valley. The war is only beginning, he tells them, a message he pounds home again that evening on TV in another apocalyptic monologue. "Our founders were willing to risk their lives, their fortunes, and their sacred honor. Are you willing to at least sacrifice your fortune and find your honor to defend freedoms that we're losing?"

The words were pretty and scary and empty all at once, and the media was paying it no mind because of something else Beck had said on the radio that morning, that an election-night joke that the new GOP Massachusetts senator Scott Brown—who all of Beck's mainstream conservative brethren were hailing as a messiah—had made about his two daughters being "available" creeped him out so much that he was worried about "a dead intern" with Brown.

It was Glenn Beck fighting to get back to his favorite character—himself, circa 1985, the glory days of the "Morning Zoo." But it was too late. All of America was his zoo now, and it had gotten way too big for the keeper to control—the wide-eyed deer and the pacing jackals and the monsters in their red sweatpants and body armor who hear something banging on their cage in the middle of the night.

CHAPTER ELEVEN

The Battle of Waterloo

"If we're able to stop Obama on this, it will be his Waterloo. It will break him."

South Carolina Senator Jim DeMint, July 19, 2009, referring to the president's health-care proposals

It is still burning in Russ Murphy's craw, sitting here in the booth of the Milford Diner, when he thinks about what he saw a few days earlier when he flipped on the TV in his trailer—to Fox News Channel, of course—and here was *America's Newsroom*, one of a daylong stream of FNC shows in which chipper blondes and their less glamorous male counterparts deliver a version of the news from your right flank. The leader of the Delaware 9-12 Patriots had a good reason to perk up when he learned that the next guest would be the onetime top political advisor to the ex-president, the man they called "Bush's Brain" and that even many liberal enemies grudgingly called a political genius—Karl Rove.

Murphy was especially interested in the topic that Rove was going to be discussing: the rise of Tea Parties and similar outfits—like the 9-12 Patriots that Murphy had established in southern Delaware—and what impact they might play on the electoral chances of Republican candidates in 2010. The GOP establishment had been rocked the day before by a poll showing that in a completely hypothetical three-way race between a Tea Party, the Democrats, and Republicans, the Democrats would win—despite the level of voter unrest over the economy and some of President Barack Obama's proposals—and the 145-year-old Republican Party would trail this so-called Tea Party that didn't even exist a year earlier.

Introduced by blond-i-ful host Martha MacCallum in an affected voice as "the Architect, himself," Rove said that such a poll testing the strength of the Tea Party was "an interesting academic exercise" but that in the reality-based world, such a hypothetical challenger would struggle to get access to the ballot in many states and also to convince voters they weren't throwing away their ballot. He said the political party that addresses the worries of these voters about massive federal debt was going to get the bulk of their votes—and then "the Architect" mentioned a little side project.

"I was in Delaware a couple nights ago and visited with a group of Tea Party organizers in Georgetown, Delaware," Rove said. "I met a nurse from a hospital, a grizzled Vietnam vet in a biker jacket, and a stay-at-home mom. Them, and a bunch of other people, but these were the leaders."

Back in the trailer, Russ Murphy's heart skipped a beat. Karl Rove, the nation's best-known political strategist, who just a couple of years ago was whispering into President Bush's ear in the West Wing of the White House, was now on the Fox News Channel talking about him, the "grizzled Vietnam vet in a biker jacket."

In one sense, this once unlikely sit-down crystallized how fast this grassroots backlash against Barack Obama had come in such a short period of time. The upshot, of course, of all the attention—the entreaties from Rove and the other GOP bigwigs, the swarm of reporters chasing quotes down in Nashville, the busloads of regular folks who helped elect Scott Brown in Massachusetts—was to raise expectations to sky-high levels, just one short year removed from a million people packing the National Mall to celebrate Obama's inauguration.

Now that the calendar had flipped to 2010 and the political tide shifted, there seemed to be no apparent way that the Democrats— Obama and his despised-on-the-right allies Nancy Pelosi and Harry Reid—would pass their signature piece of legislation, health-care reform. And when that effort was defeated, Obama would be a failed president, just like Jimmy Carter before him. So cocksure was this anti-Obama rebellion that the question they were debating at the dawn of this midterm election year was not whether the Democrats would lose Congress but whether it would be to the Old Guard of the Republican Party like Mike Castle or whether there would be a revolution of inexperienced, Tea Party–reveling "constitutional conservatives."

Which explains why Karl Rove went a-calling on Russ Murphy and friends.

The only problem was that the whole thing was supposed to be a secret. A few days earlier, Rove had come to the Lower, Slower Delaware to raise money for the state Republican Party and to urge support for Representative Mike Castle, who—having been duly chastened at the CHEER Center by Eileen M. and her cheering mob—had veered from the center lane of politics over to the right. In spite of his centrist past, Castle was hoping the anti-Obama backlash had enough froth to propel him into the U.S. Senate and the seat once held by the new vice president, Joe Biden. Ironically, the Delaware GOP Christmas gala was held at Baywood, a plush golf resort just a nine-iron down the street from Eileen M.'s modest home. Before the event, with the counsel of some local politicians, Rove granted what amounted to an audience to these new, unschooled activists—the nurse Nicole Theis, the stay-at-home mom Donna Gordon of the Delaware Tea Party, and the "grizzled" Russ Murphy.

Frankly, it's hard not to use the word "grizzled" to describe the road-tested and battle-ready Murphy. But the problem was that "the Architect's" snooty attitude toward the 9-12 Patriot and his band of amateurs really wasn't all that different from that of those college punk hippies Murphy claims harassed him back in the 1960s.

Russ Murphy was getting spit on, all over again.

"Bottom line, I sat there and it was somewhat condescending," Murphy tells you, sitting in the booth at the diner, "which I find hard at times to express to some of these people."

Murphy may not know a lot about polling and focus groups, but he knows when his band of Beck-inspired Tea Partiers has the upper hand with the GOP. Less than a year after he finished reading *The 5000 Year Leap* and answered the call from Glenn Beck to become "a September 12 man," the retired truck driver was in the driver's seat. Karl Rove needed him and his operation more than he needed Karl Rove. Christine O'Donnell, a conservative TV commentator who was quite popular with the Delaware 9-12 Patriots, was already making plans to mount a primary challenge to Castle; it was pretty unlikely that the underfunded O'Donnell could actually win, but unrest on the blue-collar right could continue to make things miserable for the lifetime patrician pol—and that could help the Democrats hold onto Biden's old seat in November, even amid a much-predicted GOP tsunami.

"They," Murphy continued, with "they" being the Republican Party establishment in Delaware—"wanted us to come there and try to use Karl Rove's image to impress us." Clearly, that hadn't worked. Now that Rove had announced the "secret" meeting to two million viewers on Fox, Murphy could report to you that while some local pols—Shaun Fink, a young activist who later joined a conservative think tank, and Colin Bonini, a GOP state senator from outside of Dover—seemed to understand the rage and frustrations of the Tea Party activists, Rove and the other bigwigs acted clueless. At one point, Murphy says, Rove grew effusive in praising the centrist Republican Castle's decades of political service—not a big selling point to an anti-incumbency mob. Murphy claimed that Bonini, the senator, had laughed out loud at those words from Rove, recalling the town hall meeting and the "birther" rant and all the radio calls attacking Castle's support for Obama's global-warming measure.

"I think Castle pretty much shot himself in the foot with these people," Murphy says Bonini told Rove. And Bonini is completely right in his assessment. Russ Murphy could care less about preserving Mike Castle's career in politics. He was on a bigger mission—from God—to save America.

"We haven't been involved in it all these years that they have and it's not our profession—but this is our county. We're not idiots," Murphy said, lingering on that last word, his voice now steaming more than the mug of coffee on the Formica table before him. "They still don't understand—it's like, when they talked about the health bill. We discussed that a little bit and it's like, 'They're making headway, there's compromise being met,' and it's like they still don't get it. The majority of the people don't want this!"

Usually in war, you don't get to pick the battles—rather, they choose you. On one level, it seemed rather odd when Jim DeMint—the junior senator from the Palmetto State, which seemed to be on the front lines of warring with Washington, just as it had been in 1860—declared that the decisive "Waterloo" would be waged over health-care reform. The South Carolinian's comment was the most memorable of a volley of over-the-top rhetoric from the increasingly usual suspects—talk radio hosts and extremist members of Congress—that painted health care proposals by Obama and friends in apocalyptic terms.

It started around July 2009, as it became clear that the new president hoped to make health care the crowning achievement of his first two years in office. That month, Michael Steele, the perpetually embattled chairman of the Republican National Committee who was elected to that job not long after Obama's inauguration, told reporters that health-care reform was "socialism" and that a "cabal" in Congress was backing it. The very next day, Glenn Beck—consciously or not—echoed Steele and called the package "good old socialism . . . raping the pocketbooks of the rich to give to the poor." Over time, of course, the rhetoric began to escalate when charges of "socialism" had lost their shock value. By August, Rush Limbaugh was casually telling his listeners that "the Obama health-care logo is damn close to a Nazi swastika logo," and by December, after months of nonstop attacks, Limbaugh was comparing Democratic health-care proposals to Nazis and Cuba and everything in between.

The escalating radio hyperbole was not nearly as surprising, however, as the way in which the stark, apocalyptic tone then carried over to the Republican members of Congress who were tasked with deciding the fate of the bill, and who in a bygone era might have sought a deal with some concessions from the Democratic majority. Instead, the right-wing politicians eagerly signed on to what was now cast as a political war of the worlds, a "Waterloo" with no retreat and no surrender.

One obscure back-bencher, GOP Representative Devin Nunes, sounded as if he were sending his audition tape in to Clear Channel when he called the Obama-backed health-care proposals the "ghost of communist dictators." Many of Nunes's colleagues followed suit in trying to up the rhetorical ante, even though when pressed in interviews they were often unable to connect their overheated verbiage either to what was actually in the bill or to their specific objections to it. "I hate to sound so harsh, but . . . this literally is a fast march towards socialism, where the government is bigger than the private sector in our country and health care's the next major step, so we oughta all be worried about it," a longtime Republican stalwart, Representative Zach Wamp of Tennessee, told MSNBC as the debate dragged on, but when pressed on the topic, Wamp tried to argue that half of the uninsured had voluntarily turned down employer coverage and that "gobs" of undocumented immigrants were receiving insurance—both claims that were contradicted by the facts.

Indeed, as the actual vote drew closer, some of the most outspoken opponents moved even farther away from the legislative process of negotiation, in favor of staging rallies and delivering fiery speeches. Representative Michele Bachmann convinced her GOP colleagues to sign onto a "Kill the Bill" rally with Tea Partiers outside the Capitol. Iowa representative Steve King fantasized about an event like the fall of Communism in Prague in 1989, when citizens overpowered the government by their vast numbers, saying, "Fill this city up, fill this city, jam this place full so that they can't get in, they can't get out and they will have to capitulate to the will of the American people." That didn't happen—only several thousand people attended the rally, where Texas Republican representative Louie Gohmert told the crowd that "I don't want to make you sick, but I brought an abortion to show you today; there's a whole lot of demons going on."

It was increasingly bizarre: some of the most powerful and privi-leged leaders of the United States were now adopting the paranoid style of the marginalized fringe as once described by Hofstadter—depicting what once would have been a difference of reasonable opinions over the government's role in health care as what the 1960s historian fa-mously called "the birth and death of whole worlds, whole political orders, whole systems of human values." By the end of the run-up to a vote, even the experienced, cooler heads of the Republican Party had adopted this clash-of-civilizations tone; Utah senator Orrin Hatch told the *Los Angeles Times* that "it's going to be a holy war."

Neither Glenn Beck nor Alex Jones could have said it any better.

By 2010, EXTREME rhetoric about health-care reform had become so commonplace it was easy to forget how strange it was that *this* bill had become the target of so much venom. For one thing, the notion of government action to cover many of the millions of Americans lack-ing health-care insurance and curbing the worst abuses of insurance companies seemed somewhat removed from most immediate issues that stirred the souls of Beck's 9-12ers and the Tea Partiers—things like preventing gun control or cracking down on undocumented im-migration. It's certainly true that the government's role in health care has been a contentious one—from the clash over launching Medicare in the mid-1960s to Bill Clinton's failed plan for more sweeping health-care reform in the 1990s. At the same time, the notion of some kind of insurance reform was consistently popular with a majority of Americans; in March 2009, during the low-decibel early rumblings of the Tea Party, a CNN-commissioned poll found 72 percent of citizens supporting an expanded government role in health care and just 27 percent (sound roughly familiar?) opposing it. What's more, many mainstream Republicans had been onboard with at least some moderate version of reform, and in fact the plan that Obama would end up pushing was a clone of one that a 2012 GOP front-runner for president, Mitt Romney, implemented as the governor of Massachusetts, at a signing ceremony attended by Senator Ted Kennedy.

On the other hand, the anti-Obama backlashers—people who had not emitted a peep when a Republican president, George W. Bush, had pushed through a pricey package of Medicare drug benefits that also benefitted Big Pharma—were now on record opposing any expanded role or nondefense expenditures from Washington. That meant that any plans for a larger federal role in health care—even though the proposal that Obama was pushing fell far short of the government-owned "single payer" plan that many liberals would favor—was right in the wheelhouse of the new Tea Party movement.

But the other main reason for massive resistance to health-care reform—called for by the radio jocks, endorsed by the activists, and adopted by the politicians—was strategic: that all the other items on Obama's to-do list, such as a serious approach to climate change and an immigration program that included any kind of amnesty, would be collateral damage to a health-care defeat. Later polling data would show that more that eight of ten of the Tea Partiers and their fellow travelers believed—incorrectly—that their views represented how most Americans feel on the issues, convincing many of the very self-delusional notion that Representative Steve King gave voice to, that "the will of the American people" was so unanimously dead set against health care that a massive angry throng might even topple the government in the streets the way the people did in Prague. Indeed, there is a sense that as the right-wing political leadership became immersed in the 24/7 bubble of Fox News and talk radio, the congressional Republicans became as convinced of the overwhelming public support for their cause as the Tea Partiers themselves, and that by denying the duly elected Democratic majority they were not just lawmakers but Saviors of the Republic.

In order to successfully carry out that Obama-thwarting strategy and capture the raw energy of the Tea Party/9-12 movements to help defeat health care, it was necessary for its newfound leaders both in the right-wing media and in Congress to twist or often ignore the facts of the actual debate, to stuff them into the box of fears and emotionally weaponized anxieties that had created the backlash in the first place. So the Obama proposal was portrayed not as a desirable expansion of health care but rather as a confiscation—not of your guns, they claimed, although God knows that would be next if this succeeded— but of your personal liberties to decide whether or not you wanted to pay for coverage. Indeed, the critics argued that the very idea of health-care coverage was outside of the Constitution and so Obama was now violating his promise to uphold it—just as the Oath Keepers had been warning that he would. And of course, the real goal was not expanding insurance coverage but redistributing wealth, because Ivy League elitists like Obama want to tax you, or ruin your good insurance, to give benefits either to the "handout people" in cities like Wilmington or the illegal immigrants and their *reconquista* of Arizona. The bottom line was that health-care reform was painted for the Tea Party set in the same terms that Russ Murphy had used to describe Obama himself: "absolutely not American."

At first, it all seemed like a giant leap of faith, with the Democrats compiling a seemingly filibuster-proof majority of sixty votes in the Senate after Pennsylvania senator Arlen Specter quit the GOP and switched parties. But then came the stunning upset victory of conservative Republican Scott Brown in liberal-leaning Massachusetts, which gave powerful force to an increasingly messianic streak among the backlashers.

In the pivotal month of January 2010, busloads of Tea Party activists and 9-12ers from up and down the eastern seaboard flooded the Bay

State to assist Brown—a once-obscure but good-looking and charis-matic state senator. The Republican's successful surge from nowhere in the polls partially reflected their door-to-door crusade, but it was also driven by widespread public anger at the very moment that U.S. un-employment was cresting over 10 percent, along with the fact that the Democrats—as is their custom, all too often—put forth a spectacularly unappealing candidate in the gaffe-prone and humorless state attorney general, Martha Coakley. That last factor was probably the deciding one, but it didn't stop the Tea Party from taking credit for Brown, or the chattering classes on cable TV from agreeing. On January 19, 2010, the boisterous crowd at Brown's victory party chanted "Forty-one! Forty-one!"—a symbol of their confidence that electing a Republican in blue Massachusetts guaranteed the final vote needed for a filibuster to kill health care. The Democrats, the backlashers reasoned, wouldn't dare try any legislative moves to thwart "the will of the people."

Meanwhile, it was no wonder that establishment Republicans began to fear the Tea Party as much as, or arguably more than, liber-als did. A few weeks after Brown's victory, GOP chairman Steele sum-moned about fifty Tea Party activists and members of related groups to Washington for a private meeting, and there was apprehension on both sides. "Steele wants to try to co-opt us, but we're coming to tell him he doesn't get it," one unnamed Tea Party leader told Fox News. "We want to return the Republican Party to its roots. We're expecting some fireworks." It all sounded exactly like what Russ Murphy had told you about his encounter with Karl Rove, that the Tea Party didn't trust the pointy-headed conservative elites much more than the liberal ones. The meeting lasted for four hours, and there's little evidence that Steele made much headway. Lisa Miller, a leader of the Tea Party in Washington, D.C., told MSNBC afterward that "we're going to have to retake the Republican Party, if you will, instead of the Republican Party absorbing us."

But as the 2010 election season began to unfold, there were also indications that the power of the Tea Party movement to get tangible results—at least the type that gets the attention of Big Media and political insiders—might be mostly limited to GOP primaries in high-profile races featuring longtime Republicans with some centrist baggage facing less-tainted candidates who were nonetheless skilled politicians. Exhibit A was the state of Florida, where at the height of Obama's post-election popularity, GOP leaders inside the Beltway decided the best way to hold on to an open Senate seat in the Sunshine State was with its middle-of-the-road and seemingly popular white-haired governor, Charlie Crist; Crist immediately doubled down on what was a horrible bet by embracing the Democratic president, both literally—in front of the camera on an airport tarmac—and figuratively by backing the $800 billion Obama stimulus package, the spark that created the angry backlash movement in the first place. Tea Partiers rallied enthusiastically behind a lesser-known upstart, the youthful and handsome Cuban-American former Florida house speaker Marco Rubio, who marched from obscurity to an almost insurmountable lead over Crist. By the spring of 2010, Crist had abandoned the Republican Party altogether to run as an Independent.

And Florida's Rubio was practically a flaming liberal compared to the Tea Party–backed Republican candidate for the U.S. Senate in Kentucky, the libertarian-minded Rand Paul. Paul is an eye surgeon and a longtime antitax activist who has one other huge asset in appealing to the right-wing backlash—he is a son of a movement hero, the 2008 and possible 2012 presidential candidate Ron Paul. In the Bluegrass State, party leaders led by the Senate Majority Leader, Mitch McConnell, lined up behind youthful secretary of state Trey Grayson, despite the fact that Grayson is a Harvard grad and former Democrat who as a young man committed the cardinal sin of voting for Bill Clinton. Paul, who wants to end the Federal Reserve Board and the federal income tax, rolled to an easy primary victory over the GOP's handpicked Grayson. One base of support for Rand Paul—not surprisingly—were the locals who flooded the Knob Creek Machine Gun Shoot twice a year; in April 2009, Paul showed up there in person and, during a break in the heavy artillery pounding, declared "we're in danger of losing all our freedoms now with an administration that is not friendly to gun owners."

Immediately after capturing the nomination, Paul did a flurry of TV interviews and demonstrated that the rigid ideology of the Tea Party does not always play well on the national stage. Most famously, he said several times that as a libertarian he wouldn't have supported the provisions of the 1964 Civil Rights Act that barred private businesses—like a Woolworth's lunch counter—from discriminating; comments he later retracted. Even more bizarrely, he said it was "un-American" for Obama to criticize the company behind the environmental catastrophe in the Gulf of Mexico—the English-owned British Petroleum. As the general election approached, it was not clear whether some of Rand Paul's past extremism would come back to hurt him. In 2008, for example, he told an audience in Montana about his belief in the North American Union —"complete with a currency, a cross-national bureaucracy, and virtually borderless travel within the Union"—that was the same discredited conspiracy theory embraced by the John Birchers, their ally Representative Paul Broun, and even more fringe elements.

But lost in the media frenzy was the growing evidence that Rubio and Paul were also outliers. In a slew of early primary races in the late winter and spring of 2010, Tea Party activists either ran for office themselves or backed friendly outsider candidates—and failed miserably, usually due to a lack of experience, money, exposure, or all three. In Obama's home state of Illinois, GOP leaders again picked a moderate for the president's former Senate seat—U.S. Representative Mark Kirk—but this time the Tea Party–backed rival received only 19 percent of the primary vote. On the same day, a Tea Party candidate for Illinois governor finished a dismal fifth. In ultraconservative Texas, a flood of novice candidates linked to the Tea Party and similar right-wing movements was itself swamped by the raw force of incumbency. Remarkably, even Ron Paul drew three Tea Party challengers in his far-right-looking south Texas congressional district, but the "money bomb"–pioneering Paul had $2.5 million in the bank while none of the rivals had even $100,000, and the incumbent not surprisingly grabbed about 80 percent of the vote.

The poster child for the harried Tea Party politician in 2010, in fact, was a Ron Paul acolyte who ran for governor in Texas, Debra Medina. A GOP county chairwoman who had never held office before, Medina ran under the radar screen and rose in the polls with support from groups like Paul's Campaign for Liberty and even the Oath Keepers, as well as a solid performance in a televised debate against the incumbent Republican governor, Rick Perry, and U.S. senator Kay Bailey Hutchison, once considered the front-runner before sentiment turned against Washington. Medina's campaign—like those of many of these other Tea Party–inspired newcomers—drew on several of the themes that had echoed from the gun fears of Knob Creek to the antifederalist cheering of Atlanta's Tenth Amendment Summit; her four main campaign planks were to fight for the rights of gun owners, to be a leading voice against illegal immigration, to crusade for the power of state sovereignty, and to eliminate all property taxes in Texas.

Meanwhile, Medina was also giving bizarre interviews to the Texas-based Alex Jones, in which she agreed with the host about "Soviet brainwashing" by the police in Texas and proudly proclaimed that she wasn't "a Bilderberger," referring to the international conspiracy theory. Polls suggested Medina was on an upward track to pass Hutchison and at least make a runoff with Perry—until she was tripped up by an unlikely source: Glenn Beck. When Beck invited Medina on his radio show, it was presumed to be a coup for her candidacy—until Beck shocked her with a question over whether she believed the U.S. government had advance knowledge of the 9/11 attacks. Medina said she didn't have a position but that "I think some very good questions have been raised in that regard"—and her momentum faltered under the belief she was a "9/11 truther."

Candidates like Medina—or even lesser-known challengers like an independent Tea Party hopeful for a Tennessee congressional seat who, facing a well-funded Republican, asked his backers to help him with a fundraiser at a bowling alley because "I'm not one of those guys who has a ton of special interest money"—helped bring into sharp relief what the new movement actually could and could not accomplish.

The Tea Party's true success in 2010 was not in electing their own people but moving incumbents like Delaware's Castle or Arizona senator John McCain—with his conservative back-flips to the right on immigration and gays in the military—to the farther right. In fact, some new and more down-to-earth activists realized that as badly as they wanted to make a difference in the big-ticket national races in 2010 and then 2012, the best path to long-term success was the slow road, at the local grassroots level.

This was beginning to play out in a couple of ways. One was the discovery that after the decade of apathy that took root during the presidency of George W. Bush, local Republican Party organizations were ripe for a takeover, thanks to a boatload of unfilled positions on the level of neighborhood precinct captain. These takeovers didn't happen only in places like Arizona, where Ron Paul diehards like Jeff Greenspan had engineered a minor coup in Maricopa County, but in many states across the country from Pennsylvania to Nevada, where right-wing "constitutional conservatives" seized the party apparatus in Las Vegas. There was, in fact, a new group promoting this—called the National Precinct Alliance—empowered by its finding that some 60 percent of the 150,000 GOP committee seats across the country were unfilled. Ultimately, Tea Party control of these Republican Party committees could lead to nomination of even more conservative candidates in future races—if that's possible. Indeed, that's what happened in Utah in May 2010, when the Tea Party elected so many delegates to a state GOP convention that they unseated the solidly conservative U.S. senator, Robert Bennett.

In Delaware, Russ Murphy and his 9-12 Patriots took another approach, focusing as much on local issues as on the national kerfuffles over health care or immigration. A few weeks after Rove unsuccessfully urged Murphy and his cohorts to fall in line behind Castle's Senate candidacy, the ex-Marine and his group stormed the state capitol building in Dover instead. Their core message was that the "Delaware consensus"—the friendly gentlemen's agreement between Democrats and Republicans in state politics on so many major issues—was a thing of the past.

"We went there as their employer, more or less, and we were giving them their assignment for the year" is how Murphy explained it later. He said "their future employment would be judged in their performances, not on their promises."

When lawmakers returned to Dover for the first day of their 2010 session, many were stunned when Murphy and other members of the group passed out a packet with what they called their "demands" for new legislation. A couple of these demands from the Delaware 9-12 Patriots centered on common good-government themes, such as passage of two long-stalled measures for voters to place initiatives on the ballot, as well as referenda on bills already passed by the lawmakers. Murphy's group was also pushing for an end to Delaware's closed primaries that prevented independent voters or party crossovers from playing a role in selecting the fall candidates.

But other demands on their list sounded as though they were hatched in the incubator of angry talk radio, especially on the topic of immigration. Here, the 9-12 Patriots were telling the Delaware lawmakers they must develop a program very much like the one that had caused public unrest and wreaked economic havoc down in Arizona, with penalties for employers who hire undocumented immigrants, broad law-enforcement powers similar to those wielded by Sheriff Joe Arpaio, and a ban on immigrants without papers from serving in the Delaware National Guard. The 9-12 Patriots also demanded that the lawmakers not pass any bills that might restrict the use of firearms.

"The demands listed are without compromise and are non-negotiable," it stated in the packet that Murphy was handing out to the elected officials. "We are going to bring these issues to the forefront and push to have the citizen/voter taxpayers hold you accountable for your lack of due consideration."

It was the arrogance of the 84-Percent Bubble that the 9-12ers lived in, where the nonstop piped-in political Muzak of Beck and Limbaugh and the wooing by the Karl Roves and the adulation from the blondes on Fox News were the source of moral certitude that for the elected officials, it was suddenly their way or the highway. Even in a small state that Obama and Joe Biden had just carried by 100,000 votes.

Not surprisingly, some of the lawmakers were flabbergasted, especially those from the more urban and more populated New Castle County, the places that 9-12er Alex Garcia had described as "the handout areas." One of them, state representative John Kowalko from the university town of Newark, harrumphed to the *Wilmington News-Journal* that the demands that Murphy was handing out were "impertinent."

The seeming power of a unified minority in Washington with just enough votes to thwart Obama was also a source of strength and, arguably, arrogance and self-importance. Even after Brown's election, the Democrats held 59 percent of the U.S. Senate, 59 percent of the House of Representatives, and 100 percent of the White House. But the GOP's forty-one Senate votes—representing, it must be noted, no more than 37 percent of the American public (thanks to Republican popularity in smaller states)—seemed paramount, because it offered just enough votes to kill any piece of legislation through the delaying tactic known as the filibuster. These representatives of 37 percent of the country wielded unprecedented powers because of something the likes of which this nation had never seen before: their ability to stick together on every single issue with the sole purpose of obstructing Barack Obama and his Democratic allies. It was an "I Hope He Fails" strategy hatched in the ratings-driven studios of talk radio, but now rigid legislative fealty to the on-air musings of Rush Limbaugh and Glenn Beck had ground Washington to a total halt.

On the last Saturday in February 2010, the Delaware 9-12 Patriots took their revolution to America's new public green. They lined the

DuPont Highway in Dover, down the road from the Kirby & Holloway Family Restaurant, in front of the Dover Mall and right next to the Pier 1 Imports. Dressed in wool flannel shirts and some in hoodies against the chill winds of late winter, Murphy and his allies stood in front of waist-deep snowbanks and let their signs do the talking—"Torture Terrorists Not Taxpayers" and "Stop Socialist's Healthcare Now!!!" (brandished by a grandmotherly gray-haired woman in big glasses who abruptly yelled into the ever-present video camera, "Stand up America and fight!") and "In God We Trust" and Obama portrayed as a donkey and "Commander in Thief." The display was greeted by a steady stream of honking horns from the midwinter shoppers.

In hindsight, the rising expectations of the Tea Party may have peaked too soon—before the health-care matter was actually resolved. All those honking horns that you witnessed in early 2010 from Scotts-dale, Arizona, to Dover had an unintended effect—waking up the actual sleeping giants. That would be the 53 Percenters, and the president they had elected a year and a half earlier.

By the end of their winter of discontent, Democrats in Washington realized they had little choice but to play the hand they had now been dealt. In December 2009, the pre–Scott Brown Senate had actually passed a version of a health-care bill that even many Democrats—especially in the House—were not happy with; but the party's strategists now realized it was the path to achieving most of their goals—covering as many as 35 million uninsured people and barring insurance companies from denying coverage to people with preexisting medical problems. If the House passed that Senate version, some of the problems could be fixed with a second bill under a process called reconciliation, in which a measure determined to have an impact on the federal deficit cannot be filibustered by the minority of forty-one senators.

There was just one more thing this strategy needed, however: the old Barack Obama. Not the one who'd been playing rope-a-dope and taking punch after punch from the Tea Party and from Fox and friends, but the passionate one who'd caused *his* people to honk their horns and dance in the streets of places like Philadelphia back on November 3, 2008, an event that now felt as if it had happened some fifty years ago.

On a Monday morning, March 8, 2010, when the last soot-covered snow piles were finally melting into the muck of oncoming spring—all these forces converged back toward Philadelphia, toward a small college campus where the city's row houses abruptly give way to the wide lawns of suburban Montgomery County, where Obama would give yet another impassioned plea for health-care reform. The president of the United States woke up this day on the lavish second floor of the White House and headed out toward *Air Force One*, accompanied by a large press corps and his West Wing entourage.

Down in his trailer outside of Milford, Delaware, Russ Murphy was also up early, around 6 a.m., climbing into a rented van and picking up a half-dozen other local activists for the roughly two-hour drive north. Murphy says it was a spur-of-the-moment thing, to fly the Delaware state flag outside the Obama rally and let the cameras know that some folks from Joe Biden's home state were vehemently opposed to health care.

Except that the captain of the Delaware 9-12 Patriots and his tiny crew never got within striking distance of their elusive foe. At first, the campus cops at Arcadia University confined Murphy and the other protesters to a parking lot far from the main event; as the morning dragged on they moved closer, to where the TV cameras were at least, and to where a reporter from the local suburban paper asked Murphy for his opinions. But he would never get a chance to look Barack Obama in the eye, as he saw the flashing lights of the motorcade climb the hill and then vanish, more than thirty yards down the road.

Inside, Obama took the stage, introduced the local dignitaries, and whipped his suit jacket off, the modern contrived version of the give-'em-hell-Harry whistle-stop, and then he leaned into the big lectern with the presidential seal. Murphy and the other protestors were just gnats outside the big house; all the cameras were trained directly on the president of the United States, and he appeared driven to remind all of the people, in the hall and watching on television, of how he got here in the first place.

And you've seen all the pundits pontificating and talking over each other on the cable shows, and they're yelling and shouting. They can't help themselves. That's what they do. But out here, and all across America, folks are worried about bigger things. They're worried about how to make payroll. They're worried about how to make ends meet. They're worried about what the future will hold for their families and for our country. They're not worrying about the next election. We just had an election.

Inside the hermetically sealed college auditorium, people whooped and cheered at the reference, at the recollection of what they had accomplished back in the recent past of MyBarackObama.com and "Yes, we can!" The TV picture on all the cable networks was framed by a representative snapshot of the America that spoke up on November 3, 2008, and had then fallen strangely mute. There was the stocky African-American in the blue suspenders, the young man with tan skin and a slight Jeri-curl, the collegiate Asian woman with the long straight black locks, the beefy man with the stark gray beard.

Everything had flip-flopped since the 1960s, now that the children of that era's conservative "silent majority" were grown up. Now they were the ones performing street theater, while onstage here at Arcadia University was America's new silent majority, which was growing in number and influence on America, instead of shrinking. And these "silent" ones roared to life now when Barack Obama told them, "I'll be honest with you. I don't know how passing health care will play politically, but I do know that it's the right thing to do."

ELEVEN DAYS AFTER the Obama rally in Philadelphia, Representative Paul Broun is rising on the House floor to speak. Like his new friends in the Tea Party, the radical Georgia congressman had staked so much on the ability to block health-care reform. Now, the passage of the bill is threatening to expose the vapidity of that saving-the-Republic-from-dictatorship argument, and a vote is a matter of hours away. Broun looks several years older than he did at the Eggs and Issues event in Hartwell, which was just three weeks earlier; he is wearing his glasses this time, and his voice is hoarse.

"If Obamacare passes," Broun says, pretending to hold an imaginary plastic card in his hand, "that free insurance card that's in people's pockets is going to be as worthless as a Confederate dollar after the war between the states—the Great War of Yankee Aggression." He emits a small and strange chuckle after saying that—frustrated and bemused by this rapid turn of events, relegating himself, at least on this night, down to a lower league, the League of the South that neo-Confederates played in, railing against the "federal empire" that followed the War Between the States.

The next morning, at 5 o'clock, Russ Murphy is up early again—standing in pitch blackness on this unseasonably warm first day of spring, as a large bus pulls into the Food Lion lot along the flickering lights of the sleeping commercial strip in Milford, Delaware. Murphy and about forty of his troops are answering the call—one of a series of increasingly desperate pleas from what passed for national leadership of the Tea Party. The strategy was to flood the streets of the District of Columbia with so many unhappy citizens that the Congress would be forced to abandon health care, just the way those Commie dictators had collapsed in Eastern Europe, without a shot being fired. The big-business-funded FreedomWorks called for a "People's Surge against Obamacare 2.0," and told members, "we will be storming the three House Office Buildings."

But the troops were getting weary—you could hear it in Murphy's voice earlier in the week as he dithered on whether to go at all. In the end, the Marine veteran decided to be there for the last battle, heading over the Chesapeake Bay on the bus with his band of Delaware 9-12 Patriots, with a stop at McDonald's to prepare for the long march ahead. The Delawareans reached the U.S. Capitol complex early, planted their large banner right near a main stage, and soaked in the right-wing vibe.

They even held a low-key meeting with Representative Mike Castle—on their side now, on this particular vote—in his office. Afterward, Murphy was remarkably mellow about the whole thing. "Everybody could see the handwriting on the wall" that the bill was going to pass, he said, and from his perspective it wasn't about stopping health-care reform anymore, but about gaining recruits for the coming battle to roll it back. The next war.

Unlike the 9-12 March the previous September, which had been pimped for weeks in advance by Beck and the rest of Fox News, there was no one erroneously claiming that 1.7 million people were on the Mall this time, because the crowds were small enough that reporters could count them the old-fashioned way. On this Saturday with perfect weather and the health-care "Armageddon" looming, the Tea Party leaders drew an estimated three thousand followers, at most. Many gathered in front of the congressional Cannon Office Building when their rally speeches were over and—lacking the numbers and possibly the gumption for "storming" the buildings—some who were not as laid-back or resigned as Russ Murphy instead hollered the bitter emotions of last resort. For all the right-wing chatter during the Obama backlash about staging a conservative "Woodstock," the baby boomer counter-counterculture instead fell back on an ugly verbal equivalent of the Weather Underground's futile 1969 antiwar vandalism rampage called the "Days of Rage"—or maybe this was the forty-five-year-old showdown between white authorities and civil rights marchers on Alabama's Edmund Pettus Bridge all over again.

"It reminded me of the '60s," Representative John Lewis of Georgia—who was beaten by cops on that Selma, Alabama, bridge in the famed 1965 march—later told reporters. Some forty-five years had passed, and now Lewis's lifelong passion had brought him to the U.S. Capitol, where he would argue that health care was a civil right, too, and vote accordingly. The right-wing rebels were on both sides of Lewis and his colleagues in the House leadership as policemen escorted them from their offices and up the steps of the Capitol, chanting, "Kill the bill! Kill the bill!" The "Don't Tread on Me" flag waved over the mini-throng—there was a young girl in a McCain-Palin T-shirt from 2008, a sour-looking woman in gray shorts holding a toy puppy in one hand and snapping digital pictures with the other, and a phalanx of white guys on the main railing, middle-aged and beefy, baseball caps pulled down tight over wraparound sunglasses—the new paranoid style. The seventy-year-old Lewis had never shied from a challenge in his life, and so he spoke back: "I'm for the bill. I support this bill, I'm voting for the bill."

"Kill the bill, nigger!"

More than one member of Congress was targeted. Another African-American, Emanuel Cleaver from Kansas City, who was right behind Lewis, called it "a chorus"—and the anger is still growing. As Cleaver himself strolled past the gathering and the white dudes with the baseball caps, something happened that was recorded for posterity on a video. The congressman stopped at the group and gesticulated as if he were swatting at a fly and exchanged words, as one of the wide-bodied men in the baseball hats lurched forward, hands cupped around his mouth like a college cheerleader but his face contorted in rage. A disgusted Cleaver turned back up the stairs, wiping something from the right side of his face.

He got spit on.

It can't be a coincidence that the greatest venom is heaped toward Washington's best-known icons of diversity. While there are few if any reports of slurs hurled at the white and centrist "Blue Dog" Democrats who actually engineered the bill's final passage, openly gay Representative Barney Frank of Massachusetts was called a "faggot" by the unruly gathering. The frenzy peaked when House Speaker Nancy Pelosi walked past, carrying the gavel that was used when the House passed Medicare in 1965. Right-wing pundits and radio callers later accused the about-to-turn-seventy first female House speaker of aggressively "antagonizing" the Tea Party. One activist who got through on a phone call to Glenn Beck radio later said "it was like they wanted something to happen."

"Yes. Yes, they did," replied Beck.

That same week, Beck—self-appointed and self-taught national historian—made the bizarre comment that John Lewis and his allies later "locked arms because they wanted to compare themselves to the civil rights activists. How dare you!"—implying unfamiliarity that Lewis is in fact the greatest still-living leader from that movement.

This, indeed, was what had changed since 1965, the year of Medicare and the Edmund Pettus Bridge: there was now a national infrastructure of conservative outrage like Beck and the Fox News Channel, with new arteries leading straight to the central core of the national debate. While the Tea Party continued to rage underneath, Iowa representative Steve King—the same congressman who'd supported "implosions" at IRS offices just after the suicide pilot attacked one in Austin—took a "Don't Tread on Me" flag and waved it from the House balcony, while others like Representative Michele Bachmann also ventured out to egg the crowd on. The incivility even spread to the House floor. When Michigan Democratic representative Bart Stupak, a leading abortion foe, rose to explain why after much agonizing and negotiation he had decided to support the bill, a GOP House member, Randy Neugebauer of Texas, shouted out "baby killer!" (although he later claimed it was "it's a baby killer," speaking of the legislation and not Stupak).

But it was all for nothing. The House passed the health-care package that night, and two days later Obama signed the main provision—surrounded by a beaming Pelosi and other supporters, while eleven-year-old Marcelas Owens, whose mother lost her health insurance and then died from pulmonary hypertension in 2007, hovered over the top of the president's desk. The ebullient scene—with people chanting that 2008 campaign slogan "Yes, we can!"—was devastating to some of the newfound conservative activists who'd fought so hard to prevent this day.

The next day, Obama went to Iowa City and sprinkled salt on the wounds of the Tea Party: "You turn on the news, you'll see the same folks are still shouting about there's going to be an end of the world because this bill passed," the president said, amid loud laughter. "I'm not exaggerating. Leaders of the Republican Party, they called the passage of this bill 'Armageddon.' " There was more laughter. "Armageddon. 'End of freedom as we know it.' So after I signed the bill, I looked around to see if there were any asteroids falling or some cracks opening up in the Earth. It turned out it was a nice day. Birds were chirping. Folks were strolling down the Mall. People still have their doctors." The joint was practically in stitches now—a dagger aimed at his opponents after all these months.

In his ranch house high atop the steep hillside in West Whiteland Township, Pennsylvania, seventy-four-year-old Al Whayland—still unemployed, still looking for a job—logged into America Online and started composing an email. It said, in part:

> We are distraught at what is being brought upon us. I read an article in a local newspaper this morning and it is the mind-set of some people (too many I am afraid) that has given the "Culture of Corruption" a window of opportunity to impose upon the American people their Socialist philosophy. A College Student said that they thought the HC Legislation was good because nobody in our Country should go without Health care. Obviously, the feeling was sincere, but woefully naive. Another person in a Senior Center stated that they were in favor of the Bill because the "downtrodden in our rich Country should be taken care of."Once again sincere, but oblivious to the consequences that will result in that happening under this horrific legislation. I don't know for sure, but I would bet on it that they don't watch, or listen to your shows, or for that matter any other show on Fox. You don't have to inform my Wife and I, as we watch you as much as possible. . .

When he was done, Whayland clicked his computer mouse and sent his imprecation to Glenn Beck.

Indeed, the damage that the long health-care battle caused in

Congress inflicted deep wounds on the chances for progress on any other measure—especially with many Republicans still terrified that any cooperation with Obama or with the Democratic majority on any issue could leave them vulnerable to a primary challenger who could harness the anger of the Tea Partiers. "There will be no cooperation for the rest of the year," a petulant Arizona senator John McCain, now knee-deep in the muck of his primary challenge from the immigrant-bashing J. D. Hayworth, told a radio station back home. "They [the Democrats] have poisoned the well in what they've done and how they've done it."

Unfortunately, the GOP had just enough juice inside the Beltway to make this a self-fulfilling prophecy. Within days of McCain's unilateral declaration of noncooperation, his closest ally, Senator Lindsey Graham of South Carolina suggested in a fit of anger that he was unlikely to help the Democrats pass either comprehensive immigration reform or climate change legislation in 2010. In other words, the Democrats may have won what Graham's South Carolina colleague Jim DeMint had called "the battle of Waterloo," but the Republicans still had enough ammunition to win a political war of attrition, and the casualties would be the silent majority of Americans who were pleading with the government to do something about the nation's twenty-first-century breakdown.

Ironically, this *was* a kind of an apocalypse—not the one that the Tea Partiers and their allies like Paul Broun had been warning about, but a different kind, a complete breakdown of Washington's ability to get anything done, even staring in the face of serious problems that required complex solutions, and some eventual compromise. These were more of the very real, and sometimes dire, consequences of angry or paranoid rhetoric filtering its way up to the top of the national debate.

DOWN IN DELAWARE, WGMD's Bill Colley had stayed off his Twitter account for a couple of days, but shortly after Obama signed the health-care bill he was back online. "It was a beautiful morning in Long Neck," he wrote, as a warm sunny spell hovered over the dunes and the gently rustling sea oats of the state's southernmost reaches. "The calm before . . . Are we at the brink of civil war?"

The passage of health-care reform had revealed the two opposite directions that the backlash against Barack Obama and his policies could now take in the wake of defeat. One was the American political equivalent of the Long March—regrouping in the political wilderness of the small towns and exurbs where the movement was centered, taking over the local GOP and electing members to the school board, and adopting the difficult mantle of patience aimed at ending the Obama presidency in 2012, or before the president could complete his mission of national transformation.

In addition, the statehouses in some of the reddest of red states moved quickly to distance themselves from Washington after health-care reform passed. That was most true in Arizona, with its extreme new anti-immigration law as well as its thinly veiled jab at Obama's birth certificate; in addition, a number of Republican state attorneys general filed lawsuits seeking to block the reform plan from taking effect—really no different from the strategies discussed at the Tenth Amendment Summit sponsored by Ray McBerry of the League of the South. The aggressive state postures were a sign that even if the Tea Parties were not nearly large enough or powerful enough to reclaim Washington, their movement was beginning to rip the fifty states apart at their seams, the ultimate self-fulfilling prophecy of them all.

And then there were a few on the paranoid fringe who wanted to take the other route, the shortcut.

When the Oath Keepers had gathered on the Lexington Green to launch their organization back in April 2009, one of the attendees— standing alongside founder Stewart Rhodes, the innkeeper Celia Hyde, David Gillie in his pressed Navy whites, and the future arrestee Marine Sergeant Charles "July4Patriot" Dyer—was a mildly notorious figure from the first militia heyday in the early 1990s, an Alabama man named Mike Vanderboegh. A self-described "Christian libertarian" and gun-rights activist who'd once been active in militia outfits like the Sons of

Liberty, Vanderboegh was now fifty-seven and living on government disability checks in a Birmingham suburb—but still used the Internet and his widely read blog called Sipsey Street Irregulars to rally a new generation of militia enthusiasts. His small group of supporters called themselves The Three Percenters (based on a historically inaccurate view of the number of colonists who actively fought British rule). The rail on Vanderboegh's blog notes: "You can try to kill us, if you can. But remember, we'll shoot back."

On the Friday before the health-care vote, Vanderboegh took to his blog to urge his followers to take their right-wing "Days of Rage" a half-step farther than angry epithets and the occasional spittle:

> So, if you wish to send a message that Pelosi and her party cannot fail to hear, break their windows. Break them NOW. Break them and run to break again. Break them under cover of night. Break them in broad daylight. Break them and await arrest in willful, principled civil disobedience. Break them with rocks. Break them with slingshots. Break them with baseball bats. But BREAK THEM.

What happened next was powerful testimony to the power of the Internet to move people—except this time, you could call it antisocial networking.

Vanderboegh's incitement to vandalism appeared on his blog at 3:55 p.m. that Friday. Sometime between then and Saturday morning, a brick came crashing through the large glass window of the county Democratic Party in Wichita, Kansas, and written on it was "No to Obama" and "No ObamyCare." It would be the first of several such incidents; in Rochester, New York, a brick that was hurled through the Democratic Party headquarters there came attached to a famous quote from Barry Goldwater, "Extremism in the defense of liberty is no vice." There was unrest in the late Goldwater's home state of Arizona, too; in addition to the earlier-noted angry death threats received by Scottsdale-area Democratic representative Harry Mitchell, another prominent state Democrat, Representative Gabrielle Giffords, representing Tucson, had her district office glass door shattered within hours of her health-care vote. Throughout the next week, these reports of threats and vandalism—mostly against Democrats, although a couple involved Republicans, too—multiplied in Vanderboegh's cyber-wake. By May, *Politico* quoted the Senate's sergeant-at-arms as saying that threats against members of Congress rose by some 300 percent in the early months of 2010—particularly, according to the FBI, death threats from male gun owners either suffering from mental illness or stressors such as unemployment, or both.

These hard-core conservatives and their very own "days of rage" should not have been that surprising. For a year now, the likes of Glenn Beck had been telling them that the backlash had the power to prevail over the dark forces of socialism (or worse), that "we surround them"—but that the consequences of failure could be catastrophic, possibly signaling the death of the Republic itself. The reality that—as Obama himself mocked—no such thing was happening was not a source of reassurance but a trigger for even greater anger. A movement that was built atop a pyramid of so much misinformation was not well equipped to deal with the contradictions of its core beliefs, even—or especially—when they became apparent to the rest of the world.

The immediate reactions were violence or denial—just as with people like Rich Poplawski, Eddie Perkovic, and Nancy Genovese, who simply refused to believe there were no "FEMA camps," or the radio callers some seventy-two years earlier who refused to believe that aliens had not landed in Grover's Mill. In a way, John McCain's vow of non-cooperation in the Senate corridors and Mike Vanderboegh's call for breaking windows sprang from the same basic instinct—which was to shut everything down, rather than deal with the traumatic nature of change. It all reeked of fear—the brand that had been ginned up on the television night after night, and the consequences of that form of terror for the American body politic could be quite harmful indeed: utter paralysis.

Even greater fears of violence were stoked when federal authorities moved in and arrested nine members of an ultra-extremist Christian militia group called the Hutaree, which was based in the battered Rust Belt regions of the central Great Lakes and which, according to a federal indictment, had been hatching a scheme to murder one law-enforcement officer and then kill multiple lawmen by attacking his funeral—which in the group's bizarre thinking would move it closer to its ultimate goal of war against the Antichrist. One poster on the Hutaree Web page had promised that "we will be the fighting force, that the devil worshipping new world order don't [sic] want to have to meet up with." The most chilling thing is it did not sound so different from the words about a "new world order" from U.S. congressman Paul Broun, when he spoke to the John Birch Society.

So this was the question looming over the right-wing reaction to Obama with his term nearly one-third completed: How serious is the threat to societal order, and how broad? What you wondered in particular was how the revival of health-care reform and a more assertive Obama was affecting the new pool of more idealistic recruits who'd been rousted from their couches by the likes of Glenn Beck—people like Russ Murphy and his Delaware 9-12 Patriots.

IT IS THURSDAY night in Milton, Delaware. The tiny town—population 1,657, named for the seventeenth-century free-speech brawler and poet John Milton—is about six miles off the main highway, which may explain the surprisingly pristine condition of its postcard-sized Victorian homes with their gingerbread-flavored porches, and its compact downtown of two-story brick façades and ornate cornices, a paradise not yet completely lost. The squat Milton Fire Department has staked out the main corner, and up on the second floor you find a half-dozen older ladies moving around large tables, the advance squad for the Delaware 9-12 Patriots here in Sussex County. The leaders are running late—raising questions about a loss of momentum. It turns out that Theresa Garcia is tied up at her real-estate business, and when Alex Garcia shows up he seems harried, grousing about how hard it's been to get out to some property he owns in West Virginia. When Russ Murphy finally arrives in his windbreaker and his tall cowboy boots, there are only about thirty minutes to spare.

A gray-haired man wearing a white Delaware 9-12 Patriots T-shirt walks up to Murphy. "Do you mind if I put these on the information table?" Murphy shrugs, and the man places brochures for the radical Oath Keepers and its ten orders about the concentration camps and the gun confiscation that its members won't obey. He is a sixty-three-year-old disabled U.S. Army veteran of Vietnam and the first Gulf War named Harold Conklin, and in a brief conversation he mixes the concerns and complaints that are so familiar by now—his anger over his belief that the government is taking over health care for all and that Obama is some kind of "Manchurian Candidate," tempered by complaints about the government health care that Conklin—who says he was exposed to the toxic Agent Orange—has already been receiving from the Veterans Administration.

Having completed his literature drop, Conklin sits down at a long table and makes small talk with two other retired vets, while a gaggle forms as usual around the cake and cookies, trying to figure out how to get the big coffee machine to work. It's weird—you came to Milton expecting the Delaware 9-12 Patriots to be in a lather about health-care reform, but folks seem more troubled by the brief lack of caffeine. As the 7 o'clock hour approaches, more than one hundred of them have clicked off Fox, ventured out, and rolled up the stairs into the fire hall—the Dover AFB retirees and the senior beachcombers of Rehoboth, television-age transients who'd suddenly discovered these like-minded people as an excuse to get off the couch for three hours.

This particular group of self-appointed patriots is more interested in building a foundation than in throwing the bricks. They now have three people lobbying their legislators in Dover, where the 9-12ers had given up on one of their goals of pushing for legislative initiative when they realized it could be a tool to make new big-government laws for the same folks up north who had elected Barack Obama and Joe Biden. And that's not all: The Delaware 9-12 Patriots—with their focus on local education—had now elected a member to the Cape Henlopen School Board, a youthful forty-something mother of three and self-proclaimed talk-radio fanatic named Sandi Minard.

After the meeting, remembering the discussions from an earlier visit to Delaware, you ask Minard if she'll be pushing to change the way that global warming is taught in the Cape Henlopen schools. "My children had to watch the Al Gore movie and I was upset with that—especially after they found it to be scientifically incorrect," she says. "They don't go back and tell the kids, and they don't go back and re-teach them." While she said she just wanted students to learn both sides, it didn't sound as if hot-button issues like climate change or evolution were a top priority for Minard. Yet at the same time, she was reading a book that was popular with some of the 9-12ers called *The Harsh Truth About Public Schools*, which argues that American education is marked by its anti-Christian bias. Several more 9-12 Patriots were running in upcoming school board elections—a strong signal that this movement planned to make an impact well past the 2010 elections.

But then there is a stark reminder of how politics is driven by the personal.

In the middle of the flow of committee reports, Murphy asks to grab the microphone back to say one more thing. He then launches into a roughly eight-minute monologue— the point of which is mostly obscure, almost certainly for intentional reasons, but with dark hints of threats to the Delaware 9-12 Patriots, both from the professional pols, the Karl Rove wannabes, who would like to co-opt them, and possibly from plotters within. Murphy speaks of another closed-door meeting he held with the political elites. "There was a move afoot,"

Murphy explains, starting with some emails, "that people with a political agenda were trying to form an umbrella group in Delaware and they were going to use the Tea Party to establish that umbrella group." He describes what happened next:

> I don't con, BS, whatever way you want to put it. They got all of those people from those emails—the leaders, the organizers, the wannabes—in one room in one meeting at an extremely long table. Every seat was occupied and there was standing room only, and then we started and then it was becoming known the people that came there told us that we needed them. They would create an umbrella group and they would show us how to win, they would show us how to make this successful because they were leaders and they'd been involved in this for years and through this umbrella group all the finances and everything would be at their control. They would decide the issues and the finances, whatever it needed to implement demonstrations . . . and, or, whatever. And then they went through some other things, and I asked them, "You wanna tell me what the difference is between what you're proposing to do and what we are ultimately against—big government? This is a grassroots organization!"

The one hundred or so people in the fire hall were all paying rapt attention to their leader now, leaning forward in their folding chairs. Murphy's diatribe had all the elements of a classic Glenn Beck radio rant—short on specifics but long on conspiracy-laced emotion and rooted in resentment, reassuring the little guy in the room that "you are not alone," that we surround them. The grizzled Vietnam veteran in the biker jacket had maybe learned a thing or two from his hero of the airwaves.

"'This is what you gotta do,'" Murphy describes these unnamed political leaders as telling him. "'We have the inside track—we have the contacts with the media and we have the contacts with the politicians that can make this work.' And they suggested that number one, we stop listening to Glenn Beck."

A shock wave goes through the fire hall—there are loud oohs, punctuated by laughter at the absurdity of it all. These unnamed political leaders—whoever they were—might as well have suggested that the Delaware 9-12 Patriots surrender their coffee and their cake, or simply give up oxygen.

Murphy continues. "But the final straw was a person who was standing halfway down the table, standing up, said this—you know, stop the Glenn Beck stuff, and 'I highly recommend that you stop saying prayers'"—again, more oohs and ahhs ripple through the room—"'at the beginning of your meeting because that insults and alienates some people.'" The accumulation of a half-century of resentments that had been boiling inside Murphy since someone turned that stove to high back during Vietnam and the uproar of the 1960s—the know-it-all doctor at the Marine recruiting office, those hippies at the Swarthmore train station—is bubbling to the top, steaming out anger as his words build to a poetic climax worthy of Milton.

"Ladies and gentlemen, I sat at the head of that table. I'm not *stupid*. I may be slow, and old, but I'm not *stupid*. I sat at the head of that table for a reason. That points to the person in charge. And when that person said you should stop saying prayers, I slammed my fist on the table, books shot up in the air. I stood up and I said, 'This is the Delaware 9-12 Patriots! And as long as I run this organization, we will say the Pledge of Allegiance at every meeting and at every meeting, we will have a prayer!'"

"Amen!" a voice cried out, and there were more whoops, and then applause.

"They" still didn't get it, and "they" never would. On the turn of a dime, this wasn't about health care, or cap-and-trade, or Barack Obama. This was all about respect—the people on the second floor of a fire hall in Milton, Delaware, understand, even if the elites in their wool suits and their glossy ties do not. This mission was not new—it dated back to the Nixon years—but what was different now was the technology and the opportunists who could bring them together, and push all this resentful energy in the same direction.

For Russ Murphy, it was all that, and something more. And that was finally beating back the thing that had haunted him through all these years—through the booze and the busted-up marriages and lonely nights under a canopy of stars on America's open highway—and that was not taking that commission to second lieutenant, not going back to Vietnam. This time, Russ Murphy will never leave any of his men, or women, behind.

Nobody knew anymore where this thing was headed—toward a second American Revolution or just the next school board election in Sussex County. Russ Murphy didn't know either, but he knew the thing that mattered: that he was finally in command.

Chapter Twelve

Orlando Magic

> You think, uh, religion is for suckers and easy marks and molly-coddlers, eh? You think Jesus was some kind of a sissy, hey? Well, let me tell you, Jesus wouldn't be afraid to walk into this joint or any other speakeasy to preach the gospel.
>
> Elmer Gantry, as portrayed by Burt Lancaster in the 1960 film

Today, this joint is an angular mass of steel and concrete, laced with commercial signage, with a name as nondescript as its state-budget-crisis architecture, the three-year-old UCF Arena in Orlando. It is the first Saturday since the spring solstice here in the near tropics, and occasionally the eternal sunshine of an 80-degree Florida day struggles to sneak past the concession lines and down the passageways into the drab concrete bowl. But for about 7,500 congregants inside the hard man-made tent, heavenly weather can wait. Brother Glenn Beck is preaching, and he is just warming up.

"I was just standing backstage and saying to myself, 'Do we have the faith to do it?'" Beck says. It is only five minutes into Beck's seven-hour-long American Revival, this long-promised political-education crusade that he has been hawking for weeks now on his radio show and then nightly on Fox, and already he is holding back the tears, looking out at this pool of middle-aged humanity shrouded in loose polo shirts and sprinkled with the salt and pepper of graying hair. "What an amazing thing this is—if we just build it, they will come. If we just follow the dictates of the Spirit. Everything is going to be fine . . . It's your turn. You have to be an evangelist for America."

It has been 421 days since Beck started riding the right-curled tsunami against Barack Obama's presidency, with his visions of a political apocalypse amid the collapse of the U.S. dollar. Now, wearing fresh-faded jeans and a dark blue shirt with epaulets, kind of a casual-Saturday-Salvation-Army look, he looks out over a mini-multitude, his most rabid fans on this end of the country who have come here to the untouristy northeast corner of Orlando, by plane and by automobile, shelling out as much as $134, with the service charge, for a lower-deck seat.

And suddenly the whole game is changing before their eyes.

"I thought this was going to be about how to organize political parties," Beck says, trying to explain what was on his mind when he hatched this whole American Revival scheme back in the fall, when he was a few miles up the road from Orlando at the Beckiest place on earth, a retirement-heavy contrived town called The Villages. "I walked off the stage [in The Villages] in a cold, cold sweat and said, 'We're wrong. I don't know where we went wrong, but this is not the direction we were supposed to be in.'" There is a catching in his throat. "And that's when faith, hope, and charity came to me. It's not about politics."

Looking out over the crowd—so many of them retirees or economic refugees from the crowded Northeast suburbs of the postwar era, and from a Catholic parish or a local synagogue, culturally far removed from the born-again fundamentalism now embedded here in the reclaimed Florida swamplands—Beck was quick to add this wasn't about religion, even as he implied you needed to have a belief in God to be an American.

"We do need to talk about faith and we do need to honor God and we do need to understand what's happening to us," he said. He segues into a rant against the social justice movement, and how Communists are using the name of God and "social justice" as a tactic to fool God-fearing Americans, and he is here in Orlando to expose that. But mainly, his message is this:

> Our foundation is God. It must always remain God. We must humble ourselves before Him and beg Him for our arrogance and quite frankly for our sloppy vigilance. [Applause] From God, we build our morals. From God, our morals and our charity comes . . . We cannot find any solutions from Washington. They will come from God, through us!

For the next two hours, Beck's accidental parishioners are exposed to a half-baked American history lesson from the leader of a movement to impose a conservative- and Christian-fundamentalist rewrite of history on the schoolchildren of Texas, a man named David Barton, who throws out disconnected facts blended with half-truths at the speed of a Florida panther chasing its prey. After that comes economic pundit David Buckner, a sometimes adjunct professor at Columbia who's parlayed his friendship with Beck into a lucrative financial practice. It is almost time for a lunch break, and now Beck is back onstage to thank Buckner and escort him off.

This is when it happens.

A woman has fallen or collapsed onto the floor—in the upper deck at the far end of the arena from where Beck and Buckner are standing—and she can't get up. There is a loud commotion—it sounds like protestors at first—until several of them work to shout in unison: "Doctor!" There is initial puzzlement etched on the faces of the two speakers, and then Beck cups his hands around his eyes and looks toward the upper deck "Can we get the houselights, please!" he says. "Section 204 is where we need the doctor? 203? 202."

About ten men and women begin striding purposefully toward the commotion. Then, brief silence, and a woman shouts out, "Say a prayer!"

The host concurs, and bows his head downward, his arms crossed hard against his chest. After about ten seconds, Beck wrinkles his nose, his eyes moist again, and begins to hum softly into his headpiece microphone. It is the melody of "Amazing Grace," that hymn of national unity and revival ever since the tent-revival days of Billy Sunday, and its soft intensity builds as the chorus of 7,500 joins in, just a few more each nanosecond, most humming like Beck and now Buckner on the stage, but a couple of thousand gently mouthing the words, "I once was lost but now am found/Was blind but now I see."

Beck opens his blue eyes toward the crowd, cocks his head. "I just love you so much—you're such a great audience," he says, voice cracking on nearly every syllable. "You're such a good group of people." He talks of waiting for the paramedics and then starts to announce the scheduled break for lunch.

A disembodied voice. "She's okay, Glenn!"

Beck smiles and gives a thumbs-up, amid sustained applause. The beatified-looking star rubs his hands together. "Can I just tell you something? I've been to a lot of events in my life, I've been to a lot of different things, but, boy, I gotta tell you—I can *feel the spirit* and I can feel America here, coming alive."

The audience rises for lunch, and now flashing on the screen is the message that people can support the upcoming rally near the Lincoln Monument in late August by texting a ten-dollar donation to the Special Operations Warrior Fund—roughly the amount that someone might throw into a collection plate at the end of a particularly moving sermon.

It is hard for a Beck agnostic to know what to make of this Orlando magic; the fallen woman is later reported as checked out and fine, but she does not return to the dank arena confines. Only one thing seems clear: saving America is suddenly not ambitious enough for Glenn Beck; his goal (maybe all along, or maybe since he woke up this morning, who knows with him?) is now saving your mortal soul.

For over a year now, Beck has been talking up the nobility of the Founding Fathers and their brainy philosophies. But his true cosmic ancestors are those giants who've worked the teeming emotional under-belly of American sin and salvation, and now Beck has synthesized it all into one manic superhero who combines the mesmerizing storytelling skills of Orson Welles and the big-tent hucksterism of P. T. Barnum and the fearmongering of Joe McCarthy and then sprinkled in ele-ments from fiction, like the insane picture-tube edginess of *Network*'s Howard Beale.

And now, at the forefront of this political movement that has been so much about reinvention for so many of its actors, the spiritual leader of the backlash is reinventing himself all over again. This means you are present for the rollout of arguably Beck's greatest character invention yet: Elmer Gantry 2.0, in the style of the greatest fictional evangelical of the twentieth century, using the multimedia gospel to paint a vision of impending hell not in the afterworld but right here in the United States, while reassuring people that it is not too late for all of us to ward off unending fire and brimstone.

What Beck must have realized when he left the stage at The Villages that day is that political revolutions are often short-lived and often end badly. Already, the failure of Beck's followers and the other random Tea Partiers to prevent the passage of health-care reform was sure to have many of them questioning their faith in the movement. It is only five days after Obama signed the main bill into law, and so America's top salesman is here with a new and improved offer . . . eternity.

THE THING IS, the masses didn't know they wanted eternity as they streamed into Orlando, instead wanting a slab of political red meat, even for breakfast. You learned that shortly before 7 a.m., when you stumbled down to the coffee-and-small-powdery-donut bar of the Days Inn–University of Central Florida. On the big-screen TV, an attractive young woman is giving the local weekend weather, a glorious array of yellow suns plastered across the screen from Daytona all the way to St. Pete. Then there are footsteps behind you, and a sense of urgency.

"Do you mind if I change that to Fox News?"

The first "Beck zombie" of the day has arrived. His name is Joseph Cerniglia, and after you go through the motions of asking him if he's here for the Beck gala, he launches into a long-winded monologue about his excursion to the UCF campus on the afternoon before—in a futile effort to somehow get in to see Friday's taping of Beck's regular Fox News TV show, which was filmed at the arena. The climax of his trip came when he wandered into the campus bookstore run by Barnes & Noble next door and ended up in an argument with the woman up front about not being able to find any of Beck's books on the shelves.

Cerniglia—age seventy, a big man with a thick gray beard, already with a spot of coffee on his polo shirt, a vague hint of his native Bronx in his voice—comes across as a Beck fan on a two-liter bottle of Red Bull, but he is not easy to typecast. It turns out that Cerniglia was a successful stockbroker in New York when he fled to Vermont in the 1980s, where he bought an orchard and a winery and then developed the popular hard cider brand Woodchuck Cider. Then he sold the successful product, and four years ago, practically on a whim, he purchased a large house in an exclusive island community near Savannah, the Landings at Skidaway Island. Starting his life over yet again, Cerniglia found the Italian-American club in the Georgia city, began a business selling antique prints—and became a huge fan of Glenn Beck in his spare time.

He has a way of making it all sound like an emotional Italian-American guy thing. "I like a man who can cry and not be ashamed," he says. "I do it myself, sometimes." Cerniglia is also impulsive. He had no plans to come to Orlando until the Thursday night just before, when he was watching Beck's show, which blended an emotional reaction to the passage of health-care reform with a passionate rant about liberals blaming him for the vandalism and death threats that followed. "It was like I was looking into his eyes and he was looking into mine," Cerniglia tells you. "He's a very sincere man."

On Friday morning, the retired vintner and his female companion hopped into his Mercedes and aimed south toward central Florida, a four-and-a-half-hour drive. Like so many other Beck fans, Cerniglia tells you that watching his show has taken him back to a youthful place that he'd lost all those years he was building a business and raising a family—of learning new things about American history, of thinking about ways to make a difference outside the confines of an executive-sized home. "I have learned more from Glenn Beck—learned more about American history and government, from Glenn Beck—than in the previous forty years of my life," Cerniglia says.

This is one of the things that Beck's legions of detractors don't quite understand—that many of his fans are desperately questing for answers rooted in the form of anything passing for knowledge. And now that Beck has gotten to them first with the John Birch–era ranting of W. Cleon Skousen and a misreading of Thomas Paine and then the fundamentalist pseudo-history of David Barton, it will be all but impossible for anyone with actual common sense to roll it back.

Cerniglia wants to get back up to the UCF Arena as early as possible, so you hitch a ride in the back of his Mercedes. You get the impression that he also sees something else of himself in Beck—the qualities that back in the Bronx where he grew up would get you labeled as a *mensch*. At the entrance to the parking deck where Cerniglia had parked the day before on his bookstore misadventure, a young man standing in front of the ticket machine sticks out his hand and says, "Parking for Glenn Beck is ten dollars."

"But I was here yesterday, and it was only five dollars."

The attendant shrugs, and repeats that it's ten dollars now that Beck is on campus.

"How do you even know I'm going to see Glenn Beck?" Cerniglia asks the young man. "Maybe I'm just coming to the campus to visit my daughter." But there was no appeal—for Beck's American Revival, all sales are final. Cerniglia and his companion pull their imported luxury car into a space—and as you say your good-byes he is still grousing about that extra five dollars. At first, you chuckle over this seemingly disconnected incident, but during a day of talking to

Beck's diehards in Orlando it occurs to you that this is a core belief, that somebody—whether it is Barack Obama or the kid at the parking garage—is always sticking out his hand, asking to take what they'd worked for all their life.

You would touch base with a couple dozen people before the show and during the breaks—mostly white, mostly over fifty, with retirees, Vietnam veterans, and the unemployed disproportionately represented. The common themes were clear: that government was seeking to grab everything that they'd worked for to give it to lazy, undeserving people, and that if they didn't act now, America would be ruined when they were no longer here to save it (the phrase "children and grandchildren" surfaced again and again). They now crowded into this concrete bowl to look at each other, to see the tangible proof that, in Beck's own words from his famous March 2009 show, "You are not alone."

A sizable number of the people at the UCF Arena are from The Villages, the private fifty-five-and-over gated community some forty-five minutes to the north of Orlando—which barely existed in the 1990s and now has more than 75,000 residents, more than 98 percent of them white and heavily Republican. Retirees arrive there from a lifetime working and raising kids in the Northeast, and several suggested that Beck—coming on in the heat of a tropical late afternoon, right before supper—offers a way to form new bonds there.

"I never realized the dangers to this country until I started listening to Glenn Beck at the behest of my friends—I had really thought he was crazy on the radio," says Marlene Goldberg, who was "a Jewish Democrat from New York" until she moved to The Villages a few years ago. Now she is a registered Republican, and she is shelling out a Benjamin and an Andrew for lower-level seats to get a Beck-approved primer on American history. A few minutes later, you return to your seat in Section 107, and here is Phillis Kluft, seventy-one, also of The Villages, who overhears you questioning someone else. Kluft rises to face you— she is rail thin, with dark auburn hair and high cheekbones that are either ruddy from the Florida sun or flush with anger as her monologue picks up steam. Divorced and left to work and raise four kids all by herself in East Haven, Connecticut, she worked several jobs to get her kids through school—but Kluft seems too worked up in her senior years for a genteel retirement in The Villages consisting of morning golf and afternoon mahjong.

"I saved money for my old age and didn't go on a vacation or buy a new car. It really galls me that these people sit on their ass and expect other people to take care of them!" thunders Kluft, who is now a leader of the Tea Party in central Florida. "I am so disgusted with this Obama bullshit!!!" About a dozen other people in Section 107—who've been gradually turning their heads as Kluft's speech builds to its climax—are now whooping in approval. This is what they'd come here for, venting their anger.

But now the star of the show had other plans.

A faith healing.

To be sure, you can't deliver the promise of heaven without the threat of hell, which Beck has successfully refashioned into an apocalyptic vision that is not otherworldly but a demonically possessed United States in a not-too-distant future. All of the attendees received a thick binder of educational materials not just from David Barton with his contrived Christianist history of the founders but, rather incongruously, an article by Karl Rove on "Making Washington Listen," as well as an ADD-addled spew of articles that cover everything from an assault on "black liberation theology" to "Thinking the Unthinkable." The last two pieces are paid advertisements—for Goldline International and for Food Insurance, asking the attendees, "Will You Be Able to Feed Your Family if a Disaster Strikes?"

In typical fashion, Beck managed during his stage appearances to do his sponsors' bidding by weaving statements of gloom about the economy and the end of the almighty dollar with exhortations for food storage, telling the audience at one point that when it comes to stockpiles, "I am incredibly prepared." Beck previewed yet another book project, this one coming out in about three months, and playing up the dire worldview that he's sold to the audience to the hilt. He told the Orlando crowd that his next book would be a work of fiction, "a story of America in a time much like today where the people are confused," with a government in crisis and the rise of a citizens' group called the Founders Keepers (sounding like a combination of the 9-12 Project and the Oath Keepers), which "leads to a battle and a civil war, and life is upside-down planet-wide." He did not reveal the title that was already listed for the book on Amazon.com, *The Overton Window*, a reference to the political theory of how to radically shift ideas of what is acceptable or possible in politics.

Such as the possibility that America is on the brink of a civil war.

In many ways, Beck's seven-hour "fusion of entertainment and enlightenment" is the world that the futurist Alvin Toffler had predicted in 1970 when he wrote his seminal book, *Future Shock*. In the depths of that earlier tumultuous era in American politics, Toffler theorized that the technological revolution that had accelerated since the end of World War II was creating massive societal and psychological upheaval as well. He argued in *Future Shock* that the rapid disappearance of our familiar touchstones—defined in many American locales by stable neighborhoods built around dependable jobs and churches or civic institutions—would cause large swaths of society to act out in bizarre and unpredictable ways. "Future shock is the shattering stress and disorientation that we induce in individuals by subjecting them to too much change in too short a time," Toffler wrote. One of the drivers of this alarming phenomenon, he predicted, would be what he called "information overload": the bombardment of information in a new media age (and he was writing this long before the Internet) that would actually inhibit the abilities of people to make rational choices.

From the stage in Orlando, it was bombs away. "If we don't face the truth right now, we'll be dead in five years," Beck declared at one point. "This country can't survive." It was the message he had been driving home for the last year, but there was no longer a need to dwell on it. Most of his audience, especially the $134 diehards, had already been scared to death for months. (At one point, Buckner asked the attendees to text in their outlook for the U.S. economy, and 80 percent were "pessimistic.") Now that the bad cop Beck had built an audience of more than ten million on radio and TV through political brimstone, the good cop Beck was here to show you the path to salvation and helpfully point out a few consumer products that could help make the journey smoother.

This was the typically Beckian twist on the Elmer Gantry saga—that the audience would get both the heavenly Sister Sharon Falconer and the hell-mongering Gantry himself, but Beck would be playing both roles. It wouldn't work, though, if Beck did not have such a keen grasp of what his mostly middle-aged-and-older audience was paying for—its deepest fears and its pent-up hopes. There was one riff during Beck's tent show in Orlando that might have sounded like a throw-away bit to a newcomer, but really cut right to what the entertainer was giving back to his audience.

"We're already being erased," Beck tells them.

This is his keynote address at the end of the long day, and now he is back in a suit and tie, pulling a small leathery book from his back pocket, the kind of notebook that Hemingway and Picasso once used for a twentieth-century version of proto-blogging. "Get Moleskines. Ever see these little Moleskine books? . . . You put it in your back pocket, and you put it in your purse. You keep it with you at all times and you write down the things that you see—that you see, that you hear, that you read, that you feel, that you experience. We are at the crossroads of history. This is an amazing time. Don't put it down electronically. Put it on paper. Keep it with you. I'm telling you—our children and grandchildren will fight over who gets Grandma or Grandpa's Moleskine—they will fight over this! You need to tell history, because whether or not you believe it yet, you're making it."

At that moment, America's top purveyor of fear reached out and glommed onto his audience's greatest fear of all. It wasn't Barack Obama or the "gun confiscation" or Marxism or socialism, or even the fear of death—well, not exactly. It was more that they were seeing the end of their stay on earth, and that as soon as they were gone America would no longer look like the familiar place they had worked to build, but instead be a landscape without factories that made things or familiar front-porch neighborhoods, a nation that would be overrun by Spanish speakers and perpetually in hock to the Chinese. It's not that Glenn Beck's audience is afraid to die, but they are afraid they will die . . . and no one will remember that they were here.

Who will tell their story? Glenn Beck, and the Moleskines, apparently.

THERE WAS A day in America when we surprisingly found in our politics a vehicle for courage, for beating back "nameless, unreasoning, unjustified terror which paralyzes needed efforts to convert retreat into advance." The issues today are very similar to the challenges that Franklin Roosevelt convinced citizens to stare down in 1933, but this time it is national courage that retreats, while fear advances on all fronts.

The reasons that we've regressed are not really that complicated. Over the last four generations, we have built a consumerist society in the United States where we have discovered that the most effective marketing tool is fear, and where winning politics is powered by that type of marketing—and where the once-solid line between politics and entertainment has become virtually nonexistent, in a 24/7 media world where we happily amuse ourselves to death.

It is only in this most recent era that the political brains completely grasped what preachers like Billy Sunday and the early pitchmen of Madison Avenue had figured out back in the opening decades of the twentieth century: that fear is able to motivate people to act in ways that patient, rational explanations and policies will never achieve.

We have seen the political fear factor improved and refined, from LBJ's nuclear-themed "Daisy" ad in the 1960s to the menacing Willie Horton spot destroying the White House ambitions of Michael Dukakis in the 1980s to George W. Bush riding the coattails of a mysterious election-eve reappearance by 9/11 mastermind Osama bin Laden to his reelection in the 2000s. But political appeals to fear—either intentional or accidental—can go only so far if the leaders who win the ensuing elections cannot produce results; that is exactly what happened when Bush won that fearmongering 2004 campaign and couldn't keep Americans safe from a natural disaster on Bourbon Street or a financial disaster on Wall Street.

In 2008, Americans were pulled like a wishbone by two profoundly different instincts. The old-line conservative politicians looked like frightened deer in the face of the headlamp-cool rationality of Obama that fall, and so it fell onto the professional amusers—Rush Limbaugh and then Glenn Beck, joined by a freed-from-responsibility Sarah Palin—to fill the void by spinning a counter-narrative that wouldn't be dragged down by the dead weight of governing and its fraternal twin, which is accountability. Looking ahead to 2012, it didn't escape some pundits that almost all of the early GOP presidential front-runners were no longer in office, freed from the cursed duties of making hard decisions.

How successful has the escalating volume of fear been? By April 2010, the Pew Research Center would find that Americans' trust in government was near the all-time lows equaled only by the times surrounding Ronald Reagan's election in 1980 and the early years of Bill Clinton's presidency; indeed, the 22 percent of respondents expressing faith in government's ability to tackle America's problems was nearly half of what it had been ten years earlier. The underpinnings of that steep decline were to be found both in Bush's many missteps and in the alarming macro-economic trends, but now we had the likes of Beck and Limbaugh to whip those brushfires in directions that were counterproductive.

And by 2010, there were actual things to be terrified about. The increasing signals that a recovery from the Great Recession was finally gaining steam only seemed to mean that companies were hell-bent on growing their profits, not their payrolls; a widely discussed analysis of the jobs picture by *Atlantic* writer Don Peck suggested that unemployment could linger over the high 8-percent level for as long as eight years. Likewise, the Tea Party movement is not wrong to focus on annual deficits and the long-term debt as a potential American albatross. But while FDR's 1933 inauguration was imbued with hope for "a brighter future," the nation was now more paralyzed by fear than inspired toward positive social change. Concrete proposals that might alleviate the actual problems, such as real reductions in health-care costs or increasing taxes on the very wealthy to a rate still below what millionaires paid during most of the Reagan administration, were demagogued to death as "creeping socialism" on talk radio and Fox. Barack Obama spent hours in verbose news conferences and detailed speeches to Congress trying to lay out the improvements on the health-care plan; conservatives nearly killed it with a two-word lie—"death panels."

As scientists explain it, the human brain is hard-wired by millennia of evolution to fear imminent-seeming threats but not abstract ones—which is why Americans can be riddled with angst over one confused young Nigerian airline passenger with explosives in his underwear, while a majority won't believe the scientific consensus that gradual global warming could cause famine and flooding. In the last thirty-five years, experts have also come to understand much better just how fear impacts politics. In a landmark 2004 piece in *The New Republic*, writer John B. Judis examined how the right wing had come to place what he called a "Death Grip" on American politics. He noted the work of Ernest Becker, who wrote the Pulitzer Prize–winning *Denial of Death* in 1974 but—as synopsized by Judis—sounds as if he'd DVRed several weeks of Beck's show some thirty-five years later:

> Becker described how human beings defend themselves against this fundamental anxiety [over death] by constructing cultures that promise symbolic or literal immortality to those who live up to established standards. Among other things, we practice religions that promise immortality; produce children and works of

art that we hope will outlive us; seek to submerge our own individuality in a larger, enduring community of race or nation; and look to heroic leaders not only to fend off death, but to endow us with the courage to defy *it*. *We also react with hostility toward individuals and rival cultures that threaten to undermine the integrity of our own* [highlight added].

The author Judis closely followed the work of three psychology professors whose recent research uncovered a powerful link between fears of mortality, the 9/11 attacks, and the ability to inspire political action. He noted that one 2002 project at Brooklyn College "showed that mortality reminders dramatically enhanced the appeal of a hypothetical candidate who told voters, 'You are not just an ordinary citizen: You are part of a special state and a special nation.'" Eight years later, it would fall not to a candidate but to a radio-and-TV entertainer to make that exact pitch. The need for this power-laden kind of "American exceptionalism" explains why so many of the Tea Party activists you spoke with reacted so viscerally to news reports—often slanted or flat-out inaccurate—that Obama was traveling to other nations to apologize for the United States or that he had bowed to the emperor of Japan.

Still, there is something else that is so important to driving the backlash against Barack Obama, and for all the trees that were killed in order to produce long print articles about the Tea Party movement in the first two years of his presidency, it was something that seemed to be completely overlooked.

Time.

Time is multiplying fear, many times over.

The Tea Party movement is heavily infused by the first wave of the baby boom, the crest of postwar American offspring that ranged in age from fifty-five to sixty-four on the eve of the 2010 elections, and many of these were retired early—some by choice, many by layoffs and other economic upheavals. The ranks of the groups like the 9-12 Project or the Oath Keepers were swelled with disabled veterans, ex-cops who'd taken a retirement package, homemakers with grown children, and the like. The differing demographics of the coalition that had elected Obama—particularly with voters younger than fifty, at an age more likely to be wrapped up in the nonstop duties of child-rearing as well as work—also meant the emerging Obama majority was less overexposed to political messages on cable TV or talk radio, and also had less free time to get on a bus for Washington to march around and carry protest signs.

Contrast that with the people you met over the course of a Tea Party winter—the Oath Keeper Celia Hyde, who started following politics on Fox when she'd lost her job, or Joe Gayan, the Wisconsin conspiracy theorist whose factory position was shipped out to China when he was only forty-eight, or Al Whayland, the Glenn Beck fanatic who'd rather be working at a desk selling mortgages at 5 p.m. than at home in front of his big-screen TV. Time was a cheap commodity for them.

But ultimately, the participants in the powerful revival of paranoid politics in America are looking for someone to blame for their predicament in life—someone who is not themselves. It's a sad commentary on human nature that people have this strange predisposition to blame the loss of hope on people who are less fortunate than them, rather than the powerful, or powerful unseen forces like globalization or new technology. But what is even more tragic is that some people in positions of authority—in government or big media or running large business ventures—manipulate that blame to further their own agenda. The solution is not to change human nature—good luck with that—but to tackle the root causes, providing citizens with the framework to work productively until the retirement day of their own choosing, as well as stable communities where people seek companionship and purpose from their neighbors instead of from a bombastic cable TV show. It would also help if the new silent majority could offer a more compelling story line than the nightly opera of fearmongering on Fox News.

Doing those things will not be easy—just as there are other questions about the Tea Party that are not easy to answer. It is becoming increasingly clear, for all the expressions of anxiety over the economy and government, that the thing providing the movement with so much of its fuel is anxiety about race, sometimes subtle and sometimes not so much. Certainly, you rarely saw the overt style of racism that flourished into the 1960s—people using the N-word, for example (its rarity is why it was so newsworthy when it was reported that it was shouted at Representative John Lewis as he went to vote in favor of the health-care bill), or arguing that a black man could never be qualified to be president.

But from the stirrings of discomfort over Obama's early speeches to the backward-looking immigration law that was enacted in Arizona, fear of The Other was rarely far from the surface. Racism isn't just a virulent human failing; it is also a purification tool that the manipulators use to promote an ugly but powerful brand of unity, the "white culture" that Beck so brazenly defended against the encroachment of Obama, who represented the "rival culture" that the psychologist Becker warned about.

The vexing matter of racism looms over another unanswered question for the majority of Americans who disagree with the backlash, a question that revolves around "the E-word": Empathy.

When it became clear that the Tea Party wasn't going to melt away from either boredom or irrelevancy, two schools of thought emerged from their progressive rivals. The path of least resistance was to bash back at these stubborn opponents as willfully ignorant and mostly racist "Teabaggers"—a cheap feel-good approach that largely serves to make the angriest liberals look not much better than their name-calling conservative rivals. The other school of thought was to look at the rank-and-file of this movement not as villains but as fellow Americans with some legitimate grievances about their place in society—economic or otherwise—who were being led toward hatred and irrationality by a merry band of right-wing pranksters.

The problem is that many of these pleas for empathy for Tea Partiers are also so saturated with the stench of condescension as to be completely worthless. The prime example was a much-discussed essay published in *Psychology Today* in early 2010 by a San Francisco psychologist named Michael Bader, with the title of "Why We Need to Have Empathy for Tea Party Lunatics," as republished on AlterNet. In the piece, Bader argues that the most out-there right-wing radicals are no different from paranoid—albeit not always politically so—patients that he sees in his practice, that these are people who suffered very real pain on a personal level and are looking for a cosmic conspiracy that will absolve them of blame for their problems.

Bader's analysis seems right on the money in some ways, but falters in others. For one thing, you can't help but think that under- or unemployed Americans like Joe Gayan or Al Whayland really *were* the victims of big-business-driven conspiracies, such as outsourcing factory jobs to China or manipulating the housing market; it's just that these are not the conspiracies the backlash is so worked up about. Also, Bader's attitude is somewhat troubling given that it's difficult to be truly empathetic toward someone when you're calling that person a "lunatic" at the same time. Try walking up to somebody at a Tea Party rally or here at Beckapalooza and telling him, "I think you're a lunatic but I understand the deep pain that you must be feeling"—and see how far that takes you. That type of elitist condescension won't counteract the right-wing movement—it is, instead, the force that gives it life.

Here in Section 107 at the UCF Arena, you are listening to Beck and his TV pals like David Barton and the constitutional conservative judge Andrew Napolitano and their seven-hour reinvention of politics as a kind of performance art, with Beck dramatizing his personal triumph over the bottle or throwing out disconnected feel-good crowd pleasers like, "If we wanted to kick their ass in the Middle East, we could have done it in a year and brought the troops home." Progressives can't compete with this sort of emotional messaging. But then, they don't even try. Liberals think that such a thing is beneath them, that by repeating those same rational but complicated, non-bumper-sticker arguments—that health-care reform can actually lower the deficit or that "green jobs" is a sounder policy than "drill baby drill" or that sometimes it's better to work with other nations than to insult them—again and again, they will somehow eventually get through to the heartland.

In the 1980s, a graduate student at the University of Pennsylvania—Jonathan Haidt, later an associate professor of psychology at the University of Virginia—tried an experiment to see how people from different social groups valued their gut feelings as compared to dispassionate reasoning. One test involved the story of an old woman who had no rags left in her house and privately cut up an old U.S. flag to clean her toilet. Those of lower socioeconomic status were repulsed by the story (Haidt used groups in both the United States and Brazil); the only group not troubled by the private flag desecration was elite university students at Penn, including several who saw it as a way of recycling. Haidt later recounted this failure of elites to understand the raw power of basic instinct in an article entitled "What Makes People Vote Republican."

Haidt's article was published before the 2008 election, before Columbia and Harvard Law graduate Barack Obama arrived in the White House to double down on the Ivy League style of this aloof and often spectacularly unsuccessful brand of persuasion. Ironically, it was candidate Obama who once told an audience in Philadelphia that "[i]f they bring a knife to a fight, we bring a gun." Just two short years later, the Obama agenda and his progressive supporters were getting pelted with a barrage of politically lethal .44-caliber slugs marked "death panel" or "Nazi" or "Communist," and the president was the one brandishing the switchblade instead.

The people who would try to coolly explain to angry, future-shocked citizens why it's practical to use an old forgotten American flag to clean the toilet are running the country now, but the people who are disgusted by such a thing are running our discourse—the people whose easy solution to terrorism is, as WGMD's Bill Colley told you many months ago, "hang 'em!" You didn't need to infiltrate Beck's concrete-and-steel theme park in Orlando to see that the purveyors of college-textbook approaches to climate change or for getting the nation over the recession hump are going to need to find a radically different brand of rhetoric to make much headway.

In a not-too-long-ago time, progressives were able to move the nation emotionally and carry the debate—that happened in the 1960s when televised images of weaponized fire hoses and police attack dogs swayed shaken Americans to finally enact meaningful civil rights legislation. But then progressive-thinking people retreated to their ivory towers, instead of using emotional appeals for the idea that the one thing that could truly make America an exceptional nation could be not our weapons but our humanity—the wealthiest nation on earth finding a way to provide affordable health care or a quality education to all. The battlefield of emotion was abandoned to the likes of Beck and Limbaugh and their followers, and we are now witnessing the carnage in the wake of that unfortunate retreat.

The challenge posed by the most regressive elements of the backlash are daunting, but the risk of pretending the situation is not something critical—that the Tea Party movement is just, in Dick Cheney's famous expression, "the last throes" of something that will peter out—is too great. The dangers of another lethal episode like Rich Poplawski's cop-killing spree, let alone another Oklahoma City, and of the gridlock that had already paralyzed Washington for months at a time, and of rogue states like Arizona enacting laws that smack of the nineteenth century, are all simply too great for the new silent majority to ignore.

That certainly means continuing to strive for more jobs and better health care and schooling and all the things that could make America once again a place of opportunity for all of its citizens. Even—especially, really—for the folks who think that Barack Obama is a citizen of Kenya or that "jack-booted thugs" are already practicing to confiscate your guns and send you to a concentration camp. That certainly means rebuilding our economy so that people like Joe Gayan and Celia Hyde aren't unexpectedly "retired" by their early fifties, and so that rootless young men like Rich Poplawski are making windows instead of making comments on a white-supremacist Web site. It also means rediscovering ourselves as a nation where adults with a heartfelt desire for learning real and accurate American history are handed something else besides a bibliography of crackpots like W. Cleon Skousen and zealous rewriters of reality like David Barton.

But progressive-minded Americans also have to keep remembering that the real enemy today isn't neighbors with different opinions, but fear and ignorance itself—and that there are brave ways to fight the needless anxieties that hold us back. The best way to fight the fearmongering of a Glenn Beck is taking on the pyramid of hucksters underneath him, the purveyors of survival seeds and gold coins that are the oxygen that support this dangerous social pathology. That means using the ways of the free market to sell ideals that are rooted in hope for America and not in apocalyptic fears. There is no reason, nor would there be any excuse, for blockading the free speech of the Tea Parties, but their worst ideas can be outspoken by those who argue against fear with facts, and by reminding us all that what has made America great has been our inclusiveness and not the dominance of any one culture. It has happened before in America—when the decency of President Dwight Eisenhower's government and truth-seeking journalists like Edward R. Murrow beat back the Red-baiting paranoia of Senator Joseph McCarthy—and there is no reason that in a patient America this will not happen again.

As the temperatures rose moving into the long, hot summer of the 2010 elections, there were a few encouraging stirrings from liberals and moderates—that they would fight, for example, against Arizona's backward immigration laws through marches and possibly boycotts. These were signs that the majority could once again be pushed out of its silent pose, just as it was briefly in the fall of 2008, not for a candidate this time but for a bigger cause.

Decent American citizens should fight these battles not with any

intention of shutting up dissenters, but because of the desire to reconnect with those dissenters in a more productive, more just, and more
civil society—because, in the words of Obama when he spoke at Arcadia University, it is the right thing to do.

However, we may well amuse ourselves to death first.

On a late Saturday afternoon in the Sunshine State, Glenn Beck is
doing his very best to do exactly that. His keynote address, approach-
ing Fidel Castro territory in length as it clocks in at over an hour and
twenty minutes, has the same dashed-off qualities as his best-selling
books, meandering from anecdote to anecdote, most of them personal—leaving the audience on the edge of its seats wondering if a belly
laugh or another crying jag is just around the corner. Which is precisely
the method in the madness of Beck. The onetime student director of the
Sehome High School production of Molière's *The Miser* is big on the
props—at one point he pulls out a sledgehammer to quote Gandhi's
violent metaphor in support of nonviolence, a Beckian paradox if ever
there was one—and big also on the two-bit theatrics. As he delivers one
of several mini-monologues, about an alcoholic low point, curled up in
a fetal position on an ugly olive-green shag carpet in a low-rent apartment, Beck addresses the arena crowd in a half-sprawl from the hard
floor of the stage. Acting. You could not help but think that Beck was
praying that somewhere way up beyond the lights of the arena, Orson
Welles was watching this moment.

And that his mother could see it, too.

Inspiring a political movement was just the means to an end for Beck,
and that end is what you are seeing today, a performance. The actual
problems of America—and its political realities—are such a small part
of his American Revival. At one point, he does warn his audience that
in a couple of weeks some experts—not political ones, mind you—were
going to come onto his Fox News Channel show and propose an actual

budget for the United States, one that would slash federal spending by 40 to 50 percent. That would mean real pain for the untrusting-of-government people who were cheering him on, people who would see cuts in their Medicare or Social Security or unemployment benefits were such a draconian plan ever to happen.

"The system is going to reset—it has to reset," Beck says—promising, like any crafty televangelist, the joys of liberating yourself from your money. "But it's just a car. It's just a home. You'll survive, and I'll make this guarantee. You will be happier." He ends on a moment of pure shtick, a throaty Jimmy-Stewart-filibuster recital of Emma Lazarus's "New Colossus," the poem forever etched inside the pedestal of the Statue of Liberty, and completely at odds with the anti-immigration fervor of the audience. Beck pleads to "[s]end these, the homeless, tempest-tossed to me/I lift my lamp beside the golden door!" But the real message to these change-averse warriors who are fighting for their country back had come earlier in the afternoon, when Beck—brandishing his leather Moleskine—assured them that the world would never forget them:

> Everything you do, everything you see, everything that's happening in America today, is history—profound, fundamental transformational history. Whether we win or lose—whether mankind's freedom is preserved, or does fundamentally transform into something I can't recognize—this will remain, and these stories must be told. You must pass our information on to the next generation. They may not think it's anything important. It will be.
> It will be.

The performance ended at exactly 5 p.m., the new national Zero Hour for paranoia. The doors of the golden-and-black UCF Arena swung open, and the masses emerged, tempest-tossed, to begin the journey back to their stucco-coated gated communities or to their factory-stripped small towns. They kept coming for several minutes—a steady, slow-moving procession of gray-bearded sons of Vietnam and golden girls of the retirement-village Tea Party set, sprinkled with Cuban-American freedom fighters and computer-discombobulated job-seekers, a wounded purple heartland of America. For a split second, they struggled to adjust their eyes—numbed by the hours of indoor gray—to the beautiful saturation of a late-afternoon Florida sun, and then they kept on moving.

They were braced to fight a war of the worlds, real or imaginary.

ACKNOWLEDGMENTS

I was interested in the Tea Party before there even was a Tea Party. It was the fall of 2008, before the presidential ballot was even cast, when I began trying to get my arms around the growing American canyon I was witnessing between the throngs—outnumbered though they eventually were—who idolized Sarah Palin and a stubbornly ignorant brand of politics, a kind of modern Know-Nothing Party, and the coolly rational (sometimes too much for its own good) younger army behind Barack Obama. Still, I didn't see the Obama backlash coming—but when it came, I knew it was a story that I had to witness in real time. It took more than a year to map out and then report on the new American right wing and to write this book—and I have never once regretted the decision to dive right in.

On my *Philadelphia Daily News* blog Attytood or my writings for Media Matters or other sites, I certainly promote a progressive (a.k.a. "liberal") point of view on most issues, and—make no mistake—my values are also reflected in some of the conclusions reached in this book. But I also want to make clear that in speaking with dozens of activists in Tea Party and related groups like the Oath Keepers or the 9-12 Project, I always tried to report fairly, to listen to what people had to say, and to report their words and their actions accurately. It was in that spirit that I made the somewhat unorthodox decision to write in the rarely used voice of second person. It's not just me trying to learn what the Obama backlash is all about, but also the vast majority of Americans . . . you.

One thing that writing *The Backlash* helped remind me is something we all need to remember, which is that we should always strive to see the humanity—even in those we profoundly disagree with. Several activists in the Tea Party movement were very generous with their time—and their opinions!—and I am truly grateful. These include Russ Murphy of the Delaware 9-12 Patriots as well as Al and Larraine Whayland, who welcomed me in their home, as did Celia Hyde of the Oath Keepers and many others.

I also want to acknowledge a number of journalists and related experts who were valuable resources—including Stephen Lemons of the *Phoenix New Times*, who is the world expert on nativist movements in Arizona; David Weigel, who was still with the *Washington Independent* when he offered guidance on Knob Creek and other matters; Alexander Zaitchik, Glenn Beck's unauthorized biographer; Max Blumenthal of *Republican Gomorrah* fame; David Altheide of Arizona State University; Larry Keller of the Southern Poverty Law Center; and Chip Berlet of Political Research Associates.

Once again, the *Philadelphia Daily News* has been very, very good to me in allowing me to do what it takes to produce a book in a relatively short period of time. This includes city editor Gar Joseph and editor Michael Days, as well as Pat McLoone, and also Wendy Warren and everyone else at Philly.com and the people who keep my blog Attytood running—Vance Lehmkuhl and Michele Tranquilli; I'm most grateful to every one of my friends and colleagues at the *Daily News*—some of the most amazing journalists that I have ever known. At the same time, once I branched into blogging, I would not have had the privilege of even daring to write a book were it not for the support and encouragement of other bloggers and related folks like Susie Madrak, Mark Karlin, John Amato, Greg Mitchell, Duncan Black, Josh Marshall, Jane Hamsher, Michael Tomasky, Joan Walsh, Keith Olbermann, Monika Bauerlein,

Jennifer Nix, Richard Blair, Jay Rosen, Jim Romenesko, Rem Reider, David Sirota, Rick Perlstein, and countless others.

This book would not have been possible without the generosity of Media Matters for America, where I am now a senior fellow. I want to acknowledge David Brock, Eric Burns, Ari Rabin-Havt, Jeremy Schulman, and Jon Sime, as well as my colleagues like Eric Boehlert, Joe Strupp, and Karl Frisch. Another person who was a huge help was my former editor Martin Beiser, who was the one who suggested making this book more of a road trip, which made it a much more exciting project.

Will Lippincott of Lippincott Massie McQuilken, my literary agent, has been there every step of the way for me—both helping me to shape a very raw idea into the book you are holding now and then advocating for me far better than I ever could. I'm sure this will be the second of many, many projects together. I'm also grateful to the people who work with Will, including Rachel Vogel and Jason Anthony.

But no one has been more enthusiastic about this book—probably more enthusiastic than me, on some days—than my editor, the aptly named Matt Harper at HarperCollins. His thoughtful editing—often conveyed in his trademark lengthy phone calls—gave this book the shape and the focus that it sorely needed, and I'm incredibly thankful for that.

I'm also thankful for the support of my family, including my parents Mary and Bryan Bunch, the latter who continues to serve as my best sounding board. And especially my wife, Kathy Boccella, who encouraged my bizarre road trips and tolerated many other hassles, and my children, Julia and Jesse, who frequently distract my work—but only to provide joy.

RESOURCES

The complete endnotes for *The Backlash* are available online—including hyperlinks to any news sources that are posted on the Internet. The Web address for the online endnotes is http://www.philly.com/philly/blogs/attytood/TheBacklashendnotes.html.

In addition to the specific articles cited in the endnotes, several books, articles, or blogs were invaluable resources for me and are excellent sources for delving deeper into the right-wing movement in America and related topics. These include:

Alexander Zaitchik has written the definite biography of the rise of Glenn Beck: *Common Nonsense: Glenn Beck and the Triumph of Ignorance* (Wiley, Hoboken, NJ, 2010). His articles about Beck and the influence of W. Cleon Skousen, the author of *The Five Thousand Year Leap*, are also available at Salon.com.

My reporting on Arizona was heavily influenced by the online reporting of Stephen Lemons of the *Phoenix New Times*, who is the expert on the nativist movement in the Grand Canyon State. His blog is (mysteriously) called Feathered Bastard. It's at: http://blogs.phoenixnewtimes.com/bastard.

David Weigel has covered the rise of the Tea Party and related right-wing activities for three publications, most recently the *Washington*

Post. He was a helpful resource and even a Super Bowl–watching companion, thanks to the blizzard of '10; and you can read him at Right Now: http://voices.washingtonpost.com/right-now.

OTHER WORKS

Bader, Michael. "We Need to Have Empathy for Tea Partiers," *Psychology Today,* March 5, 2010, http://www.psychologytoday.com/print/39146.

Blumenthal, Max. *Republican Gomorrah: Inside the Movement That Shattered the Party.* New York: Nation Books, 2009.

Haidt, Jonathan. "What Makes People Vote Republican," *Edge: The Third Culture,* September 9, 2008, http://www.edge.org/3rd_culture/haidt08/haidt08_index.html.

Hofstadter, Richard. *The Paranoid Style in American Politics.* New York: Vintage, 2008.

Judis, John B. "Death Grip: How Political Psychology Explains Bush's Ghastly Success," *The New Republic,* August 27, 2007, http://www.tnr.com/article/death-grip.

O'Brien, Luke. "Judson Phillips Threw a Tea Party, and Trouble Came," AOL News, February 5, 2010, http://www.aolnews.com/politics/article/judson-phillips-threw-a-tea-party-and-trouble-showed-up/19345884.

Postman, Neil. *Amusing Ourselves to Death: Public Discourse in the Age of Show Business.* New York: Penguin, 1986.

Toffler, Alvin. *Future Shock.* New York: Bantam, 1984.